City Design

City Design

Modernist, Traditional, Green, and Systems Perspectives

Jonathan Barnett

 Routledge
Taylor & Francis Group

LONDON AND NEW YORK

First published 2011
by Routledge
2 Park Square, Milton Park, Abingdon, Oxon OX14 4RN

Simultaneously published in the USA and Canada
by Routledge 711 Third Avenue, New York, NY 10017 (8th Floor)

Routledge is an imprint of the Taylor & Francis Group, an informa business

Typeset in Univers by Florence Production Ltd, Stoodleigh, Devon
Printed and bound in Great Britain by TJ International Ltd, Padstow, Cornwall

British Library Cataloguing in Publication Data
A catalogue record for this book is available from the British Library

Library of Congress Cataloging-in-Publication Data
Barnett, Jonathan.
City design: modernist, traditional, green and systems perspectives /
Jonathan Barnett.
    p. cm.
Includes bibliographical references and index.
1. City planning—Environmental aspects. 2. City planning. I. Title.
HT166.B373 2011
307.1''216—dc22   2010023607

ISBN13: 978–0–415–77540–3 (hbk)
ISBN13: 978–0–415–77541–0 (pbk)

* Includes material from Jonathan Barnett's *The Elusive City*
(Harper & Row 1986) (copyright Jonathan Barnett).

Contents

Acknowledgments

I wish to thank Dongguk University in Seoul and particularly professors Hong-Ill Kim and GwangYa Han for inviting me to give a series of lectures where I could present and discuss the central ideas in this book, and also my students at the University of Pennsylvania who have helped me test, expand, and revise my perspectives.

Introduction

Three city-design challenges

The world is urbanizing faster than current city-design practice can keep up, climate change has introduced a new dynamism into what once appeared to be a stable environment, and there are controversies and uncertainties about the basic theory of city design, as shown by the failure to create a coherent rebuilding plan for the World Trade Center site after the terrorist attack in September of 2001. These are three of the most important challenges to effective city design today.

The challenge of rapid urban change

At the beginning of the twentieth century, cities housed only 15 percent of the global population. Today more than half the people in the world live in urban areas, some in traditional cities, some in the kind of decentralized development often criticized as urban sprawl, and some in unplanned squatter settlements. Rapid urbanization has been accompanied by exponential population growth. The number of urban dwellers today exceeds the number of people living in the entire world as recently as 1960.[1] While much of the new urbanization is taking place in Asia, Africa, South and Central America, the United States is expected to add more than a hundred million more people during the first half of the twenty-first century. Most of that growth is expected to take place within ten multi-city regions in such places as Florida, Southern California, and the Pacific Northwest, while elsewhere rural areas and some older cities lose population or grow slowly. Even where population growth is slow, rapid urbanization continues in response to migration out of older areas and increased demand for housing created by the smaller sizes of individual households. Spreading urbanization takes place even in European countries with stable or shrinking populations.

At one time cities could be expected to remain recognizably the same for centuries. Urban change speeded up at the beginning of the nineteenth century with the interaction of railroads, factories, and rapidly increasing population. Even so, about 1910, at the beginning of the worldwide city-planning movement, it was possible to believe that traditional street and park design strategies that went back to the Renaissance could bring order and beauty to urban central areas, and what was then the new garden-city concept could evolve to manage urban change in suburbs and new factory towns. This consensus was soon challenged by the modernists, originally a small radical group, who believed that modern cities should be built on hygienic principles to maximize sunlight and open space, using what were then the new technologies of highways and steel-framed towers to sweep away the accumulation of the past. Modernist rejected the traditional relationships between buildings and streets in favor of a separate grid of traffic ways enclosing large blocks where buildings are located for optimal sun exposure. After the great economic depression of the 1930s and the horrific disruption of World War II most city designers switched to a simplified version of modernist design ideology, relying on automobile trans-portation, tall buildings, and park space as the way to rebuild and expand cities, although some traditionalists objected, and a few visionaries urged much more radical systems technologies.

City designers have had substantial influence over urban commercial centers, communities for rich people, and mass housing for the poor, but have only been able to change urban development at the margins, as large parts of any city had been constructed over previous generations and regional growth trends embodied many decisions outside the control of designers.

Now the scale and speed of urbanization and decentralization has turned the management of urban growth and change into an entirely new problem. Urbanization is happening so rapidly in China that city districts can be constructed or rebuilt in a few years, and whole new cities created. By government decree, Shenzhen has grown from a fishing village in 1979 to a metropolis of more than 9,000,000 people. It is routine for planners and designers working in planning institutes in China to see their maps and sketches translated into reality at a scale and speed that earlier generations of frustrated visionaries would never have believed possible. The cities of the United Arab Emirates like Dubai, Abu Dhabi and Doha are also growing fast, acquiring their glittering skylines in little over a decade. Cities like Bangkok, Jakarta, and Mumbai changed out of recognition in the last half of the twentieth century. In some places cities or parts of cities are growing with no design at all: Robert Neuwirth estimates that a billion people, perhaps a third of all urban dwellers, and almost a seventh of the world's population, live in squatter settlements where there is very little control over design and development.[2] Where new buildings do follow a rule book, the locations where development takes place may still be outside of any design and planning system. The US housing industry builds an average of about 1.5 million houses and apartments a year, 2 million a year at market peaks and 1.2 million a year when times are bad for building.[3] Much of this construction takes place in master-planned communities of several thousand units, and all of it requires approvals by the local government. However, very little of this new housing implements a community or regional design, but instead responds to available land and the initiatives of individual builders. In Canada, a country with an economy comparable to the United States, there are stronger policies to make individual developments fit into a larger picture. In the Netherlands, the Scandinavian countries, and Singapore, large areas, if not the whole of each country, can be said to have been constructed according to an overall design. In Korea, the United Kingdom, and most western European nations there are strong local design controls, national planning concepts, and a new interest in what is called *spatial planning*, another name for regional design. However, as the world speeds towards a population of nine billion people by mid-century, the influence of the city designer is still marginal in large parts of both the developed and developing world, even while the built environment is being reconstructed and expanded at a pace and scale that require direction.

Climate change as a challenge to city design

Traditionally city designers had been able to assume that the natural environment was a stable background for their work, its forces understood and controllable through engineering. More recently the entire trend of urban development is being revealed as unsustainable, not just because of the waste of resources created by spreading urbanization and decentralization, but because the climate of the earth itself has become far more dynamic. The destruction of much of New Orleans by Hurricane Katrina in 2005 has become an important indicator of what to expect from global climate change, although this particular tragedy need not have happened. New Orleans had relied on flood walls and levees built by the US Army Corps of Engineers. They should have protected the city from a storm of Katrina's intensity but both the engineering and construction turned out to be defective.[4] The subsequent failure to provide the resources needed to rebuild and protect New Orleans revealed that there is no longer a political consensus in the United States—where a majority now live in places that used to be suburban or rural—for maintaining traditional central cities, even when the destruction of a big part of an important city was clearly the fault of a Federal government agency. Officials in vulnerable coastal locations like Boston, New York, and Miami have begun to look at what would happen to them if they were hit by a comparable disaster. Big parts of Miami and Miami Beach are only a few feet above sea level, and are thus exposed to a direct hit by a storm surge, even one less intense than Katrina. A direct hit on New York City by a hurricane striking at high tide would send a wall of water over lower Manhattan, flooding subways and vehicular tunnels. The airports would be under water as well. Boston is equally at risk in the wrong set of circumstances. Would these cities be written off the way large parts of New Orleans have been? And what happens to all coastal cities as the world's climate changes?

There is now consensus that climate change induced by human activities is a real and serious problem, and is happening faster than was predicted only a few years ago. Some of the scenarios for what could happen if the average surface temperature of the oceans rises more than two degrees Celsius are truly horrifying.[5] Preventing the worst potential climate consequences from industry and urbanization will clearly have to become a city-design priority, and this will mean less dependence on automobiles, more preservation of the natural environment, and much more concern about the location and orientation of buildings for energy efficiency.

Adapting cities to the effects of climate change will be another priority. Some ocean temperature increase has already taken place and more is already inevitable. Sea-level rise is a component of climate change that is relatively easy to predict. Sea levels rise because warmer water occupies more volume, and because land-based glaciers are melting. A conservative prediction is a worldwide rise in sea levels of half a meter by mid-century and at least a meter by 2100. This amplifies the threat to coastal cities already at risk from storm events. For example, according to this prediction, much of Miami Beach will be below sea level in 2100.[6]

Planning for future sea-level rise will change the way designers think about cities. Pudong, the new skyscraper district of Shanghai, was largely fresh-water wetland up until 1990. In retrospect it was not a good place to make such a big urban investment. The low-lying islands being created by dredging off the coast of Dubai don't look like such a good investment decision either.

The Netherlands, where 55 percent of the country is already below sea level, is clearly on the front line of climate change, under threat from rising sea levels and also from increasing amounts of river water coursing through the country because Alpine glaciers are melting. After a terrible storm in 1953, the Dutch created a system of storm-surge barriers that guard the Eastern Scheldt delta and Rotterdam harbor. Television news stories of people flooded out of their homes in New Orleans and other Gulf Coast communities have caused the Dutch to take another look at their fortifications, particularly dikes that might contain construction from hundreds of years ago. They are also looking at ways to accommodate periodic flooding from rivers by channeling the waters into park areas or farmland. The City of Rotterdam has released a plan for making the city climate-proof. These efforts are supported by a national policy to protect the whole country from the worst possible event: the 10,000 year storm. In that context the idea of paying for whatever is necessary to protect the country from storms has been taken out of politics, giving it a similar status to the military budget in the United States. There may be discussion about the value of specific programs, or the amount of spending in a given year, but the idea of defense is not at issue. The government in Britain funded a storm-surge barrier in the Thames to protect London after a destructive surge from the same 1953 storm that caused such damage in the Netherlands. Design is now under way to raise the Thames Barrier to deal with rising sea levels. A barrier is under construction to protect Venice from flooding. Most countries, however, are a long way from a consensus about protecting coastal cities and about how to pay for it. Rebuilding in Gulfport and Biloxi, east of New Orleans and also hard-hit by Katrina, goes forward without any investment in protective measures beyond what can be done on individual properties.

Climate change is also predicted to increase the duration and severity of drought. Although specific predictions are difficult, places that suffer from drought now, such as Australia and the American south-west, can expect that the problem will become worse. Making cities sustainable in areas subject to drought will require major changes in city and building design. It is probable that people will look back in amazement at the days when purified drinking water was used to irrigate lawns and flush toilets.

Failures of city design after 9/11

The attempts to rebuild New Orleans after Hurricane Katrina, and the probability of more such disasters as the world's climate changes, show that there are large gaps in city-design practice as it relates to working with and understanding the natural environment. Another disaster, the destruction of the World Trade Center Towers on September 11th 2001, revealed the inability of local institutions and a wide range of respected design professionals to respond effectively to a major city-design problem.

Originally the Lower Manhattan Development Corporation and the Port Authority of New York and New Jersey, the two agencies tasked with managing the rebuilding, intended to draw families of the victims, community leaders, design professionals, and interested citizens into a consensus-building process that would be the inspiration for a place that represented both renewal and healing.

Public participation is used routinely in the United States to deal with major changes in city design and development. It is a well-established process that usually begins with the basic issues, which at the World Trade Center site would have included whether to rebuild at all, and, if so, how much should be built, how best to memorialize the victims, and what kinds of development would be most appropriate. Discussions can become unstructured and divisive. Success comes when the participants have become so familiar with the possible choices that they are impatient to make a decision. This can easily take a year. The sponsoring agencies did not contemplate such an open process or such an extended time frame. The agencies selected an experienced urban design and planning firm, Beyer Blinder Belle, who were given six weeks to define a set of design alternatives that could be discussed at an unusually large public meeting scheduled for July 2002, to be facilitated by America Speaks, a non-profit organization which specializes in conducting public forums. The intent was to narrow the alternatives to three immediately, and develop a final site design by the end of December. The agencies required that any plan replace all the square-footage that had been destroyed, because of the contract between the Port Authority, which owned the land, and the leaseholder for the destroyed buildings, Silverstein Properties. This decision eliminated many potential alternatives and was a significant issue that needed to be discussed with the public. It wasn't.

The July 2002 meeting was held at New York City's convention center with some 4,300 participants.

John H. Beyer presented six design alternatives focusing on the public space that would be a memorial to the victims. They were called Memorial Square, prepared with input from Cooper Robertson + Partners who were working for the owners of the World Financial Center office buildings to the west; Memorial Plaza; Memorial Triangle; Memorial Garden, with input from Skidmore, Owings & Merrill working for Silverstein Properties; and finally Memorial Park, and Memorial Promenade, alternatives designed by Peterson/Littenberg, a firm which had been retained as consultants by the Lower Manhattan Development Corporation. Each alternative included the same amount of potential development, in response to the requirement that the rebuilding match the area destroyed in the terrorist attack. The buildings were portrayed as generic boxes, stand-ins for the architecture that would surround the memorial and be created later by others.

Inviting thousands of people to discuss the alternative merits of complicated open-space concepts with no prior preparation would never be a good idea, and in the tense atmosphere of rebuilding after a great tragedy it was a disaster. People couldn't tell the six open-space concepts apart. What they could see were the generic mass models that were placeholders for future building designs, and which understandably looked very similar, as each alternative had to show the same amount of office space. So none of the alternatives received a strong preference, and the designs received a bad press, notably a *New York Times* editorial describing them as "dreary, leaden proposals that fall far short of what New York City—and the world—expect to see rise at ground zero."[7]

The World Trade Center design process did not include a 20 to 30 person working committee, representing everyone with an interest in the outcome, which usually parallels the big public meetings for this kind of participatory decision-making. For the World Trade Center site a working committee would have included representatives from the Lower Manhattan Development Corporation, the Port Authority, Silverstein Properties—a crucial participant in any discussion about what should happen next—as well as representatives of victims' families, leaders of community organizations, leading New York design professionals, and representatives for people who live and work in the local area.

It is not unusual for the first public meeting in a participation process to go badly, particularly when public emotions run high. In another situation, the designers could have gone to the working committee, discussed what had gone wrong, and established the conditions for a more constructive public meeting the next time. For the World Trade Center site it would have taken a lot of courage to continue with the promised public participation process in the face of such outright rejection, and the two agencies didn't have it. They abandoned any official method of involving the public and the important stakeholders in a design and development decision process and announced that they would hold a worldwide architectural design competition.

Almost 500 teams of architects and other design professionals offered their qualifications, and in September, 2002 seven groups of architects, all well known, were chosen to develop sketch designs. The lead firms were:

- Foster + Partners
- Studio Daniel Libeskind, with Gary Hack and George Hargreaves
- Skidmore, Owings & Merrill with SANAA and Field Operations
- a collaboration of Richard Meier, Peter Eisenman, Charles Gwathmey, and Steven Holl
- a collaboration called THINK led by Rafael Vignoly, Frederic Schwartz, Shigeru Ban, and Ken Smith
- United Architects—a collaboration among Foreign Office Architects, Greg Lynn FORM, RUR Architecture, Kevin Kennon, and UN Studio
- Peterson/Littenberg

Establishing this competition generated great excitement. It was an inspiring moment for architects, planners, and urban designers to see issues that they cared about discussed on news broadcasts, the front pages of newspapers, and in magazine cover stories. Two books that capture the time when it was possible to believe that something significant was happening are Paul Goldberger's *Up From Zero,* a lively account of the whole planning process, and *Imagining Ground Zero* by Suzanne Stephens with Ian Luna and Ron Broadhurst, which includes the graphic presentations for the official proposals for the World Trade Center site, and many of the unofficial proposals as well.[8]

The architects proved to have much better abilities to communicate with the press and the public than the city designers. Daniel Libeskind, head of one of the two teams selected as finalists in December of 2002, presented a group of buildings of distinctive prismatic shapes in graduated sizes. The tallest, which Libeskind called the Freedom Tower, was to be 1,776 feet tall at the top of its mast. Libeskind made much of a retaining wall deep below ground that survived from the original World Trade Center saying that it should be left visible as a reminder of its heroic role keeping back the waters of the Hudson River to the west even after the disruption of the attack. He also explained that at precisely the day and hour at which the terrorists had flown a plane into the first tower, a shaft of sunlight would penetrate between his new towers and illuminate the retaining wall and the space in front of it.

The other finalist team, THINK, proposed two skeletal steel structures of approximately the height and shape of the destroyed World Trade Center office towers, with a museum housed within the skeletal towers at what would be about the 35th floor. The office space required by the program was accommodated in a surrounding ring of relatively conventional office buildings, which had a variety of floor plans but were all to be the same height, about half as tall as the skeletal structures. This design separated the powerful symbolism required for the memorial from the demands of the real-estate market, and the uniform height for the surrounding wall of office buildings was a workable urban design concept.

In contrast to the symbolism of Libeskind's Freedom Tower, defiantly taller than the destroyed World Trade Center and at 1,776 feet supposedly evoking the spirit of the American Revolution, the skeletal towers projected a mixed message of defiance and regret. More important, they represented an investment of at least half a billion dollars, with no supporting source of income, plus a long-term commitment to maintain the structures and operate the museum.

Libeskind's design was selected, but that turned out to be a meaningless decision.

The problem with Libeskind's design was that it depended on the distinctive, geometric shapes he had given to each of the buildings. There was no generic underlying principle. The best way to implement his proposal would have been for Libeskind to be the architect for all the buildings, unlikely in a development of this scale unless the buildings were to be constructed at once. The development program was only about preserving the long-term rights to build; it was a serious misunderstanding to assume that 11,000,000 square feet of office space was likely to be built immediately. Most of the competition designs that were eliminated relied even more heavily than Libeskind on a single continuous construction program, which made their proposals infeasible. The THINK design could have allowed for many different office-building architects and developers, provided they would observe the height limitation and uniformly flat facades proposed. The design by Peterson/Littenberg, which unlike the others used a traditional vocabulary of axial and symmetrical building relationships, could also have been translated into design guidelines for development extending many years into the future.

Larry Silverstein, the developer who had held the lease for the World Trade Center towers, had the right to redevelop the site and did not choose to implement Libeskind's design. He had his own architects, Skidmore, Owings & Merrill (SOM), and he had given them clear instructions, which did not resemble the concepts that SOM and SANAA had submitted in the competition. There was a brief period in which Libeskind and SOM were said to be collaborating, but the only remnants of Libeskind's design were the name, Freedom Tower, and the mast height of 1,776 feet. The Freedom Tower name has since been discarded. The other buildings on the site, also being developed by Silverstein Properties, were entrusted to several famous architects, who also paid no serious attention to Libeskind's concept as urban design guidance for the whole site. The Port Authority had no interest in sacrificing millions of square feet of sub-grade space in order to leave the retaining wall exposed to sunlight, and a second competition was held for the memorial open space, with the winning design selected in January of 2004.

I.1

This model photograph shows the buildings being constructed on the World Trade Center site after the failures of the public participation process and the international design competition. While the model shows individual works by some of the finest design firms, they do not add up to a coherent work of city design. Starting from the left is One World Trade Center by Skidmore, Owings & Merrill, then, in the background, Seven World Trade Center, also by SOM, then 200 Greenwich Street by Foster + Partners, 175 Greenwich Street by Rogers Stirk Harbour + Partners, and 150 Greenwich Street by Maki and Associates. In the foreground are the two sunken courtyards of the National September 11 Memorial designed by Michael Arad and Peter Walker to recall the original footprints of the World Trade Center towers. The pavilion in between is part of an associated memorial museum designed by Davis Brody Bond Aedas. Between the Foster and Rogers buildings is the transportation terminal designed by Santiago Calatrava.

This model photograph (Figure I.1) represents the official plan devised after the failures of the public participation process and the design competition. Starting from the left is One World Trade Center by Skidmore, Owings & Merrill, behind it Seven World Trade Center, also by Skidmore, Owings & Merrill, and then 200 Greenwich Street by Foster + Partners, 175 Greenwich Street by Rogers Stirk Harbour + Partners, and 150 Greenwich Street by Maki and Associates. In the foreground is the National September 11 Memorial designed by Michael Arad and Peter Walker with an associated memorial museum designed by Davis Brody Bond Aedas. Between the Foster and Rogers buildings is the transportation terminal designed by Santiago Calatrava. The space between the SOM and Foster buildings is the site of a possible future performing arts center. The buildings and memorials are the work of some of the finest design firms, but the plan doesn't realize the high expectations that were created when rebuilding began. It is similar to the design entitled Memorial Plaza, one of the six alternatives rejected after the public meeting in July 2002, and characterized by the *New York Times* as "dreary, leaden proposals" (Figure I.2).

I.2
This model photo shows one of the designs for the World Trade Center site rejected at a large public meeting in July of 2002, and characterized by a *New York Times* editorial as "dreary, leaden proposals that fall far short of what New York City—and the world—expect to see rise at ground zero."

The debate about modernist and traditional city design

An important subtext of the controversy over rebuilding the World Trade Center was an assumption that it required architecture whose forms had special significance. The iconic building has become a central commitment of modernism. Modernist concepts, described in the next chapter, have dominated city design since World War II. Criticisms of modernist city design have grown intense as more and more of it has been built around the world: especially its failure to accommodate historic preservation and conserve existing neighborhoods, its role in promoting social inequity by concentrating poor people in the least desirable areas, the disruption created by highways running through the center of cities—another central modernist concept—and the destruction of the natural environment as urbanization spreads over larger and larger regions. Traditional city design, which the modernists defined themselves against, had recently been used in planning Battery Park City, immediately adjacent to the World Trade Center site. The Battery Park City Plan,[9] with its emphasis on traditional parks, streets, and blocks, had been a large influence on the initial six plans for rebuilding the World Trade Center that were shown at the public meeting in July of 2002. The assumption that the memorial space was the important design determinant and the buildings would follow later was not supported in the meeting, or by the critical reaction afterwards. Unfortunately there turned out to be no shared assumptions about how to design a coherent and distinctive group of buildings that could be implemented by different architects over an extended period.

Traditional city design, which does include a set of shared expectations for future buildings, has been making a comeback in historic European cities, for example, the rebuilding of the central parts of Berlin with modernist buildings constrained by traditional guidelines, the precinct around St. Paul's Cathedral in

London where a modernist plan implemented just after World War II has been replaced with new buildings that hold the street walls in the traditional way, and a new low-rise center for Den Haag in the Netherlands. In the United States, starting in the 1980s, there has been a movement to revive traditional city design for suburban planned communities. Some of its proponents, banded together as the Congress for the New Urbanism, founded in 1993, have also been advocates of a return to traditional classical architecture. What is new about the new urbanism is the idea that cities took a wrong turn when modernist city-design concepts became dominant: New Urbanism is actually a slogan for going back to a past where city design is perceived to have worked better. The principles of new urbanism don't require classical architecture, but it is an easy way to follow them. Traditional classical architecture is anathema in most schools of architecture and also for most architecture critics. This esoteric architectural debate spilled over, sometimes in surprisingly vituperative language, into the published criticism and discussions of rebuilding the World Trade Center site and helped paralyze decision-making.

Another aspect of traditional city design was its compactness, as much of daily life before automobiles took place on foot. Sprawling urban development has created a new interest in compact, walkable business centers and neighborhoods, which can be supported by new transit and high-speed rail initiatives that can counteract uncontrolled urban growth. The search for compact and walkable urban forms has caused designers to look back at traditional city-design principles, without needing to use classical design for the buildings. This approach will be discussed in Chapter 2.

The green argument against modernist city design

While orienting buildings for optimal exposure to light and air has always been a fundamental part of modernist planning doctrine, the modernist method of dealing with the natural environment has been to subdue nature through engineering. Sites can be bulldozed to make them level, wetlands can be filled in, and streams that are in the way of development can be rechanneled into underground culverts. Such uses for technology were challenged by Ian McHarg in his manifesto *Design with Nature*,[10] first published in 1969, in which he pointed out that failure to work within the constraints of natural systems invited retribution: landslides, floods, subsidence of buildings. McHarg's book helped reinforce earlier ideas about garden cities and suburbs, preserving the natural environment through green belts, and site designs that worked with the natural contours of the land. More recently, as the natural environment has proved to be a much more dynamic system than even McHarg had envisioned, designing within the constraints of natural systems has become understood as essential for sustainability, both for slowing down or stopping climate change and for adapting to the new situations climate change produces. The United States Green Building Council is a private organization, which, since its founding in 1994, has quickly grown to have international influence through its certification system for professionals and projects, the Leadership in Energy and Environmental Design (LEED) program. The initial emphasis of the LEED program has been on improving the energy efficiency of individual buildings, but it has begun to turn its attention to larger-scale development by issuing standards for neighborhood design. This move is likely to be followed by standards that embody some of the green city-design principles discussed in Chapter 3.

The search for more systematic urbanism

The big problem in implementing all city designs is the relationship between the original city designer and the people carrying out the component parts of the design, who may not set to work until many years after the completion of the original concept, and could be following different design philosophies and operating under changed economic circumstances. City design requires a control system that is strong enough to preserve the original concept and flexible enough to be adaptable as situations change. One of the first such systems was a statutory relationship between street width and the height of buildings that has been in force in Paris since the eighteenth century. During the reconstruction of Paris that began in the 1850s, this system was elaborated to include facade controls that produced the congruity of buildings along the great boulevards still admired in Paris today. A version of the Parisian system was used to guide development in Boston's Back Bay, and the relationship between building heights and street widths was built into New York City's first zoning code, adopted in 1916, and from there has influenced many other codes. Zoning itself can be considered a primitive form of systems city design, as it is consistent in a variety of situations that influence the form of the city, although only in a general way. During the 1960s there was a worldwide interest in developing megastructural and mechanical systems that could be extended to whole cities and regions. While they proved impractical as city design, these kinds of building systems continue to influence the design of airport terminals, shopping centers, and multi-use urban centers. More recently research into computer-aided pre-formative design, in which systems are developed which in turn create building and city designs, has outlined a promising area of research, although still a long way from implementation. Systems city design is explored in Chapter 4.

Chapter 5, the concluding chapter, addresses how city design can meet the challenges of modern urbanization, and help create sustainable cities. It also suggests a way of looking at city design that accepts the existence of a wide range of design theories.

Modernist city design as first defined by a small group of architects in the 1920s continues to be the default position for city design around the world. The big new cities that have grown up within the last generation, like Shenzhen in China and Dubai, Qatar, and Abu Dhabi in the Emirates, are almost entirely designed according to modernist principles. Modernism has to be the reference point for considering the future shape of cities, and this is where we begin.

1 Modernist city design

The architects who created modernist city design more than eighty years ago believed, like other artists at the time, that to be modern requires a revolution against the past.[1] They saw their revolution creating a collective society where everyone would have housing that meets minimum standards for sanitation, light, and air. The poor would move out of crowded basements, attics, and airless courtyards and join the rest of the social order in blocks of apartments surrounded by green space. New technology—that is, the technology that was new in the 1920s—inevitably would reshape the whole city. Most of the older urban areas would need to be swept away to eliminate slums, open up wide new streets and highways for automobiles, and create green space. Factories should move out into special industrial districts and office workers cluster in downtown towers. New buildings were to be shaped by steel frames and wide expanses of glass. Modernism in city design is as determinist as Marxism in assuming that past history is a dustbin and future history will prove it to be inevitable.

Much of this modernist revolution has now happened. Anywhere you see rows of apartment towers surrounded by green space, or by parking lots, you are seeing modernist city design. Where highways are the main means of travel, with wide and widely separated streets designed for speedy traffic not pedestrians, or where tall office buildings are grouped on a paved platform: this is city design according to modernist principles. Modernism had a formative influence on post-World War II reconstruction in Europe, the former Soviet Union, and Japan. In English-speaking countries, the influence of modernist city design is seen most often in planned housing developments for low-income people, in the design of downtown urban renewal, and in new urban centers on the edge of metropolitan areas, but it has also had a pervasive influence on highway and street planning. Today the official plan for every city in China embodies these design ideas. You see them in Korea in planned new communities, in Thailand, Singapore, and now in Vietnam. Until recently this kind of city design continued to be the norm everywhere in the former Soviet Union, and in the countries within the Soviet sphere of influence in Eastern Europe. You can see it in Scandinavia, Central and South America, Africa, Indochina, India, and the Middle East.

Yesterday's revolutionaries, seeking the antidote to urban slums, did not foresee that modern technology would help transform so many of the working-class masses into members of the middle class. The modernist city with its streets designed for fast traffic and open spaces planned as large parks is still intended for people who toil long hours, six days a week, in factories or offices, with the other day left free for a big meal, and a family stroll in the green spaces the planners would provide. City dwellers are assumed to have little discretionary time or income for shopping and entertainment, only the most basic education, few cultural interests, and not much energy left over for sports. Nor do you see any provision for religion in modernist city designs. The architects and planners who devised the modernist city understood that they themselves would continue to have dinner parties in their private houses or spacious apartments, would patronize restaurants, shops, and department stores, and spend evenings at movies, plays, and concerts. They would travel on vacation and spend their weekends at country houses. It just did not occur to them to plan for many other people to enjoy this way of life.

Modernist city design was formulated primarily by the Congrès Internationaux d'Architecture Moderne, or CIAM, a series of conferences founded in Switzerland in 1928 by a small coalition of modernist European architects. It was publicized by an even smaller group of architectural historians, journalists, and educators. Two of its principal organizers were Le Corbusier, the name adopted by a Swiss-born architect practicing in Paris (his original name was Charles-Edouard Jeanneret-Gris), and Sigfried Giedion, a professor of art history in Zurich. Le Corbusier was the most forceful proponent of modernist design in the group, and Giedion, as the Secretary General, organized the meetings, imparted coherence to the published proceedings, and wrote influential books portraying his CIAM colleagues as participants in a new historical direction, while leaving out other developments that didn't fit.

The CIAM was intended to redefine the expectations for official architecture and city design all over the world. Traditional urbanists were not invited to participate, and modernists whose work was considered too expressionistic or individualistic were also excluded.[2] Accounts of the conferences reveal that there were still clashes of personalities, splits along geographic and linguistic lines, disagreements and dissension from what were later to be seen as CIAM positions, and a general naïveté about how both government and private investment decisions are made, but in the end the CIAM has to be considered to have had an astonishing success.

The technical, social, and economic forces that have spread modernist city design around the world were much more powerful than the small group of architects and planners that made up the CIAM, but these people had a sense of mission.

They recognized the trends early and they worked hard to shape them in ways that could be easily replicated. They knew that the group of government officials, influential journalists, professors, and practitioners they needed to reach was relatively small and they found ways to reach them. They circulated exhibitions; they published proceedings, reports, and studies. It is remarkable how much current development continues to parallel concepts advocated in CIAM publications written by Le Corbusier, Giedion, and later by Harvard architecture professor, Jose Sert, although the CIAM had lost its sense of certainty after World War II and had ceased to exist by 1960. Government officials, real-estate developers, practitioners, and many professors of architecture and planning still act as if modernist city design is the obvious choice, although the original ideas about revolutionary mass housing and collectivist planning set forth at CIAM conferences, if they hadn't long been forgotten, would be seen today as no longer relevant in many parts of the world, and not the best answer for the people who need improved living conditions.

Developments leading to the CIAM

The CIAM was part of a campaign for a modern architecture that became effective in the 1920s but has origins earlier. Some historians find the first impulses towards modern architecture in the mid-eighteenth century, when the industrial revolution began and traditional ideas were challenged by new rational and scientific principles. Others trace a genealogy of building and structural innovation through the nineteenth century including the use of steel frames and large sheets of glass. Some historians see the buildings of US architect Frank Lloyd Wright in the years before World War I as the foundations for modern architecture in the 1920s; others give primacy to innovations in Europe.[3] An early attempt to devise what would in retrospect be considered a modernist city was the Cité Industrielle, by Tony Garnier, a Frenchman who won the Grand Prix de Rome in 1899, and used his time at the Villa Medici to develop a theoretical project for a factory complex and workers' housing rather than studying Roman ruins. The drawings were first exhibited in 1901 and Garnier continued to add to them until the project was published in 1917 (Figure 1.1). Garnier designed his buildings to be constructed of reinforced concrete and left out almost all traditional ornament derived from historical forms, particularly in the designs for housing the factory workers. Garnier's project is also related to the model factory towns that are part of the development of garden cities, discussed in Chapter 3. Garnier, who in the 1920s was an architect in Lyon, was invited to the first CIAM meeting but did not attend.[4]

One impetus towards the creation of the CIAM was the outcome of the 1927 competition to design the League of Nations headquarters in Geneva. The winning design was a traditional symmetrical and palatial building faced in stone, but several members of the selection committee had favored the entry by Le Corbusier and his cousin Pierre Jeanneret proposing an unsymmetrical building complex that expressed

its construction of steel, concrete, and glass and would have been the largest and most prominent example of this new approach to architecture, had it been selected. There were other modernist entries, including proposals by Richard Neutra and Hannes Meyer. Among the founders of the CIAM there was a fleeting hope that the result of the League of Nations competition could be reversed, and a determination that big government design decisions would have a different outcome in the future.

The highway and the free-standing tower are central components of modernist city design. They replace the traditional building and street relationship, derided by modernists as the *rue corridor*, with its frequent intersections and relatively low buildings constructed parallel to front property lines. Instead, blocks must be large, so that traffic has to stop at the minimum number of intersections, and buildings should leave as much open space as possible and need not follow the geometry of the streets. This prophetic sketch of tall towers along an elevated highway (Figure 1.2) was made by Le Corbusier in 1922 as part of his polemical exhibit, La Ville Contemporaine. At the time tall buildings were always part of existing city blocks. No limited access highways existed in 1922 either. Le Corbusier is imagining them by analogy to railways. Le Corbusier drew his towers all the same height and shape, which gives his city design a coherence that has seldom been achieved when the cities of towers he helped inspire were actually built. The developers and architects of the American skyscrapers that Le Corbusier admired were competing to create the tallest and most distinctive buildings. Buildings along highways today are likely to be highly competitive in their design, but the lack of sidewalks and pedestrians is just as foreseen by Le Corbusier.

Le Corbusier exhibited another set of city designs in 1925 (Figure 1.3) which shows central Paris entirely demolished and replaced by uniform towers organized

1.2
Le Corbusier's prophetic 1922 drawing of sixty-story office towers along an elevated highway. At the time no such buildings or highways existed anywhere.

Modernist city design

1.3
Le Corbusier's famous 1925 proposal to replace the center of Paris with tall towers grouped along an express highway. A few historical buildings like the Louvre and Notre Dame would be permitted to remain.

along a highway. Notre Dame, the Louvre, and a few other buildings are described as preserved for what Le Corbusier called sentimental reasons. This drawing demonstrates clearly that modernist city design assumes that existing cities are unsanitary, poorly organized, and impossibly congested and should be demolished and replaced. While central Paris is still much as it was in 1925, this drawing predicts what was to happen to many urban centers in the furtherance of modernism, including making the highway interchange the central urban experience. Le Corbusier published his concepts of city design under the title *Urbanisme* in 1925. This book was translated by Frederick Etchells and published in London in 1927 as *The City of Tomorrow and Its Planning*.[5] It was also published in German in 1929.

The buildings that appear in Le Corbusier's drawings of future cities follow principles of modern architecture, which he helped to invent. A defining characteristic of modernity is that the building should not look as if it were built during an earlier historical period. Le Corbusier tried to demonstrate architectural principles that transcend traditional design in his book *Vers une Architecture* of 1923, also translated by Etchells as *Towards a New Architecture* and also first published in English in 1927. A German translation had already appeared in 1926. Le Corbusier exhorted architects to think in terms of mass, surface, and planes, and illustrated how these abstract qualities inform designs for such modern constructions as grain elevators and factories, as well as locomotives, automobiles, and ocean liners. While he wasn't saying that buildings should have windows like factories, or that stairs and balconies should have railings like steam ships, this was the way his gallery of images tended to influence other architects. Le Corbusier was not immune from these influences himself. He also analyzed the proportional systems that informed the design of some famous historical buildings, saying that the proportions could be followed without their original architecture.

However, the most important design principle of modern architecture is to separate enclosure and support. The demand for bigger and taller buildings in congested nineteenth-century cities, particularly in New York and Chicago, had led to the development of steel and steel-reinforced concrete frames to transcend the limits of traditional construction. The steel "skeleton" permits heights far taller than the tallest masonry cathedrals or church towers, and also can create open interiors, interrupted only by columns, where partitions can be placed as needed rather than as required for structural support. The exterior can become a weatherproof skin held in place by the building's supporting frame, which means that windows can be continuous—in contrast to the limited window openings in a wall which is part of the supporting structure for the building. Architects of tall buildings before the 1920s usually hid their new construction techniques behind masonry walls that—while they were really held in place by the frame—looked traditional. The modernist architect sought to express the new structural freedom, although steel still had to be encased by masonry because it was otherwise vulnerable to fire.

1.4
Le Corbusier's diagram of the separation of enclosure and support in buildings that have a modern column and floor slab structure. The exterior walls, no longer supporting the building, can become "curtains" of lightweight materials, including large sheets of glass.

In the margin of *Vers une Architecture* (Figure 1.4) is a sketch for what Le Corbusier called a "domino" house, that is a house or apartment that could be a unit of mass production. Prefabrication follows from the separation of enclosure and support. The steel columns and beams come to the building site as component parts that have been manufactured in a steel mill. It was logical to assert that other major building components could be made in factories and delivered to the site as well, although more than eighty years later prefabrication mostly supplements traditional building rather than replacing it. When the separation of structure and support became modernist doctrine, the design ideas derived from it were also applied to individual houses and other small buildings where the building was not prefabricated and where traditional construction was the most practical alternative, The flat roof follows logically from the separation of enclosure and support, as a frame structure only requires a roof which is similar to the intermediate floors. Only a long-span structure, like an arena or an auditorium, requires a different kind of roof. However, flat or nearly flat roofs are more vulnerable to leaks than a pitched roof which sheds rain and snow.

Le Corbusier sometimes added two other elements derived from his ideas about city design to his version of modernist architecture: Omit the ground floor enclosure, so that only the structural supports and the entrance to the building prevent open space from continuing underneath the building, and use the roof to replace the land lost to the building footprint.

Other origins of modernist city-design principles

Most early modernist buildings were either houses for wealthy patrons or government-sponsored low-income housing. While social housing was built in many European countries after World War I, German government agencies during the 1920s made an exceptional commitment to building subsidized housing for low-income tenants. Most of it was in conventional cottage styles, but some of it was more experimental, employing large windows, flat roofs, and leaving out all historical ornament. The Weissenhof housing project atop a prominent hill in Stuttgart, completed in 1927 as part of a much larger development of pitched-roof, cottage-style housing, was built as a demonstration of modernist architecture and as a set of prototypes ostensibly intended for low-income tenants. Ludwig Mies van der Rohe, one of the important figures in the formulation of modern architecture, was the architect in charge, and mostly got his way in the selection of the other architects. The majority were German; but Mies was able to include such important modernists from other countries as Le Corbusier who lived in Paris but was Swiss, and J.J.P. Oud from the Netherlands. He also left out many well-known German architects who in his view were not modernist enough, as well as prominent German modernist Eric Mendelsohn, and all the government architects, such as Ernst May, the city architect of Frankfurt, who were actually building workers' housing at the time. Mies assigned the sites and programs to the participating architects,[6] awarding himself the largest building and the most visible location, where he demonstrated the

1.5
The original study model for the Weissenhof housing project shows a conceptual organization that resembles a Mediterranean hilltop town.

principle of the separation of enclosure and support by providing open-plan apartments that could be subdivided in different ways.

Mies's interest in building was much stronger than his interest in city design. While Weissenhof demonstrated that a group of architects could work together using a similar set of objective forms with flat roofs, plain wall surfaces, and large areas of glass, it also revealed a lack of any organizing city-design principle. Mies's original study model (Figure 1.5), which was probably developed with Hugo Haring who at the time shared office space with Mies and who was interested in naturalistic and expressionistic forms, shows a vague resemblance to an Italian or Provençal hill town. However, as built, Weissenhof is simply a collection of individual structures on separate building lots along rectangular connecting streets (Figure 1.6). Haring had originally been included as an architect but was dropped by Mies after a dispute about control, which may have included the overall plan. Sigfried Giedion excused the result by explaining that the original site design "unfortunately could not be realized for commercial reasons."[7]

During the 1920s Mies also prepared architectural projects which have become famous for illustrating the design potentials of modern technology, but also reveal the modernist assumption that the existing city could be disregarded, as it soon would be replaced. The photomontage of Mies's project of 1927 for a bank building in Stuttgart shows a simple glass wall that was actually far in advance of the technology that would have been needed to build it (Figure 1.7). While the architectural concept may have been inspiring, the montage anticipates the all too familiar picture of a modernist building completely unrelated to the existing city context. The stone walls of the building in the foreground belong to the railway station designed by Paul Bonatz, which had just been completed when the photomontage

1.6
Weissenhof as built relies for continuity on a shared vocabulary of flat roofs and planar walls, which turned out to be insufficient to create a successful city design.

was made. Bonatz was only nine years older than Mies, but the railway station is clearly portrayed as part of a past that can be disregarded. The transparent design by Mies for the Adam Building in the Leipzigerstrasse in Berlin, designed in 1928, (Figure 1.8) is also far ahead of the actual building technology of the time, and again totally unconnected to the surrounding city.

The most significant organizing principle that developed out of the more experimental German housing projects in the 1920s was uniform orientation of buildings in widely spaced parallel rows. This design strategy was a corrective to the dismal courtyard housing where most poor people lived in German cities. Sometimes the parallel rows were placed for optimal orientation of the apartments, but often they derived from the geometry of the surrounding streets. Modernist ideas about separating pedestrians from traffic and creating widely spaced streets left the placement of the buildings as the dominant feature of city design. Otto Haesler's housing development at Kassel-Rothenberg from 1930 to 1932 (Figure 1.9) takes an objective criterion—optimal orientation—to the point of regimentation. Almost all the walk-up residential buildings face the same way. In keeping with modernist concepts about the separation of people from traffic, all the buildings are reached by footpaths. Of course, low-income tenants in 1930 were not expected to own automobiles.

Richard Neutra, an Austrian architect who had worked briefly for Eric Mendelsohn, moved to the United States in 1923 where he worked in a Chicago office, Holabird and Roche, on the construction of actual tall buildings, and then worked for a short time for Frank Lloyd Wright. Neutra then moved to Los Angeles where he designed a famous early-modernist house with a steel frame and large areas of glass for Dr. Philip Lovell, completed in 1929. Neutra also worked on a series of theoretical plans for cities that he called Rush City Reformed. He included fragments of his designs for a city of parallel rows of slab-like buildings with elevated pedestrian walkways and highways for fast-moving cars in his *Wie Baut Amerika?* (Figure 1.10), which was otherwise mostly about American building methods, with much space devoted to construction photos of the Palmer House Hotel in Chicago, which Neutra had worked on for Holabird and Roche. *Wie Baut Amerika?* was published in Germany in 1927 in a relatively large edition for an architectural book, 4,400 copies, and it received considerable attention among architects.[8] It is not clear who influenced who in imagining cities and housing projects of parallel linear buildings, but these ideas were current among the architects who came together in the CIAM. Neutra was invited to the first and second CIAM meetings but did not attend until the third, where his Rush City drawings were on exhibit.

German architect Ludwig Hilberseimer produced during the 1920s amazingly reductionist architectural projects that looked as if they were drawings of the concrete frames of buildings still under construction. He also applied similar thinking to reducing cities to their essentials, publishing a book about city planning, *Gross Stadt Architektur*, in 1927. Hilberseimer was also interested in parallel rows of buildings as the basis for city design, as shown in this 1927 drawing of a highly abstract urban

1.7
1927 photo montage by Ludwig Mies van der Rohe illustrating a proposed bank building in Stuttgart and the now all-too familiar problem of a new building designed without reference to its existing context.

1.8
This 1928 project by Mies which was far ahead of the building technology of the time, but also totally unconnected to the surrounding city.

1.9
The site plan for Otto Haesler's housing development at Kassel-Rothenberg from 1930 to 1932 shows the modernist propensity to treat the site as a picture plane and the layout of buildings as an abstract composition.

Modernist city design

1.10
Richard Neutra: *Rush City Transformed*, as published in his book, *Wie Baut Amerika?*, in Germany in 1927.

1.11
Ludwig Hilberseimer's proposal for a generic east–west urban street from a book he published in 1927. An impersonal and abstract urban environment is seen as the ideal for a modernist city.

1.12
Walter Gropius and collaborators, the Bauhaus in Dessau, shown soon after its completion, probably in 1926.

environment that makes no allowances for personal choices or even the identification of an individual business (Figure 1.11).[9]

The second CIAM meeting was devoted to the design of the smallest livable housing units and took place in Frankfurt in October 1929 at the invitation of the city architect, Ernst May, who was in the process of designing and building extensive low-income suburbs for Frankfurt where simple two- and three-story modernist buildings were organized largely on the garden-city principles considered in more detail in Chapter 3. The CIAM meeting happened to start on the same day the New York stock market crashed, beginning the worldwide economic depression that would bring down Germany's Weimar government and open the way to Adolph Hitler's dictatorship. The first day of the conference included a presentation by German architect Walter Gropius advocating high-rise buildings as housing for all families, including low-income ones:

> The large high-rise apartment building will have the biologically important advantages of more sun and light, larger distances between neighboring buildings, and the possibility of providing extensive connected parks and play areas between the blocks . . . [it is the] building type of the future for large residential populations.[10]

At the time the few existing apartment towers were all designed for people with discretionary income who could afford the costs of the large staffs needed to manage such buildings. Le Corbusier's polemical designs for towers were meant to be workplaces like American skyscrapers. The residential buildings in his city designs were mid-rise apartment hotels for the professional class and row houses for workers. None of the many low-income German housing projects developed after World War I had elevators. Ernst May and many others at the conference were strongly opposed to high-rise housing for the poor, but it would ultimately become part of the CIAM legacy, and the cause of many urban problems.

Gropius was a significant managerial figure in the development of modern architecture. He had become known just before World War I when he and Adolph Meyer had designed a factory administration building and an exhibition building, both making use of glass walls suspended from the supporting structure. In 1919 Gropius had become the head of an arts and crafts school in Weimar, renamed the Bauhaus, which he turned into an important center for the development of modern art and industrial design. Gropius moved the school to Dessau in 1925 and the buildings his office designed for the school were an opportunity to display modernist architectural ideas (Figure 1.12), although architecture was not taught at the Bauhaus until 1927 when Gropius brought the Swiss architect Hannes Meyer to Dessau to start an architecture program. At the time of his participation in the second CIAM conference Gropius had resigned as director of the Bauhaus after disputes with Dessau city officials, turned over the administration of the Bauhaus to Meyer, and moved to Berlin. Gropius was to provide crucial support for CIAM activities after he was appointed a professor of architecture at Harvard in 1937, and department chair in 1938. He brought Sigfried Giedion to Harvard in 1938 where Giedion delivered the lectures that became *Space, Time and Architecture*, first published by the Harvard University Press in 1941. Giedion set modern architecture and planning within a CIAM perspective as the culmination of progressive movements in art and technology, and his book was a standard text for many years. It has taken other scholars many more years to separate the partisanship and propaganda in this work from its considerable contributions to the histories of both architectural technology and city planning. Giedion helped elevate Gropius's stature as an architect by downplaying the importance of Gropius's many partners and collaborators. Gropius also let it be understood that he was a refuge from Nazi Germany. In fact Gropius worked hard to maintain an architectural practice under the Nazi regime, hoping that modernism would be accepted as a national architecture as it had been in Fascist Italy, but Hitler accepted modernism only for industrial buildings. Even after Gropius moved to England in 1934, he traveled back and forth to Germany several times. He cleared taking the job at Harvard with Joseph Goebbels' Ministry of Propaganda, explaining that "I . . . see my mission at Harvard as serving German culture."[11]

Hannes Meyer directed the Bauhaus from Gropius's departure until 1930, shifting its direction from art and industrial design towards architecture and planning. He hired Ludwig Hilberseimer in 1929 to teach city planning. In 1930 Meyer, who was certainly far left in his politics and was probably a communist party member, was forced out of the Bauhaus by Dessau officials and moved to the Soviet Union under the mistaken impression that Stalin would continue to be tolerant of modernism. Ernst May and other left-wing modernist architects also went to the Soviet Union around this time. Ludwig Mies van der Rohe became the director of the Bauhaus and continued until the Dessau City Council was taken over by the Nazis in 1932. Mies tried to keep the Bauhaus going as a private architecture school in Berlin but was soon forced to close by the Nazi regime.[12]

Rationalizing the design of the whole modern city was the subject of the third CIAM conference which took place in Brussels in November, 1930 at the invitation of Victor Bourgeois, designer of La Cité Moderne in Brussels, whose plain buildings and flat roofs may well have made it the first overtly modernist housing district when it was completed in 1922.

Le Corbusier's designs for La Ville Radieuse were displayed and presented at this conference. In 1929 he had made a lecture tour of South America and had sketched plans for transforming Rio de Janeiro, São Paulo, Montevideo, and Buenos Aires. Earlier in 1930 he had also made a trip to Moscow, had seen plans submitted in a competition for a decentralized garden city, and at the request of the competition organizers had made comments on them. His ideas about cities had continued to evolve from his initial Ville Contemporaine of 1922, a symmetrical city with tall office buildings in the center, surrounded by residential districts and then a green belt, with the houses of workers and industry located outside the green belt and beyond the drawing. In La Ville Radieuse the cross-shaped office towers are clustered at the top of the drawing rather like the head of a human figure. There is a central park-like spine filled with public buildings, with residential districts for all social classes on either side. The workers now live in the central city, not out beyond the green belt. Instead parks are used to separate each component of the city. Industrial buildings form the legs and feet. Analogies to the human figure were explicitly made by Le Corbusier when he published his designs for La Ville Radieuse, in 1935 (Figure 1.13).

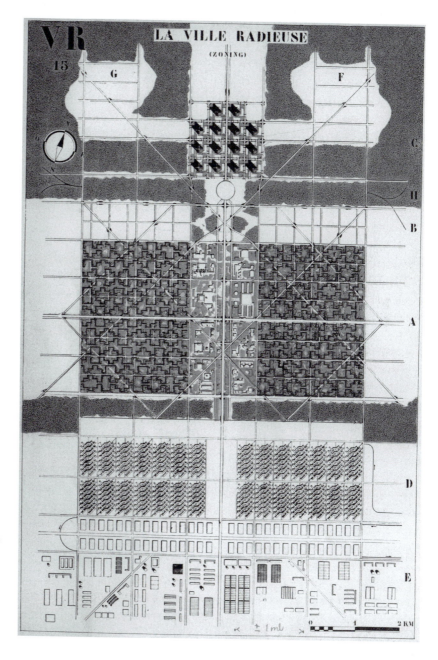

1.13
Le Corbusier reformulated his plan for an ideal city in his *La Ville Radieuse* published in 1935. He compared this diagram to a human figure, with office buildings for a head, a residential body, and industrial legs and feet.

Modernist city design

The proceedings also included another presentation by Walter Gropius advocating tall buildings for housing, as opposed to contemporary German standards for housing which favored individual houses, and limited most apartments to three stories, with no more than four in the largest cities. The diagrams (Figure 1.14) he presented document his thesis that high-rise buildings provide more access to sunlight and air and can "deconcentrate" the city without "dissolving" it, which he observes is the result of relying on individual houses. The walk-up apartment offers "neither the advantages of the house nor those of high-rise apartments." This argument, a direct challenge to the achievements of German three- and four-story social housing during the Weimar Republic, would eventually be widely accepted, as seen in the building regulations mandating exposure to sunlight in force in many cities today, particularly in Asia. Gropius's advocacy was based entirely on the physical advantages of living in towers, without any analysis of the social and managerial needs created by high-rise living.[13] Gropius was writing at a time when the household shopping for people of his social class was done by servants. Perhaps this is why it did not occur to him that when you walked out of a building you needed more than open space for a pleasant stroll or access from your garage to the highway. Interestingly, he saw no reason to revise this presentation when it was republished in 1956.

1.14
Diagrams by Walter Gropius illustrating advantages of tall residential buildings. Making light and air a dominant criterion for city design continues to be influential, particularly in China, Korea, and Japan.

Modern architecture, but not city design, displayed in the United States

Modern architecture was first promoted in the United States in 1932 by the *Modern Architecture International Exhibition* at the newly formed Museum of Modern Art. The curators were Henry-Russell Hitchcock who was then 29 and Philip Johnson who was 25, working for the first director, Alfred Barr, who was only 30 himself. Hitchcock had already published a book, *Modern Architecture: Romanticism and Reintegration,* where he argued that modernist buildings by Le Corbusier, Mies, and J.J.P. Oud represented the reintegration of architecture into a coherent relationship between design and construction, following a confused period of romanticism marked by the decoration of buildings with ornament derived from earlier historical periods. Philip Johnson met Alfred Barr, who had been teaching at Wellesley College, when Johnson attended his sister's graduation ceremony. Barr persuaded Johnson to make a tour of modern European architecture including the Weissenhof housing during the summer of 1929, before he had finished his undergraduate degree at Harvard. The next winter Barr introduced Johnson to Hitchcock, and the two of them made a tour of new European architecture in the summer of 1930, which led to the book that was to become *The International Style.* Over the next winter the idea of an exhibition of modern architecture took shape and Hitchcock and Johnson went back to gather more information and meet with architects during the summer of 1931.[14]

Somehow these young enthusiasts managed to miss the origins of modernist city design, which was almost entirely left out of their exhibition and book.

The first CIAM meeting in 1928 had been mostly about organization, and the second and third meetings were not until the fall in 1929 and 1930. Hitchcock, an architectural historian, was more interested in built examples that he could classify, and, as a believer in the theory of style, may well have thought that architectural coherence would by itself solve the problems of city design. Johnson was easily bored and discussions about the optimal spacing of buildings and the best block sizes to accommodate traffic would have had little interest for him.

Instead of introducing modern architecture as a means of creating modern cities, Hitchcock and Johnson concentrated on Hitchcock's thesis that these new buildings represented the redemption of architecture from a long period of stylistic promiscuity. In the introduction to their book, *The International Style* published by the Museum of Modern Art to accompany the exhibition, Alfred Barr wrote that the authors "have proven beyond any reasonable doubt, I believe, that there exists today a modern style as original, as consistent, as logical and as widely distributed as any in the past."[15] Hitchcock and Johnson themselves said in their opening chapter: "The idea of style, which began to degenerate when the revivals destroyed the disciplines of the Baroque, has become real and fertile again. Today a single new style has come into existence."[16]

The members of the Congrès Internationaux d'Architecture Moderne, if asked, would have preferred a title like *International Architecture,* which Gropius had already used for one of his books, or *Modern Architecture,* a title used by Bruno Taut for a book he published in England in 1929. Hitchcock and Johnson did not include any buildings by Bruno Taut, a modernist architect with significant completed buildings in Germany, perhaps because he had already published a comprehensive book on their subject three years earlier. Taut writes about a new architectural movement which he illustrates with buildings that have become familiar in subsequent histories of modern architecture. However, for Taut the guiding principles of modern architecture are efficiency, utility, and integration of construction with design; he dismisses style as inherently superficial.

The predictions of singularity and universality that would justify the use of the word "style" were never likely to be fulfilled. Even to make the prediction in 1932, the exhibition had to leave out almost all the modernist work that was being built at the time in Russia, much of the work of prominent German modernists Hans Scharoun and Erich Mendelsohn, and omit the anti-geometric theories of Hugo Haring. Frank Lloyd Wright was given a prominent position in the exhibition, but, to his justified annoyance, Wright was treated as the spiritual ancestor of the new modern style, rather than as a practitioner actively pursuing a different type of design.

The architects who were presented in both the exhibition and the book as leaders of the new style were already going in different directions by 1932. The curving fieldstone wall of a student hostel in Paris that was shown in the exhibition was a clue that Le Corbusier was starting down the road that would lead to his expressive chapel of Notre Dame du Haut at Ronchamp; J.J.P. Oud was to design buildings that we would now call Art Deco; Mies was increasingly influenced by the organizing principles of traditional, monumental architecture, as seen in the Seagram Building (designed, as it turned out, in collaboration with Philip Johnson). By the 1950s the firm headed by Walter Gropius was using neo-Islamic architectural forms and ornament in proposals for the University of Baghdad.

The exhibition and its catalogue were more inclusive than the book. The initial section of the catalogue is given to Frank Lloyd Wright and is equal to the sections given to Gropius, Le Corbusier, Oud, and Mies, and there are also comparable presentations for four additional American firms: Raymond Hood, Howe & Lescaze, Richard Neutra, and a young Chicago firm, the Bowman Brothers, scouted by Johnson to add more American architects to the exhibition, although the work shown was never built. In the book there are more examples of European buildings that met the authors' stylistic criteria: nothing by Wright and only a few examples of work by US architects. City design was acknowledged in the exhibition by a section on housing, introduced in the catalogue with an essay by Lewis Mumford. This part of the exhibition was organized by Mumford's protégé Catherine Bauer, who was to publish an important work, *Modern Housing*, in 1934. Clarence Stein and Henry Wright, designers of the Radburn planned community, also contributed to the housing section. We will come back to Stein and Wright in Chapter 3 for their work in developing the garden suburb. Johnson made sure that a model and drawings of Otto Haesler's housing at Kassel-Rothenberg with its linear parallel rows of uniform buildings dominated the housing section, and that the vaguely traditionalist architecture of Radburn was not on view, just the site plan. Le Corbusier's *Urbanisme* can be found in a bibliography within the catalogue although the drawings were not published and were not exhibited. One of Neutra's Rush City drawings is in the catalogue, but apparently was not in the exhibition.

There was little to show that modern architecture was being produced by people who were also concerned with the big issues of city design. The exhibition transformed work intended to revolutionize society into an attractive presentation of architectural innovations, which went on to circulate to thirteen other museums. The display of individual buildings as objects of connoisseurship at a fashionable museum has continued to influence the way modern architecture developed in the United States, leading to important repercussions worldwide as modernism in architecture has been redefined as the creation of unique works of art.

The CIAM Charter: manifesto for designing the modern city

Political turmoil in Europe postponed the fourth conference of the CIAM, The Functional City, until 1933. Cornelis van Eesteren, the head of the public works department in Amsterdam, had become the president of the CIAM in 1930 and much

1.15

Van Eesteren's 1934 plan for Amsterdam South replaced Berlage's traditional city design with superblocks and single-use zoning.

of the emphasis on functionalism as a way of understanding and planning the city came from him. His office was working on a new plan for the southern and western expansion of Amsterdam, completed in 1934, which superseded the more traditional 1902 plan by H.P. Berlage. Berlage's plan of corridor streets, squares, and axial relationships had become the setting for some of the best experimental architecture of the 1920s and 1930s, but van Eesteren incorporated what had already been built within a plan for highway corridors, rectangular superblocks, buildings in parallel rows, and the rigid separation of housing from industry and other uses (Figure 1.15).[17]

The fourth Congress, originally planned to be held in Moscow, ended up being held on a cruise ship sailing from Marseilles to Athens and back again. The participants used this meeting to write a manifesto about the design of the modern city, generally known as the Athens Charter, a name given to it by Le Corbusier. It begins with the prescient statement that city and region are becoming one unit. The four critical areas for planning were defined as dwelling, work, recreation, and transportation, with historic preservation grudgingly extended as a fifth category for "buildings or groups of buildings that are remnants of past cultures." Most people were expected to live in apartments, and tall buildings were to be used where there were high densities, in order to free the ground for recreation and permit the apartments to receive direct sunlight. Apartment buildings were to be grouped in neighborhoods, the size of the neighborhood determined by the catchment area for an elementary school—reflecting ideas put forward by Clarence Perry in the 1929 *Regional Plan for New York City*. Workplaces were to be located where they minimized transportation requirements but did not adversely affect neighborhoods. Streets would be sized according to their function, with highways for high-speed traffic at the top of the hierarchy. Parks would be regional in scale and were mapped so they would be in between other uses. The CIAM Charter describes a manufacturing city, very like Le Corbusier's Ville Radieuse, with its factory zone separated from the housing for the workers by ample parks, and with streets and highways for autos forming the main mode of transportation. The charter did not address the political, educational, and cultural functions of the city. Commerce was also not considered a functional element, with no definition of retail districts, or any expressed understanding that office buildings were not just workplaces, but also centers of exchange for commodities, financial instruments, and ideas. Later deliberations of the CIAM were to add the civic center as a functional element, to include office buildings, a concert hall, and possibly a museum. These buildings are shown as individual objects asymmetrically arranged on a raised platform.

The charter was not published in a widely circulated form until late 1942 when it appeared as *Can Our Cities Survive?, an ABC of urban problems, their analysis, their solutions, based on the proposals formulated by the CIAM*.[18] The book is by Jose Luis Sert, a CIAM member from Spain by then living in New York, and the CIAM is listed as Sert's co-author. The copyright is held by the CIAM. There is an introduction by Sigfried Giedion which makes sure the reader understands that it was he who invited the original group of CIAM participants to the initial meeting in 1928. There is also a foreword by Joseph Hudnut, then the dean of Harvard's School of Architecture, saying that he was a strong believer in the content of the book although: "It will be considered strange that I should find in a program for civic betterment . . . the basis for a new architecture . . ." This defensive statement indicates how thoroughly the understanding of modern architecture in the United States had been separated from its city-design context in Europe. Sert organized the book to amplify and illustrate the charter statements, which he calls The Chart, not a charter, with the exception of the section on historic preservation which he does not illustrate, explaining that it "was introduced by the Italian delegates who had to deal with these problems frequently." The text of the charter, or chart, is given as an appendix.

Another version of the charter was published in France by Le Corbusier, in 1943, during the Nazi occupation. Le Corbusier left his name off the first edition which is credited to CIAM France. The book has an introductory essay by novelist and playwright Jean Giradoux, who had been a career diplomat, minister of information in the last French government before the war, and was still in the Foreign Office. Publishing the charter was probably part of Le Corbusier's campaign to be recognized by the Vichy government as someone who should direct urban development. (Le Corbusier escaped being branded as a collaborator only because the occupation authorities were not interested in his efforts.) Anthony Eardley published an English translation of Le Corbusier's *Athens Charter* in 1973. The involvement of Giedion in Sert's book indicates that his is the official version, although Le Corbusier did correspond with Giedion when he was preparing his own publication, which has much explanatory rhetoric not present in the text Sert provides.[19]

Post Charter projects before World War II

Le Corbusier visited the United States in 1935, where he made his attention-getting remark to reporters about New York's skyscrapers: that there were too many of them and they were too small. As was his habit when he visited cities, Le Corbusier prepared his own sketch plan for Manhattan. His proposal was to tear most of it down, leaving only part of Central Park (indicated on the sketch by the letter P) and the Wall Street district (W), on the assumption, which he makes explicitly, that a smaller number of larger towers surrounded by open space would be more valuable than the existing buildings. (The R in the middle of the drawing may refer to Rockefeller Center, then under construction, although it is not drawn in and appears to be about twenty blocks too far north. While Rockefeller Center was composed of tall buildings, its street and block plan and traditional axial organization would not have been modern enough for Le Corbusier. (For a discussion of Rockefeller Center as traditional urbanism, see p. 91.) In his sketch, Le Corbusier replaced Manhattan's streets and avenues with much larger superblocks that would permit Y-shaped tall buildings, each with their own massive parking garage. "The pedestrians will have the freedom of parks over the whole ground area and the cars will travel from skyscraper to skyscraper at a hundred miles an hour on one-way elevated roads placed wide distances apart" (Figure 1.16).

The plan does not show Manhattan's train and subway system, which makes the skyscraper densities possible; and demolishing most of the existing buildings to create open space would cause unacceptable human and economic dislocation. Le Corbusier was well aware how destructive his ideas were. He called his 1930 sketch plan for Algiers an artillery shell that would shatter current concepts of the city. On the other hand, he had the audacity to make design proposals at a city-wide scale. There were few to compete with him; certainly such proposals were impossible for responsible public officials. Le Corbusier's little sketches and terse statements prefigure the way many real cities have developed. Assuming that old buildings are antiquated and should be replaced, separating tall buildings from each other within large open areas, and designing urban areas around high-speed roads and massive parking decks are all ideas that have gained wide acceptance.

Le Corbusier's 1937 plan for Buenos Aires leaves the existing city in place beneath a new network of widely spaced highways that divide it into sectors. Perhaps, on reflection, Le Corbusier had concluded that it wasn't necessary to remove all previous development. A new business center is shown constructed in the harbor, the whole waterfront is redeveloped, including a waterfront stadium, and some districts are shown as reconstructed with buildings on a new, much larger scale. All the ingredients of what was later to be called urban renewal are already present in this proposal (Figure 1.17).

During his New York visit, it would have been possible for Le Corbusier to have met Robert Moses, a powerful public official already well advanced in his career as a highway builder, and who later was to implement urban renewal on an almost Corbusian scale. Moses was an important figure in the design and construction for the New York World's Fair of 1939–1940, for which planning began in 1935. Moses and Le Corbusier could have looked out over New York together from the windows of the World's Fair offices high up in the Empire State Building, but there is no record that the two ever met.

The General Motors Pavilion at the Fair included a model of "The World of 1960," a hypothetical city designed by Norman Bel Geddes. Bel Geddes, originally a stage and lighting designer and best known for his industrial designs, had been considered for inclusion as an American modernist in the Museum of Modern Art's International Style Exhibition. Bel Geddes's model concentrates public open space in a great central park, like New York City, and like Le Corbusier's Ville Contemporaine of 1923, but unlike later CIAM and Corbusian formulations. His tall buildings are set in a context of smaller buildings, and are less diagrammatically organized than Le Corbusier's and more like what the private real-estate market would be likely to produce. Like Le Corbusier and the work of CIAM members such as Cornelis van

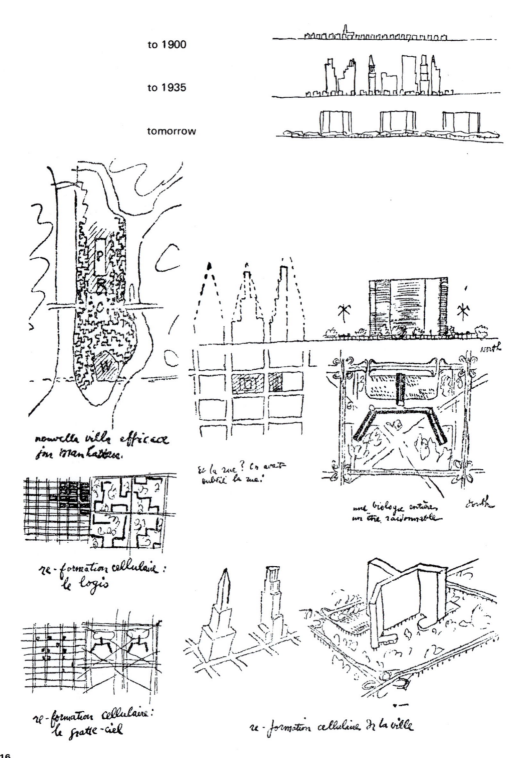

to 1900

to 1935

tomorrow

1.16

Le Corbusier's 1935 proposal for replanning Manhattan as a city of superblocks, tall buildings surrounded by green space, and high-speed streets. Le Corbusier could have met Robert Moses on this trip, but apparently did not.

1.17
Le Corbusier's 1937 plan for
Buenos Aires. All the
ingredients for post-World
War II urban renewal can be
found in this photomontage.

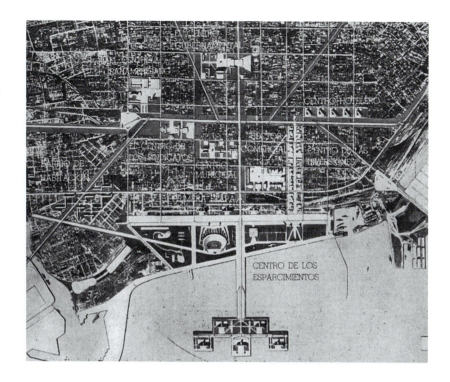

Eesteren, Bel Geddes shows the urban area divided into sectors by major highways, an idea that was central to the vision of the future that General Motors was promoting (Figure 1.18).

Parkchester is a development of fifty-one buildings with more than 12,000 apartments built by the Metropolitan Life Insurance Company on a mostly vacant 129-acre site in the New York borough of the Bronx between 1938 and 1942. A shopping district with 200 stores was also included. The architects were a board of design composed of several prominent New York City practitioners, including Richmond Shreve, the senior partner in the firm that had designed the Empire State Building, and landscape architect, Gilmore Clarke, a favorite of Robert Moses. Except for the shopping, Parkchester was all towers, ranging in height from seven to thirteen stories, one of the first and certainly the largest housing project in the United States to be designed as towers in parkland up to that time. The apartment buildings were arranged in four quadrants around a central traffic circle. While the plan was more picturesque in its arrangement than the parallel rows of low-rise buildings found in some Weimar housing, and favored by CIAM's president Cornelis van Eesteren, and also less geometric than Le Corbusier's office towers, it was clearly an application of the tower in the park for housing, as proposed by Gropius, but not yet built in Europe. Parkchester was rental housing for the middle class: the plan included garage parking for 4,000 cars and another 1,300 at-grade parking spaces at a time when many families did not yet own cars. Metropolitan did not permit African Americans to rent at Parkchester or any of their other projects.

Modernist city design   **31**

1.18
"The World of 1960," a model by Norman Bel Geddes displayed in the General Motors Pavilion at the 1939 New York World's Fair. Except for the regular separation of tall buildings, this was a remarkably accurate prediction of the decentralized city the automobile would help create.

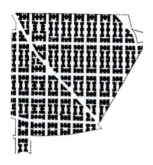

1.19 a and b
Comparison of the plan for tall buildings oriented for light and air and surrounded by open space at the Parkchester Development in the New York City's borough of the Bronx with typical development that would have been permitted by the zoning code at the time. The comparison is a little unfair as parks and open space can be created within a street and block system.

1.20
Williamsburg Houses in New York City, a slum-clearance project of the Public Works Administration designed in 1935 by an architectural team headed by Richmond Shreve that also included Arthur Holden and William Lescaze, who was a pioneer of modernist architecture in the United States. Note that the buildings are rotated away from the streets for optimal sun exposure.

The design required an exception from the street and block pattern that would have been required by a normal application of the New York City zoning code. The comparison of permitted development to the actual design is somewhat unfair, as it would have been possible to create a better traditional site plan within the code limits, but it is clear why towers in parkland were an appealing alternative[20] (Figure 1.19). Parkchester appeared to many people at the time to be the prototype for future development in the United States: large rental complexes built by institutional investors. In the next few years Metropolitan Life went on to build more tower-in-park rental projects, including Park La Brea in Los Angeles, Park Merced in San Francisco, and, after World War II, Stuyvesant Town and Peter Cooper Village, some of the first urban renewal projects in New York City, where Metropolitan's segregation policies first became an issue because public money had been used by Robert Moses to assemble the land. There were also many garden apartment projects built by institutional investors like Metropolitan, which we will come back to in Chapter 3. However, the huge increase in middle-class home ownership created by the Federal Housing Administration and the Veterans Administration, meant the end of projects like Parkchester for the middle class in the United States. Instead it became a prototype for subsidized low-income housing, a serious public policy mistake, as the tower in the park turned out to require a substantial management commitment that usually was not within the means of the public housing authorities.

The first subsidized housing units for low-income tenants built in the United States before World War II were almost always walk-up apartments like their social housing counterparts in Europe. An early example is the Williamsburg Houses in New York City, a slum-clearance project of the Public Works Administration designed in 1935 by an architectural team headed by Richmond Shreve that also included Arthur Holden and William Lescaze, who was a pioneer of modernist architecture in the United States (Figure 1.20). The buildings are rotated off the street grid by 15 degrees to optimize their orientation as favored by the CIAM. The result was to detach the buildings from the surrounding city. The combination of housing towers surrounded by open space and detached from the street system was to become a design formula after World War II.

A fifth CIAM Congress devoted to housing and recreation was held in Paris in 1937, but by that time the group was losing its cohesion. Many of the original German members had moved to the Soviet Union to escape the Nazis, and then, finding Stalin equally inhospitable to modernism, had dispersed to other countries. Some returned to Germany and were able to make the compromises needed to find architectural design work under the Nazis.[21] Gropius was in the United States, after first moving to England in 1934 and Mies had gone to Chicago in 1937 to head the architecture department at what was to become Illinois Institute of Technology.

English CIAM members had started their own organization, the MARS group. Ostensibly the initials stood for the Modern Architecture Research Group, but the S was never explained. The god of war was somewhere in the founders' minds, probably not the god of world war, but of factional contention within the CIAM. The MARS group's best-known product was a plan for the London metropolitan region that would have driven a great expressway through the city just to the north of the most historic central area. Business districts were to extend in an east–west corridor on either side of the historic center. Linear residential districts, each housing up to 600,000 people, and separated from each other by regional green belts, would be placed at right angles to the central development corridor and connected by a circular highway running around the perimeter of the metropolis. This diagram looks like vastly inflated cul-de-sacs from a garden-city neighborhood. The plan was completed in the early 1940s, while the bombing of London was going on, which might explain the willingness to write off most of the existing city. Ludwig Hilberseimer was pursuing similar ideas at this time. He had followed Ludwig Mies van der Rohe to Chicago to teach at IIT.[22] In 1944 Hilberseimer published a series of drawings showing corridors of parkland separating neighborhoods of housing laid out in rows which he accurately described as "the ruralization of the metropolis."[23] Such disregard for existing development patterns has meant that these demonstrations of CIAM theory applied to regional planning have had little influence.

The first implementation of modernist city design

World War II gave European countries an immediate need for reconstruction on an unprecedented scale. Pre-war cities had been overcrowded and congested; rebuilding was an opportunity to improve living conditions. The existence of modern technology made large-scale and tall buildings possible, while restoring older buildings using the handcrafts of a previous era seemed both too expensive and too time-consuming. The CIAM discourse had prepared architects and planners to conclude that reconstruction should be an opportunity to create modern cities, with far more open space at ground level, with highways reaching into the center, and with tall buildings for both offices and housing. Faith in this modern image of the city was strong despite the existence of few built examples, a response to the powerful images created by Le Corbusier, to the conferences, exhibitions and books organized by the CIAM, and to the version of modernism created in Sweden.

During World War II, neutral Sweden was one of the few places where building construction continued. After the war, when reconstruction was barely beginning in many European countries, the Swedes were creating a new business center for Stockholm and developing new planned suburbs, which became widely emulated models. Sven Markelius, one of the architects invited to the initial meeting of the CIAM, was the chief planner for Stockholm from 1944 to 1954. He directed the planning for the downtown Hotorget district in the 1940s. The Sergelgatan, the principal street in the area, became a pedestrian precinct running through a two-level shopping concourse. Along the concourse on one side was a series of five parallel office towers. Pedestrian bridges linked the roof terraces above the shopping. This combination of a shopping precinct, pedestrian bridges, and an orderly arrangement of office towers was to become an influential image (Figure 1.21).

Vallingby, a planned residential community and the town center for a cluster of other planned communities in suburban Stockholm, like the Hotorget, was designed by the Stockholm Planning Office in the 1940s. Vallingby was originally thought of as the heart of a self-sufficient garden city, but like later Stockholm satellite towns, it has developed essentially as a high-density garden suburb. The clusters of apartment towers average around twelve stories, and are sited informally as if they were clusters of smaller buildings. Vallingby's shopping and office district centers on a casually organized pedestrian precinct with circular fountains and playful light fixtures designed to recall trees. The architecture is equally informal, with a mixture of different surface materials and variations in height programmed to create the appearance of a village-like group of buildings that grew up over time. The architecture is modern in the sense that there is no applied ornament, and the design is derived from the expression of modern structural components. It is not heroic or futuristic: "sensible" is an adjective that readily comes to mind. In England's *Architectural Review* and other publications the critical category used for Swedish modernism was empiricism, with emphasis on the acceptability of Swedish design for ordinary people (Figure 1.22).

Official decisions about reconstruction in Great Britain had begun while the bombs were still falling; they included the comprehensive County of London Plan of 1943 by Patrick Abercrombie and J.H. Forshaw, and the Greater London Plan of 1944 by Abercrombie, neither of which had any resemblance to the work of the MARS group. The County of London Plan included concepts for rationalizing the railway system, a new series of concentric ring roads, and the recognition of London's traditional community structure, with a public open space and road plan being used to define and separate subdistricts of the city. The Greater London Plan included a proposal for a green belt around the county of London and the construction of a series of planned satellite communities beyond the green belt, a concept owing much to the model established by Ebenezer Howard. (For an extended discussion of Howard and his influence, see pp. 120–127.) Both plans included detailed designs for specific areas that, as in Swedish planning of the same period, combined the city-design ideas of interwar European housing precincts with the more informal layouts associated with garden-city plans (Figure 1.23a and 1.23b).

The rebuilding of central Coventry, the reconstruction of the East End of London, and the central shopping and office districts of the first English new towns all helped define the image of the modern city that emerged in the post-war period. Like the Swedish examples, they were sensible rather than monumental or charming.

The reconstruction of Rotterdam yielded another significant urban image: the Lijnbaan shopping precinct and the buildings associated with it. Designed by J.H.

1.21
The five parallel towers of the Hotorget district in Stockholm, which became a model for post-World War II reconstruction. There is a resemblance to Neutra's Rush City (Figure 1.10).

1.22

The center of Vallingby, a planned railroad suburb of Stockholm, a model for what was called in Britain "The New Empiricism," a modernist plan that was sufficiently un-doctrinaire to be an attractive place.

van den Broek and Jacob Bakema, the buildings are more geometrically controlled and more closely associated with the concepts promoted by CIAM than the Sergelgatan is; but there are strong analogies in the scale and character of the pedestrian precinct, and the way nearby tall buildings are set back at right angles to it (Figure 1.24).

How Le Corbusier might have treated a similar commission can be inferred from his 1945 proposal for the rebuilding of Saint-Die. This proposal was too dismissive of existing realities to be built, but it had a significant influence on other architects. A highway runs straight through the center of the city, forming a spine that connects all its elements. Large apartment blocks are set at right angles to the central highway and are surrounded by informal gardens. There is a civic center, a rectangular raised plaza with a single tall office tower, a museum, an auditorium, and other civic buildings, each a separate structure surrounded by open space, but carefully composed in a grouping that resembles abstract sculpture, or the arrangement of shapes in an abstract painting, with the plaza as the picture plane. The civic center is a significant addition as it does not fit into the CIAM's four functional categories, although it had long been recognized as a central element for traditional city plans. The organization of individual buildings, with the most important given individual significant forms and grouped on a raised plaza was to become a hallmark of post-World War II modernist design (Figure 1.25).

Le Corbusier, polemicist for the modern city, had only limited success in obtaining a significant role in actual post-war reconstruction. His major reconstruction commission was an apartment house in Marseilles which he called a Unite d'Habitation, by which he meant that the structure would be virtually a small city in itself (Figure 1.26). There was an internal shopping "street" about halfway up the

Modernist city design

1.23a and b
Patrick Abercrombie's 1944 plan for rebuilding London included designs influenced by the more empirical modernism being produced in neutral Sweden, which continued to have a peacetime economy during the war.

1.24
The Lijnbaan shopping
precinct and the buildings
associated with it
reconstructing a heavily
bombed section of central
Rotterdam, designed by J.H.
van den Broek and Jacob
Bakema.

1.25
Le Corbusier's 1945 proposal
for the rebuilding of Saint-Die.
It was not built, but it had a
strong influence on other
architects. The central
platform with civic buildings
designed as separate objects
is an addition to the
vocabulary of the modernist
city.

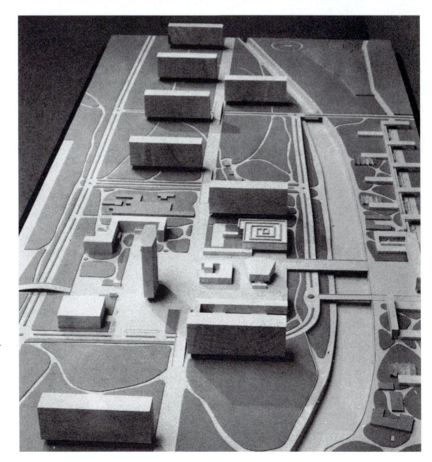

building and a theater, gymnasium, and nursery school with playground on the roof. The whole structure was raised several stories off the ground on massive supports, a Corbusian concept that permitted external space to continue under the building but also isolated it from its surroundings. Le Corbusier modified the half-dozen later buildings he designed on a similar pattern, omitting the shops. If the shops had been more conventionally located on the ground floor, they might have drawn customers from the neighborhood; but a single building was not a sufficiently large trading area to support them.

The Unite was designed as a prototype, but proved too expensive and idiosyncratic to become a universal government policy, although it had a major effect on British housing design, notably in the work of the architect's department of the London County Council. The character of many housing and planned communities in Great Britain changed. They became more geometrically abstract and tougher in design, with heavy use of exposed reinforced concrete in the Corbusian pattern.

In much of the post-war European reconstruction an image of a potential modern city coexists uneasily with the remaining old buildings. Gaps in street frontages are filled in with structures that have plain facades, large windows and, often, a studied asymmetry, but the older street patterns and building masses are retained. In newer districts, particularly in the socialist countries of Eastern Europe, the ideas advocated by the CIAM degenerated into a stereotyped formula for city design. There were two types of housing: four- or five-story walk-ups or eleven-to-thirteen-story elevator buildings. The buildings were usually placed at right angles to streets and separated from each other by a distance approximately equal to their height. The number of apartments in a housing complex would accommodate sufficient families to support an elementary school, an idea the CIAM had borrowed from Clarence Perry and the American garden-city movement. While the ingredients of the formula are rational, limiting city design in this way creates environments of unrelieved dullness, which came to be rejected by people who have any choice about where they live.

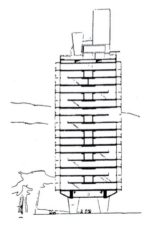

1.26
Section of Le Corbusier's Unite D'Habitation, an apartment house in Marseilles which included a hotel, a shopping arcade on an upper floor, and a nursery school on the roof. The split levels permit double-height living rooms, although the apartments are very narrow. The shops were moved upstairs so that open space could continue under the building, but the building is not big enough to support the shops and the shops are too isolated to attract outsiders.

Modernist city design in the United States after World War II

The United States emerged from World War II with a growing interest in modernizing cities to deal with traffic congestion and the deterioration that accumulated during the depression years. Although the United States had been spared bomb damage, the building clearance policies instituted in many American cities during the 1950s could produce a similar result. The Housing Act of 1949 greatly expanded publicly subsidized housing and provided Federal funds for buying and clearing "slum" properties. Following a series of court cases it became possible to use these Federal funds to assemble land, and even subsidize it, not to rehouse poor people expelled from areas found to be slums, but for market-rate housing and for office and retail buildings, a process which became known as urban renewal. All public housing and urban renewal projects that used Federal funds had to be approved in Washington, so they all met the same standards, set by government officials and academic and professional advisors. For public housing, building spacing and orientation requirements interacted with guidelines for the maximum amount of land-cost per unit to create taller and taller towers surrounded by green space on large tracts of formerly urban land.

Urban renewal reviews were more site-specific, but they tended to favor rectangular towers arranged on a plaza to form an abstract asymmetrical pattern. A plan that helped to define the image of desirable urban renewal was a proposal for railway yards in Boston's Back Bay, made in 1953 by a team of architects, headed by Walter Gropius, which included Pietro Belluschi, Carl Koch, Hugh Stubbins, and Walter Bogner. It bears a strong resemblance to Le Corbusier's plan for Saint-Die, but adapted for American conditions. As at Saint-Die, the central group of buildings is on a raised podium, is dominated by a single office tower designed as an elongated hexagon, and faces an auditorium with a distinctive exterior shape. Also like Saint-Die, the external spaces are created by large horizontal building masses. The principal differences are that within the podium is a garage for 5,000 cars, there is a large internal shopping center, and the scale of the external spaces is modulated by smaller, lower buildings, as at the Lijnbaan (Figure 1.27). The site ultimately became the Prudential Center, designed by Charles Luckman, which looked quite different, but had similar component parts. Another early urban renewal plan, Penn Center in Philadelphia, was built in place of the old "Chinese Wall" of railway tracks which divided the western portion of the city center. It did not follow the original 1952 design plan proposed by Edmund Bacon, the director of the City Planning Department, which set forth a series of three parallel office towers not unlike the

1.27
Model photo of a design for railyards in Boston made in 1953 by a team of architects, headed by Walter Gropius, which included Pietro Belluschi, Carl Koch, Hugh Stubbins, and Walter Bogner. This was the top winner in the first of the *Progressive Architecture* Design Awards. The platform with its widely spaced towers and a prominent object building is reminiscent of Le Corbusier's project for Saint-Die.

proposed **Back Bay Center** development
for Stevens Development Corporation

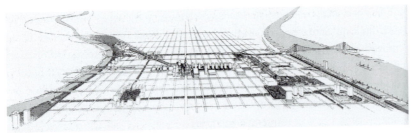

1.28
Illustration from the 1963 Plan for Center City Philadelphia: modernist towers, and, on the right, land cleared for parks around historic buildings.

arrangement of the Hotorget or the towers of the Lijnbaan. Bacon's plan also called for the demolition of City Hall, leaving only the tower, in order to connect West to East Market Street through the central square, showing a modernist disdain for historic buildings and the modernist priority for road connections. The development as built, although muddled and undistinguished, left City Hall intact. Penn Center's strong point is that it restored the City's block system and was not on a raised platform. Its pedestrian connections were underground on the model of Rockefeller Center, a more suitable solution than the modernist raised platform for pedestrians, as there is a subgrade transit system, so the pedestrians already have a reason to go down a level (Figure 1.28).

Constitution Plaza in Hartford was one of the first uses of Federal Title 1 funds for commercial urban renewal. Its site was created by demolishing the existing Front Street urban neighborhood. The project survived a court challenge in 1954, although substantial completion took another ten years. It followed the more familiar modernist formula of a raised platform with isolated tall buildings arranged on a pedestrian plaza (Figure 1.29).

Limited access highway design in urban areas was pioneered by Robert Moses in his multiple official roles in New York City and State, frequently implementing highway concepts laid out in the New York Regional Plan of 1929. Important links in the system were completed before World War II and many more were in progress by the 1950s.

After the passage of the Interstate Highway Act in 1956 a network of highways was begun to link all urban centers. Sometimes new highways were driven through the center of the city, as in Boston or Seattle; in other places, like Kansas City and Cincinnati, highways were planned to encircle the downtown business center. Victor Gruen was commissioned to develop a plan for downtown Fort Worth, published in 1957, as a result of an article he had written for the *Harvard Business Review* on the applicability of regional shopping center designs to the revitalization of existing downtowns. Gruen had already been the architect for two prototypical shopping centers: Northland in suburban Detroit, and Southdale in suburban Minneapolis. The Fort Worth plan suggested using the proposed expressway system to form a ring around the business center, rather than cut through it. Within the ring, parking garages would intercept traffic and streets within the entire central district would become pedestrian precincts—with no point less than a six-minute walk from one of the garages. The buildings downtown would be a mixture of existing structures

1.29
Constitution Plaza in Hartford, Connecticut, which replaced an older urban neighborhood with towers on a raised plaza, using Federal money for land acquisition.

Modernist city design

1.30
Model photograph of Victor Gruen's plan for Fort Worth, Texas, which would have turned the center of the city into a pedestrian precinct, surrounded by expressways.

and new buildings, some of the groups of new structures resembling the Back Bay plan. A pedestrian bridge system between buildings formed a supplemental pedestrian network (Figure 1.30). The highways as built formed a more conventional interchange south-east of the city center; and Gruen's plan was never implemented. However, an inner ring road and a pedestrianized downtown was an influential diagram and the concept of the downtown mall to help the urban retail district compete with suburban shopping centers was to become an almost axiomatic part of modern city design.

Edmund Bacon tried to apply the Fort Worth concept to downtown Philadelphia in the early 1960s, apparently without realizing that Philadelphia's central district, two miles long by a mile wide, was far too large to become the pedestrian precinct he illustrated in many different variations (Figure 1.31). Fortunately the southern link of the inner ring was thwarted by public protests, as in many other cities, where the inner ring eventually stirred up enough opposition to prevent complete implementation.

The Boston Government Center, based on an urban design plan by Kevin Lynch and developed further by I.M. Pei and Partners, was one renewal project that retained some of its original design character. A traditional monumental plaza on a large scale, with a state office building playing the role of the bell tower, it had a strong enough character to transcend differences in the design of individual buildings between concept and execution. The Embarcadero Center in San Francisco also retained important features of its original concept, including a common raised plaza level that extended over many blocks and was connected by bridges.

Thus in the years following World War II, US housing, commercial redevelopment, and highway design had all been mobilized in support of modernist images of the city, innovations which were ratified by development regulations that would apply to all buildings.

A comprehensive revision of the New York City zoning law was completed in 1961 and became a prototype for many large-city zoning codes. As in urban renewal and subsidized housing, the design concept behind the ordinance was the tower surrounded by open space. Freestanding towers were encouraged by a

1.31
Victor Gruen's Fort Worth highway ring concept was applied by Edmund Bacon to Center City Philadelphia in the 1963 plan. Center City is much larger than downtown Fort Worth and could never become a pedestrian precinct. Despite the caption included in this illustration, the design of the expressways did not contribute to a desirable physical environment. The southern expressway on the left was stopped by a public outcry.

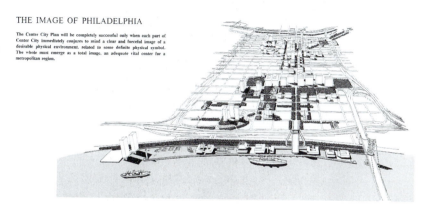

THE IMAGE OF PHILADELPHIA

The Center City Plan will be completely successful only when each part of Center City immediately conjures to mind a clear and forceful image of a desirable physical environment, related to some definite physical symbol. The whole must emerge as a total image, an adequate vital center for a metropolitan region.

Modernist city design

20 percent floor area bonus for a public open space at ground level. The architectural image behind the regulations for office buildings was derived from the Seagram Building by Mies van der Rohe and Philip Johnson, completed in 1958, and the Chase Manhattan Bank tower by Skidmore, Owings & Merrill, completed in 1960. In both cases the tower was a simple rectilinear mass set free of the surrounding street system by a paved public plaza. Towers in parks on the Parkchester and Stuyvesant Town model were also built into the open-space ratios and building spacing requirements for high-density residential buildings in the 1961 zoning.

The last days of CIAM and the birth of urban design

After World War II, instruction in most schools of architecture switched to a modernist curriculum, more or less similar to the model created by Gropius at Harvard. The architectural journals emphasized modernist buildings that avoided ornament, expressed their structural frames, and had large areas of glass. The professional architect soon found that any building that didn't follow these examples was considered out of date. The "functional city" based on zoning that separated housing and work, relied on automobile transportation, and allocated open space primarily for recreation became widely accepted by planners. Housing in towers separated by open space became a mainstream architectural idea. These concepts, identified and advocated by the CIAM when it was a small group of pioneers, were now widely accepted. With acceptance of basic assumptions came a divergence of views, with architects in England, for example, divided between the "empiricism" of Swedish modern architecture and what came to be called the "brutalism" of the much tougher post-war architecture of Le Corbusier.[24]

The first CIAM meetings after the war responded to the acceptance of modernism first with confusion and then with contention. Members objected that what they had said in earlier meetings often turned out to have little effect on Giedion's reports of what took place. Many members also found the charter simplistic and made it clear that it had never been a consensus document. Le Corbusier, anticipating criticism, suggested that CIAM devote itself to producing a new Charter of Habitation, which would be much wider in scope than the previous charter, but the members could not agree either on what should be in it, or on how to produce it.

After the war Jose Sert[25] had succeeded van Eesteren as the president of the CIAM, and Sert proved unwilling or unable to give the meetings the strong direction that, at least as reported by Giedion, CIAM had once had. In 1953 Sert succeeded Walter Gropius as the dean of Harvard's Graduate School of Design, and began spending much of his time in Cambridge, Massachusetts, while most of the CIAM membership was in England and western Europe. Gropius, busy with his American architectural practice, and Le Corbusier, also busy—although not as much as he would have liked—were willing to step aside and let a younger generation take over; Giedion accepted the change less willingly. Two of the younger architects poised to take over were Peter Smithson from England and Aldo Van Eyck from the Netherlands, both of whom were willing to use direct personal attacks and invective as a way of putting forward their arguments. In 1959 they and other relatively young, like-minded architects seceded from the CIAM and established Team Ten, named for the tenth meeting of the CIAM which took place in Dubrovnik in 1956. The older generation asked that the name CIAM no longer be used, a condition the younger generation willingly accepted. Team Ten continued to meet until 1977, but it had little influence on city design beyond the work of its members.[26]

In 1956, Jose Sert, who must have already decided that the CIAM was a write-off, organized the first of a series of annual conferences on urban design at Harvard that invited a wide range of people from around the United States who had ideas about the future of cities, including architects, landscape architects, and planners, but also critics and historians like Lewis Mumford and Jane Jacobs, and public officials, like Edmund Bacon, the planning director of Philadelphia at that time. It was Sert who decided to define the issue as a process, *Urban Design*, rather than an end product like *The Functional City*. Sert refrained from saying *Civic Design*, a widely accepted term, but associated with traditional urbanism.[27] The conference was an informed discussion; it did not produce a manifesto. In 1960, Harvard under Sert's direction added a graduate program in urban design to its degree programs in architecture, planning, and landscape architecture. Other schools soon followed. Rather than trying to convert political leaders to a four-point program, or produce definitive city designs at group meetings, Sert situated urban design within the context of other professional disciplines which had now all accepted basic elements of modernism.

Significant form: Eero Saarinen and the grapefruit

According to Eero Saarinen's wife, Aline,[28] they were having breakfast one morning when Eero took his grapefruit half, turned it upside down on the plate, and cut it into the shape of a triangle. He then took it to the office. The grapefruit half became MIT's Kresge Auditorium, completed in 1955, a thin concrete dome clad in copper and supported on three points (Figure 1.32). The Kresge dome is an example of what used to be called in modernist architectural discourse *significant form*. The term was originally used by Bloomsbury art critic Clive Bell[29] to assert that what made a painting into a work of art was not the story told or the scene described, but the abstract organization of the painting itself. Architects, confronted by modernism's prohibition against using classical columns or gothic arches to give symbolic significance to buildings, turned to engineering and geometry as a source of form and meaning. In the memorial volume of Saarinen's drawings and philosophical statements, edited by Aline Saarinen, there is a sketch of his design for the MIT chapel, which shares a modernist plaza with the Kresge Auditorium.

1.32
The Kresge Auditorium at MIT
designed by Eero Saarinen
and completed in 1955.
Significant form derived from
engineering but, according to
Aline Saarinen, was inspired
by a grapefruit half.

Saarinen has made a marginal note on the drawing asking himself whether its cylindrical shape with a sculptural bell tower on top is "too reminiscent."[30]

A clear discussion of significant form as a theory of modernist architectural design can be found in Peter Collins' 1965 book *Changing Ideals in Modern Architecture*[31] where he describes it as the logical outcome of the Bauhaus method of basic design instruction, adopted as part of the first year curriculum in most architecture schools, and of the identification of abstraction with modernism. Collins also cites Le Corbusier's chapel at Ronchamp (completed in 1954) as an example of significant form, particularly because the building is derived from modern structural materials. However, few architects could match Le Corbusier's ability to bring together painting, sculpture, and architecture in an original abstract composition, and most examples of significant form are derived from geometry and engineering. The Sydney Opera House design by Jorn Utzon won a competition in 1957, although the building was not completed until 1973 (Figure 1.33). Eero Saarinen was a member of the selection committee for the competition and reportedly insisted on Utzon's series of shell-like canopies, which conceal the actual performing arts functions within, until he wore down the practical objections of other committee members. Utzon's original elliptical shapes, carved out of balsa wood for the competition model, were created intuitively, but were rationalized so they could be built by London-based engineer Ove Arup, launching his firm on its career as the enabler of significant form.

Theoretical discussions of significant form in architecture have been swallowed up by discussions of the application of signs and signifiers to architecture, similar-sounding terms derived from semiotics and relating to a different set of issues. Some theorists have used the term monumentality, or the "new monumentality" to discuss something like the same objectives as are denoted by significant form, but monumentality carries with it overtones of traditional architecture and urbanism.

1.33

The Sydney Opera House by Jorn Utzon, a powerful example of significant form which won a competition in 1957. Eero Saarinen was a member of the selection committee and persuaded his colleagues to choose it.

More recently the phrase "iconic building" has been used. However described, it remains a powerful architectural strategy for designers when they need to shape a prominent building. It has been especially influential in the development of skyscrapers.

The designs that were exhibited at CIAM meetings showed tall buildings as standardized products, rectilinear structures all the same shape and height, which became the design strategy almost always used in government-supported housing projects. Le Corbusier varied the rectangular building block by adding sun-screens, but for Ludwig Mies van der Rohe the variations were only in the choice of building materials and the size and shape of the blocks. This photomontage of a 1959 design by Mies, for sites assembled by Robert Moses on the lower Manhattan waterfront, shows rectangular towers on raised plazas, a concept that according to modernist city-design principles was appropriate for all situations[32] (Figure 1.34).

However, private investors in office towers sought an identifiable image for their buildings, and, to a lesser extent, so did developers of hotels and apartments. Until World War II, the way to create such an image was to use ornament: Gothic, Renaissance, or the streamlined shapes often called Art Deco. At first the rectangular forms of modernist towers were themselves a useful novelty, but the novelty wore off by the 1970s. The first reaction was a return to an abstract version of historical forms: a broken pediment at the top of the tower, multiple Palladian windows, or massing borrowed from a Flemish guildhall—all strategies employed by Philip Johnson who in his later architectural practice became a leading shaper of distinctive office towers for private investors. These heresies from modernist doctrine were referred to by architectural journalists and critics as post-modernism, borrowing a term from philosophy and literary criticism where it meant a departure from current

1.34

A proposal for lower Manhattan by Ludwig Mies van der Rohe made in 1957. For a modernist, a tower on a level plaza was the right solution regardless of the circumstances. Chicago History Museum.

certainties, as opposed to a return to previous certainties, which is what the term describes when used about architecture. Unfortunately, the scale of most modern towers is too big for pre-industrial historical designs, even when reduced to abstractions. Their incongruity soon became obvious.

What did seem to work as a conceptual organization for tall buildings was expressing forms derived from engineering, such as using the structural skeleton as the exterior of the building, as in the original World Trade Center Towers in New York City, or creating a multi-story opening through the top of a super-tall building to reduce the effect of wind forces.

Technologies have now opened up possibilities for significant form unimagined by Le Corbusier or even Eero Saarinen, such as many recent buildings by Frank Gehry, beginning with his Guggenheim Museum in Bilbao. Their design is abstract, and their form is intrinsic to the structure and materials, which means they are still in keeping with modernist theory.

The search for significant form through structure has become more and more daring until the form now drives the engineering. One outcome has been the China Central Television headquarters building in Beijing by Rem Koolhaas and his Office of Metropolitan Architecture, at the time of writing left incomplete after a devastating fire. One of the architects, Ole Scheeren, explained the design as a response to the banality of ordinary tall buildings which he now considers outdated.[33] The CCTV tower defies gravity, requiring engineering based on advanced computer simulations which would not have been possible only a few years ago (Figure 1.35). According to a press release from Arup, the engineers for the CCTV headquarters,

1.35
CCTV Tower in Beijing by the Office of Metropolitan Architecture completed in 2008: as in Le Corbusier's 1922 vision it is a tower beside an elevated highway, but the tower is an example of significant form, these days usually called an iconic building.

> the building is formed by two leaning towers, which are bent 90 degrees at the top and bottom to meet, forming a continuous 'tube'. An expressed diagrid system is adopted on the external faces of the building to provide a tube structure in resisting both gravity and lateral loads, where the pattern of diagonals reflects the distribution of forces in the tube surface.

The most recent trend in the search for iconic imagery for buildings has been to look to forms generated on a computer by various algorithms. Rather than using algorithms to solve problems of organized complexity, as discussed in the Systems Design chapter, much of the purpose of algorithmic architecture appears to be to generate a systematic range of forms, one of which will be selected by the designer as an organizing concept.[34]

Limitations of modernist city design become evident

As zoning regulations were revised to relate building design to open space rather than to streets, an incremental version of the tower-in-park city was created in many places. Towers in parks, like Le Corbusier's drawings of sixty-story office buildings in the Ville Contemporaine, or the Unite d'Habitation, were not design concepts that lent themselves to incremental development within an existing city. The result was often to open up views of undesigned party walls, and to create buildings that were not related to one another, amid discontinuous pockets of open space.

Implementation of urban renewal in city centers proved to be a slow process, in which the original overall design often became unrecognizable, reducing the original concept to a series of unrelated developments on individual renewal parcels.

Implicit in most modernist city designs from the Ville Contemporaine onward was the belief that the entire existing city should be replaced by an environment in which individual buildings were far more separate than they had been before. It is thus not surprising that the most usual effect of modern city-design concepts has been to fragment development and to set up conflicts between new buildings and the pre-existing city. Groups of subsidized housing have tended to be located in accordance with the tower-in-park principle, separating them from the surrounding urban context. Most urban renewal plans have ended up with relatively little design continuity among the buildings, and the placement of each building has often been determined by abstract geometric arrangements only understandable from the air or from a long distance away. Zoning ordinances enforce fragmentation on individual developments by giving open space at ground level and setbacks primacy over relationships to streets and surrounding buildings.

To learn what a completely modern city is like we can turn to Chandigarh and Brasilia, both built as new communities under the strong influence of Le Corbusier. Chandigarh was originally to be designed by Albert Mayer and Matthew Nowicki, but Nowicki was killed in a plane crash in 1950, before the designs for the city had been more than just begun. The government of the Punjab went to Maxwell Fry and Jane Drew to ask them to assume Nowicki's role as architect for their new capital. Fry and Drew suggested that they also bring in Le Corbusier, who in turn brought in his cousin Pierre Jeanneret. Fry, Drew, Jeanneret, and Le Corbusier met in India, and before Albert Mayer arrived, Le Corbusier took Mayer's plan, which was a relatively loosely drawn garden-city concept, and transformed it into something much more closely resembling his Ville Radieuse proposal of 1935.

According to Maxwell Fry, Mayer was not fluent in French, so Le Corbusier ignored him completely when he did arrive at the working meeting. Mayer had placed the capitol in a park at the north-east corner of the site; Le Corbusier pulled it to the center of the north side of the city, squarely on a monumental axis. Mayer's plan had two parkways running north–south, flanking the business center, and a large number of gently curving streets; Le Corbusier converted the plan to a sector system with a large rectangular grid. Again, according to Fry, Le Corbusier sketched out his new design on the analogy of the human body, calling the capitol the head, the business center the stomach, and so on, suggesting that a similar process of thought went into the Ville Radieuse plan, which seems to have a head, shoulders, a torso, and legs. [35]

Modernist city design

Enough of the original garden-city concept remains that a visitor to Chandigarh is more conscious of the landscaping of the principal streets than of the generally mediocre buildings. Le Corbusier's real mark as a designer has been as the architect of the capitol complex. The secretariat, legislative, and court buildings have been completed, but, at least partly because the governor's palace was never built, the grouping of structures is separated by distances too large to permit them to read as an ensemble (Figure 1.36). The fragmentation that characterized modernist intervention in existing cities thus is also present at Chandigarh.

The concept for Brasilia is essentially the work of two architects who were both heavily influenced by Le Corbusier: Lucio Costa, who completed the initial master plan in 1957, and Oscar Niemeyer, who has designed most of the significant buildings and prepared design controls for other development. The key element of the plan for Brasilia is the central highway, which forms a symmetrical, bow-shaped curve across a broad plain and becomes the spine for a series of sectors. The capitol district is at the center point of the highway curve and at right angles to it; in plan it looks rather like the fuselage for the swept-back wings of an airplane. The city is rigidly zoned to separate different types of land uses. The residential districts are a repeating pattern of apartment blocks along the spreading wings. The central buildings are widely separated rows of towers, punctuated by iconic buildings like the legislature and the cathedral. Winding roads lead to apartment towers located in the surrounding hills. Beyond a green belt are the shanty towns and slums originally started by the construction workers, which unfortunately now house a large proportion of the population. The shanty towns are gradually being improved, with electricity and plumbing hook-ups to enable residents to upgrade where they live. There is a strong parallel to the illustrations for Le Corbusier's 1922 Ville Contemporaine where the workers were to be housed beyond the green belt with the edge of their districts barely visible, and clearly not considered, at the very edge of the drawing.

Brasilia also has some of the design consistency of one of Le Corbusier's visionary drawings. Tall buildings of similar size and shape are placed in a regular

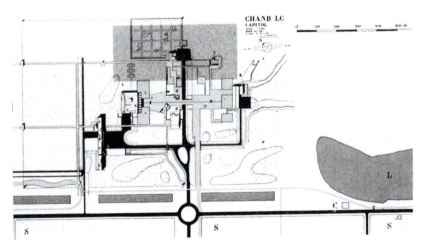

1.36
The government complex at Chandigarh designed by Le Corbusier: a modernist site plan forming an asymmetrical composition with the terrain abstracted to form a level picture plane. As the governor's palace in the center has not been built, the ensemble shown in the drawing is not complete.

Modernist city design

1.37
A view of the governmental center of Brasilia, a fully realized, modernist city with symmetrical building organization at its core.

pattern and set in sweeping areas of open space. The automobile is the major means of communication. While it may be premature to arrive at a definitive judgment of a community that has been begun so recently, Brasilia does seem to present significant proof that the modernist city formulation leaves out some of the essentials of a vital urban area (Figure 1.37).

The continuing power of modernist city design

A generation ago, it was possible to think that the influence of modernism in city design was declining. A strong critique of modernism in favor of the traditional city with its walkable streets and squares came from Jane Jacobs, and later from Jan Gehl and William H. Whyte. Other critiques of the modernist penchant for clearing away older buildings came from both the increasingly strong historic preservation movement and the proponents of community participation in planning. Within modernist theory there was a reaction against one-size-fits-all doctrine in favor of policies related to regional and cultural character. What was called post-modernism by some architecture critics also favored the return to traditional building ensembles based on axial relationships, vistas, and facades modulated by arches or columns. Housing towers for low-income people were found to be socially dysfunctional, as famously demonstrated by the demolition of the Pruitt-Igoe housing project in St. Louis in 1972 and the well-publicized social problems of high-rise new towns in France and high-rise council estates in Great Britain. The spread of garden suburbs represented a more relaxed and ad hoc relationship of buildings to landscape, although what was happening could aptly be criticized as suburban sprawl. The beginnings of the environmental movement questioned the modernist assumption that engineering technology could solve all relationships between the natural and the built environment. The proponents of megastructures argued for a more systematic method of city design based on infrastructure rather than individual buildings. We will come back to these important issues in succeeding chapters. However, while alternatives to modernism became influential in Europe and in English-speaking countries, during the same time period, modernist city design, much as defined by the CIAM, has gone on to transform the rest of the planet and continues to reshape all urban centers.

Rapid urbanization under strong central control, particularly in Asia and in South and Central America, and in the oil-rich countries of the Middle East has followed modernist city design, perhaps because it was an established available template. More developed countries have seen modernism reasserted in the new mixed-use urban centers in traditional downtowns and "edge cities."

Seoul, Singapore, Jakarta, Bangkok, and Taipei, which retained a recognizable village and precinctual structure as recently as the 1970s, have become cities of modernist towers, criss-crossed by congested expressways. The residential tower block has become pervasive, partly because the fast-increasing population requires a denser use of the land, and partly because the residential tower had already become an established building type backed by the prestige of modernist theory. The first generation of denser housing followed the modernist pattern of five-story walk-ups and eleven-story towers, usually in groups of similar design and uniform height arranged in regular rows. Another pervasive building type has been the traditional shop house or row house transformed into CIAM-style workers' housing with concrete party walls, and larger modernist windows at either end, except that the ground floor continued to express the identity of individual retail businesses with signs and lights. As some urban dwellers have become richer, they have moved to a new generation of towers, taller, with larger apartments, and more individuality of design.

The effects of affluence on modernist city design can be seen particularly in the cities of the Emirates along the Persian, or Arabian, Gulf, where small original populations, relatively few pre-existing buildings, and low domestic energy prices permitted rapid growth according to modernist principles as required by central planning agencies. Large-scale blocks have been laid out in the desert, with wide streets to accommodate multiple lanes of automobiles. The first generation of building formed relatively low-scale apartment and villa districts within the grid, with offices and hotels built along principal streets. The latest development, supported by rapidly rising oil prices, has been marked by denser districts of high-rise housing and offices and a much higher proportion of tall buildings aspiring to significant form, as illustrated by the skyline of Doha in Qatar (Figure 1.38). The Burj Al Arab in Dubai, said to be shaped like a sail, and the Burj Dubai, planned to be the tallest building in the world, are other examples of significant form in the Emirates. The Waterfront

1.38
The skyline of Doha in Qatar, United Arab Emirates. Modernism's need to create iconic, original buildings on every site produces a discordant result.

1.39
Proposal by the Office of
Metropolitan Architecture for
the Dubai waterfront, United
Arab Emirates.

1.40
The Agbar Tower, a significant
form in Barcelona by Jean
Nouvel. While it fits into its
edge-city context, it also
transforms the historic skyline.

1.41
The Swiss Reinsurance Tower
in London, by Norman Foster:
also a significant form, and
definitely not a response to
context.

development in Dubai, planned for a future 1.5 million people, looks from the model photos to continue the modernist formula of a grid of wide streets forming superblocks filled with separated towers (Figure 1.39), but it is also to include a contrasting square island of walkable streets and closely spaced buildings, designed by Rem Koolhaas and the Office of Metropolitan Architecture. This district is to be dominated by a spherical structure with an eye-like opening taking the concept of significant form back to Jungian primal iconography.

There is now a worldwide competition among cities to have the tallest towers with the most distinctive shapes. This trend is giving a modernist shape to even the most traditional cities.

The Agbar Tower in Barcelona designed by Jean Nouvel adjacent to a large traffic intersection is perhaps the most prominent object in a low-rise city. The new tower is taller and more massive than the Sagrada Familia church by Antonio Gaudi. Earlier interpolations of modern buildings into Barcelona had been careful to maintain the scale of the city's traditional urbanism. While the immediate surroundings of the Tower are as modernist as any location can be, it now gives the city a modernist skyline. The significant form created for the Agbar Tower is supposedly based on an engineering analysis of how to reduce wind forces against the building, but the tower clearly carries other symbolic messages of power and assertiveness (Figure 1.40).

The Swiss Reinsurance Co tower in London by Norman Foster, similar in design concept to the Agbar Tower, introduces a powerful modernist object into the densely developed traditional urbanism of the City of London unlike Canary Wharf in London's East End which, like La Défense in Paris, segregated tall buildings in a separate district (Figure 1.41).

While a super-tall tower in New York or Chicago is a difference of degree, and a skyline of tall office buildings is characteristic of all American cities except Washington, DC, suburban locations in the US until the 1980s rarely had tall buildings. Joel Garreau coined the phrase "edge city" to describe urban office and retail centers in formerly suburban or undeveloped locations.[36] He identified more than 130 such places in the United States alone, based on his own observations, leaving out many comparable locations in metropolitan regions he hadn't visited. Garreau was interested in edge cities as a social phenomenon and does not discuss their design, but edge cities demonstrate that modernist city design, as identified and codified by CIAM participants in their charter, has become so diffused into everyday investment, engineering, and zoning practice as to be the standard way to shape urban centers. Edge cities are almost always located close to a major expressway and often where expressways intersect, so the highway becomes a defining element much as predicted by Le Corbusier. The street design gives primacy to traffic movement, also as advocated by Le Corbusier and the CIAM Charter. Local streets are wide and far apart, forming large-scale superblocks, to minimize the number of intersections. Land uses are separated, so that offices are in one place, retail malls in another, and apartments somewhere else. Office buildings and hotels are separate towers surrounded by parking, not located along streets. Le Corbusier showed parking lots at the base of his tower designs in the 1920s, but nowhere near as many spaces as it turns out are needed. The retail mall is not a CIAM formulation, having been devised by Victor Gruen and others after World War II, but its enclosed, separated structure, located on a superblock and entirely surrounded by parking, follows modernist city-design principles. As edge cities grew up ad hoc, the product of individual projects by separate developers with zoning as their only control, they usually lack the green spaces that in modernist city design should separate residences from other uses. But metropolitan regions, in the United States and elsewhere in the world, are now punctuated by clusters of modernist towers.

Until Deng Xiaoping came to power, interpolations in existing Chinese cities conformed to the CIAM principles that had been adopted by China's Russian advisors: long, thin walk-up buildings and occasional multi-story elevator blocks, all arranged in parallel rows. The controlling document for today's much more rapid and comprehensive development, the land-use plan, is similar from city to city, as master plans are designed to specifications that apply nationally and are approved by a central authority. The plans continue to institutionalize modernist city design. They show a clear separation of land uses, wide spacing between streets leading to large block sizes, a reliance on highway-based systems of transportation, and open space provided as large regional parks. These plans also follow modernist doctrine in giving little or no priority to preserving the existing built environment, except for a few outstanding historic monuments. Chinese cities also have strict building separation and placement regulations relating to access to sunlight. Complying with these laws requires regularly spaced separate towers. The modernist tendencies in the regulations are reinforced by widespread desire among purchasers of apartments that the living areas face south, in accordance with traditional feng shui beliefs, which usually means that all the towers face in the same direction. These preferences are not so influential in the design of office and public buildings where designers have more freedom to seek significant form.

By the time of the 2008 Olympic Games, the Chinese government had largely completed remaking Beijing from a traditional compact, low-rise city into a modernist metropolis, ignoring recommendations from professor Wu Liangyong of Tsinghua University and others that the modern portion of Beijing should be a separate area, like La Défense in Paris. Beijing is now filled with clusters of towers. Some two million people have been relocated from traditional one- and two-story Hutong districts, which have been demolished and replaced by modern residential and office buildings. The Temple of Heaven, an important historic structure, has been preserved, but its traditional urban context has been demolished and replaced with parkland, so the Temple and its associated ceremonial courtyards are now incidents in a modernist regional park. Beijing today is dissected by broad traffic boulevards and radial super-highways, and is surrounded by more ring roads than Houston. Important new buildings use modern construction methods to create significant form. The new National Center for the Performing Arts on Tiananmen Square, designed by French architect Paul Andreu, places four large performance halls under a single dome covered in sheets of titanium. Andreu takes the isolation of a symbolic structure typical of modernism to the extreme of surrounding the building with a moat. Other symbolic monuments, in addition to the CCTV tower mentioned earlier, include several of the sports venues for the Olympics. A stadium is always an iconic building, but the main Olympic stadium, designed by the Swiss firm of Herzog and de Meuron, with Arup as the structural engineers, achieves its unique enclosing structure, known familiarly as the Bird's Nest, from new engineering only possible with today's computers. Similarly the Aquatics Center for the Olympics by the Australian firm PTW, with Arup as the engineers, is enclosed by a space-frame filled with translucent panels that give the impression they are made of water: again an example of the modernist doctrine of significant form created by novel uses of engineering and technology. It is true that the location for the Olympics continues the axis of Tiananmen Square out at the fourth ring road, but an axis at this scale is like the central axis at Brasilia, it is no longer traditional urbanism.

At one time Brasilia and Chandigarh were the examples of cities that came closest to fulfilling the objectives of the CIAM; today the list includes Beijing and Dubai, and significant parts of most other cities.

2 Traditional city design and the modern city

In June of 2009 the investment agency of the government of Qatar withdrew its application for a luxury housing development on the site of the Chelsea Barracks in London. This move was seen in the press as a victory for Prince Charles, the heir to the British throne and an advocate for traditional architecture and city design. The proposal for the 52,000 square meter site was a modernist design prepared by Rogers Stirk Harbour + Partners, founded by Richard Rogers, recipient of just about all the honors which can be granted to an architect.[1] The proposal had been through more than two years of controversial planning hearings, and, despite strong opposition from nearby property owners in this wealthy part of London, appeared to be only weeks away from final approval. The newspaper headline:

Prince wins victory over Rogers in battle of Chelsea Barracks
Modernist £1bn redevelopment plan dropped by Qatari royal family after letter from Charles[2]

The prince had written that the proposed buildings were an "unsympathetic and unsuitable" neighbor to the Chelsea Hospital, a symmetrical quadrangle with flanking subsidiary courtyards designed as residences for old and disabled soldiers by Christopher Wren, a seventeenth-century royal architect. A more "sympathetic" neighbor, preferred by the Prince, is an infirmary designed for the Hospital by Quinlan Terry for a site adjacent to the Wren buildings and completed in 2008. Terry's building is clearly not by Wren, but it is symmetrical and faced with brick, with some elements of a classical vocabulary and traditional window openings. Terry also volunteered his own alternative for the barracks site, in opposition to the proposals by Rogers.

2.1
The Rogers Stirk Harbour design for the Chelsea Barracks site was a series of parallel buildings in a strict modernist layout comparable to German social housing in the 1920s, except that the Rogers buildings were much closer together.

The Rogers design was a series of parallel buildings in a strict modernist layout comparable to German social housing in the 1920s, except that the Rogers buildings were much closer together (Figure 2.1). This unusual layout for luxury apartments was a response to the requirement for more than five hundred units on a 13-acre site. The more usual modernist solution would have been towers, ruled out by proximity to the campus of the Chelsea Hospital and by government height restrictions. After complaints from neighboring residents, the design was revised to open up a wider park space between the ends of the parallel buildings and adjacent properties, and to introduce some facade variations facing this park (Figure 2.2). However, the essentially repetitive and uniform character of the design remained the same. The alternative by Quinlan Terry (Figure 2.3) resembled nineteenth-century college quadrangles at Oxford or Cambridge. It was much less rigorously organized than anything Wren would have designed. It was also just a sketch, and there is no indication that it could accommodate the same number and size of apartments as the Rogers design. Terry's alternative was a winner over the Rogers design in an internet poll conducted by a British building magazine, although there was a good possibility that neighboring property owners contributed disproportionately to the poll results.

The Qatari investors probably used Prince Charles's letter as an excuse to revise a project which had become uneconomic because of a sharp decline in the housing market. They have since appointed a team of less well-known modernist

2.3
An alternative sketch design for the Chelsea Barracks site volunteered by traditionalist architect Quinlan Terry.

2.2
After strong opposition from neighboring property owners, the Chelsea Barracks site design was revised to open up a wider park space between the ends of the parallel buildings and adjacent properties, and to introduce some facade variations.

architects[3] to prepare a new development concept, working with a committee of local residents. Prince Charles's foundation was involved in the selection process for the new team, making it more difficult for the Prince to oppose the ultimate result. Well-informed investors, the Qatari Diar Development Company would know that the Prince has no official power and a reputation for eccentric enthusiasms.

At the same time the Prince was taking sides in the controversy about the Chelsea Barracks he was also calling for the eradication of gray squirrels:

> The Prince of Wales has asked landowners to wipe out grey squirrels from the countryside to protect red squirrels and to save native woodlands. He told the Country Land and Business Association (CLA) that it was 'absolutely crucial to eliminate the greys.'[4]

Modernist city design has replaced the kind of traditional urban vocabulary used by Christopher Wren, sketched by Quinlan Terry, and promoted by Prince Charles. However, the Chelsea Barracks controversy illustrates a growing interest in the principles of traditional city design as a way to correct some of the problems with modernist cities, particularly massive new structures that seem to overwhelm existing development and the groups of modern buildings that fail to provide a comfortable environment for pedestrians. Christopher Wren is a good starting point for considering both the promise and the problems of traditional city design.

Wren's plan for London

Christopher Wren was one of the founders of the Royal Society, England's academy of science, a leader of the transition from knowledge derived from writings that went back to the ancient Greeks to investigations where hypotheses had to be verified by experiments or mathematical proofs. He was thirty-four years old and a professor of astronomy at Oxford when word reached him that a fire in the city of London on Sunday, September 2, 1666 had destroyed 433 acres, almost the whole of the city, before the fire was contained late the following Tuesday night.

Wren was also already known as an architect. He was a likely candidate to become the head of the Royal Office of Works, and his designs for the reconstruction of London's old St. Paul's cathedral had been submitted just six days before the fire. Wren saw immediately that there would be a great opportunity to reshape London according to the best current city-design principles. He made the preliminary surveys for replanning London while the ruins were still almost too hot to walk on and were filled with dangerous piles of debris and hidden cavities, and was able to present his plan to King Charles II and his council on September 11, 1666, barely a week after the fire was put out.[5]

Wren's plan was as radical a departure from the existing English city as the symmetries and carefully reasoned proportions of Renaissance architecture were from the more informally organized Tudor or medieval buildings that had made up the City of London before the fire. Wren was careful to make the new streets link up to the old wherever buildings stood undamaged, but instead of the old winding streets, he proposed two new straight avenues starting in a triangular plaza in front of a rebuilt St. Paul's and leading directly across the walled city, one to Aldgate and the other to the Tower. A third avenue would start at Newgate, on the western side of the city, and meet the avenue to Aldgate at a large oval plaza that would be the setting for a new Royal Exchange. Around this plaza would be all the other financial institutions—the mint, the excise office, the hall of the Goldsmith's Company and so on.

The entire north frontage of the Thames across the burned area was to be reorganized in a new formal system. At the entrance to London Bridge, Wren proposed a semicircular plaza with straight avenues fanning out from it. Two of these new streets would lead to small circular plazas along the main avenues from St. Paul's to the Tower, and other straight streets would radiate from them. A third circular plaza with straight streets radiating from it was planned for the burned area to the west of the city walls. The district around St. Paul's, between the two sets of radial streets, was treated as a series of almost rectangular blocks, their angles adjusted somewhat to fit into the overall scheme (Figure 2.4).

The king was sufficiently impressed by Wren's plan, and by two other plans put forward a little later, one by John Evelyn and one by Robert Hooke, to decree that no rebuilding should begin in the city until an overall reconstruction scheme had been drawn up and approved.

The king created a committee of six to draft the standards for rebuilding. He appointed three of the members, including Wren, and he let the London merchants choose the others. Robert Hooke, a colleague of Wren's from the Royal Society, was one of the three nominated by the City merchants. The committee first tried to persuade all property owners in the burned part of London to submit an accurate

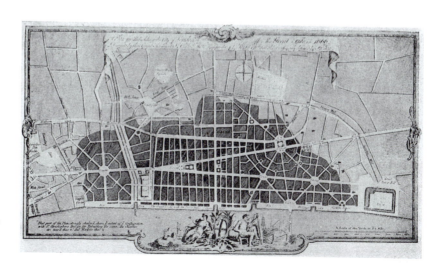

2.4
Christopher Wren's plan for rebuilding London after the Great Fire of 1666, according to what were then the latest city-design principles. The darker-shaded portions of the map indicate the areas of the city that were burned out.

survey of their land, a necessary precondition for the exchange of property to implement a new street system. Only 10 percent of the owners complied, and it became clear that the king was not going to provide an alternative by paying for the rest of the survey. Charles II, who had been brought back as king only six years before, after the Commonwealth period that followed the execution of his father, Charles I, was sensitive to the limits of his authority. London's merchants were strongly against the complex realignment of properties that new plans would require. Recovery would be quicker if everyone could simply rebuild on the old foundations. Moreover, the country was in the midst of a war with the Dutch (this was the war in which the British seized New Amsterdam in 1666 and renamed it New York), and there was no money to spare. Wren's plan also required reducing the number of parish churches and rebuilding others on new sites, disturbing concepts because people thought of city geography in terms of the parishes. The committee was forced to plan the reconstruction of London on the old street pattern, with wider rights of way and new requirements for more fireproof buildings, which included setting up uniform standards for four classes of houses. Robert Hooke ended up as the directing force for this more conservative but still difficult reconstruction.

Where Wren's city-design ideas came from

As Wren was a scholar and scientist before he became an architect, he learned the essentials of architecture from books. The transmission of architectural ideas through printed books and engraved drawings and maps was gradually to displace the medieval system in which architectural ideas were transmitted from master to apprentice and followed the movement of architects and master craftsmen from one building site to the next. The invention of printing made it possible for a designer to assimilate and use an entirely new mode of architectural expression, so that English architecture in the seventeenth century, under the influence of scholarly architects like Inigo Jones and Christopher Wren, went straight from buildings that were close to the late medieval tradition to the revival of design concepts from Greek and Roman architecture that had been developing in Italy and France for centuries. Jones and Wren were also able to select their favorite elements from any point in the pattern of historical development, from the simplicity of the early Renaissance to the complexities of Baroque architecture contemporary with their own lifetimes.

Wren's ability to think about cities as a series of connected spaces, linked by vistas along avenues, relates to the rediscovery of perspective by Italian artists in the first part of the fifteenth century. The ideal cities that formed the background for painted scenes were translated first into stage scenery, then into garden design, and later into actual city squares and streets, and as this evolution took place, concepts of space also evolved from individual squares surrounded by buildings to sequences of spaces linked by avenues. The first comprehensive replanning of a city according to these new pictorial principles had been carried out in Rome by

Pope Sixtus V and his architect, Domenico Fontana, between 1585 and 1590. Sixtus V was not the first pope to undertake changes in the city of Rome, and he took care to incorporate earlier designs into his overall scheme. One of the most important of these predecessor designs was the rebuilding of the plaza at the city end of the bridge that connects Rome with its citadel, Castel Sant' Angelo. The streets leading out of this plaza were regularized into a radiating pattern during the reign of Pope Paul III (1534–1549). The design of the plaza is related to Renaissance concepts of stage scenery such as the permanent set designed by Palladio's pupil Vincenzo Scamozzi for Palladio's Teatro Olimpico in Vicenza, which is perhaps the most famous example of its kind. It shows, through a central arch and four side doors, glimpses of seven streets lined with buildings whose uniform cornice lines vanish in an exaggerated perspective. The theater was completed in 1585, the same year that Sixtus began the transformation of Rome (Figure 2.5).

The key element of Sixtus V's plan for Rome was a succession of long, straight streets, the changes of direction marked by piazzas with central obelisks. The streets linked the major pilgrimage destinations through sections of Rome that had been essentially uninhabited for centuries (Figure 2.6). Sixtus and Fontana also planned and built a new aqueduct which restored water service to the districts that the new streets opened up to habitation. The construction by Sixtus V of the Piazza del Popolo at the entrance to Rome was intended to make that plaza into a theater that enjoyed vistas down the streets that fanned out from it, like the glimpses of city streets at the Teatro Olimpico, although the concept of the piazza was not fully realized until the nineteenth century (Figure 2.7).

The uniform streetscape evoked by the Teatro Olimpico was also implied by the long, straight streets of Sixtus's Rome, although these streets, constructed

2.5a and b
The permanent set designed by Palladio's pupil, Vincenzo Scamozzi, for Palladio's Teatro Olimpico in Vicenza shown in plan and in a photograph. Through the doorways, the viewer catches glimpses of streets lined with buildings whose uniform cornice lines vanish in an exaggerated perspective.

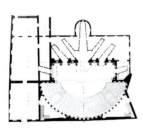

2.6
Sixtus V's plan for Rome was a succession of long, straight streets, the changes of direction marked by piazzas with central obelisks.

2.7a and b
The plan of the Piazza del Popolo at the entrance to Rome was intended to make that plaza into a theater that enjoyed vistas down the streets that fanned out from it, like the glimpses of city streets at the Teatro Olimpico, although the concept of the piazza was not fully realized until the nineteenth century. The Piazza has been restored as shown in a recent photograph.

mainly through underpopulated or abandoned parts of the city, had no buildings along much of their length for many years.

Uniform street architecture was not an essential element of earlier Renaissance concepts of architectural space. Sebastiano Serlio's often published sequence of theater sets, from his architectural textbook, *L 'Architettura*,[6] shows an ideal streetscape of Renaissance buildings as a suitable backdrop for tragedy, a more realistic mixture of medieval and Renaissance structures as a setting for comedy, and a landscape vista as the satyric scene. Even in the tragic street scene, the buildings are by no means uniform, reflecting the individuality of buildings in most ideal cities painted during the "high" Renaissance (Figures 2.8–2.10).

Michelangelo's design for the Capitol at Rome, begun in 1536, about the time Serlio's treatise was first published, is an important step in giving architectural

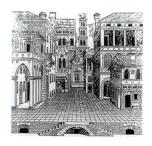

2.8, 2.9, 2.10
Sebastiano Serlio's drawings
of a street with a mixture of
medieval and Renaissance
structures as a setting for
comedy, a more idealized
streetscape of Renaissance
buildings as a suitable
backdrop for tragedy, and a
landscape vista as the satyric
scene.

2.11
Michelangelo's influential
design for the Capitol at
Rome, begun in 1536, uses
the placement of buildings to
exaggerate perspective views.

uniformity to external urban spaces. The placement of the two flanking buildings to create an exaggerated perspective, the architectural vocabulary of colonnade and colossal order, the organization of the pavement pattern around a central sculpture, all were to prove influential (Figure 2.11). Giorgio Vasari's later design for the courtyard of the Uffizi Palace in Florence, with its buildings canted to produce an exaggerated perspective and its uniform cornices and moldings, may have been a direct influence on the set design of the Teatro Olimpico.

Lewis Mumford has suggested that the long, straight street and the concept of uniform, repetitive facades may have been a response to the introduction of horse-drawn carriages into cities, which began at about this time. A pedestrian or an individual on horseback can negotiate a more complicated street pattern and has time for a more idiosyncratic perception of a city than a passenger peering from the window of a swiftly moving coach.[7]

Uniformity of spatial enclosure, so hard to obtain with buildings, could be realized much more easily in garden design. Long vistas, extending the architectural system of a great house, could be enclosed by walls and plantations of trees and enlivened by pools, fountains, and cascades. The rondel, or rond-point, was originally a clearing in a forest created as a setting for the ceremonial hunts that took place at court. The circular opening designed by Andre Le Notre for the forest at the end of the long axis on the garden side of Versailles, with radiating avenues leading from it, turned the rondel into an ornamental device for dealing with the intersections of long axial vistas. In addition to the long, straight garden avenues enclosed by

plantations of trees on the garden side of Versailles, the side of the palace that faces the town forms a forecourt where three avenues converge in a fan-shaped pattern that is similar to the streets originating at the Piazza del Popolo (Figure 2.12).

The gardens at Versailles can be seen as a kind of city plan, because they represented a controlled environment for the centralized power of the court. The rond-points and radiating avenues at Versailles and other French gardens were added to the apparatus of plaza and vista already created in Rome to become the vocabulary of city design in Wren's plan for London.

Roman plazas with radiating streets appear in Wren's plan at the two most important entrances to the city: the foot of London Bridge and the top of Ludgate Hill in front of the newly positioned St. Paul's, a gateway to the walled city that is a close analogue to the entrance to Rome at the Piazza del Popolo. The way St. Paul's is placed at the origin of two major avenues indicates that Wren was familiar not only with the map of Sixtus V's Rome but also with the way Carlo Rainaldi's twin churches, begun in 1662, frame the streets entering the Piazza del Popolo.

There is no evidence that Wren ever journeyed to Rome, but he did make a long visit to France in 1665. The development of the gardens at Versailles actually did not begin until the year after Wren made his plan for London and two years after his visit to France, but Wren may have seen Le Notre's plans while they were in preparation, and he would have known Le Notre's modifications to the Tuileries gardens and his design for the gardens at Vaux-le-Vicomte, where analogous motifs are employed.

Wren, a royalist from a prominent royalist family, was attracted to design ideas employed by autocrats. But Sixtus V, the absolute ruler of the Papal States as well as pope, confined most of his town-planning efforts to parts of Rome that were essentially uninhabited. Louis XIV asserted his symbolic primacy over France

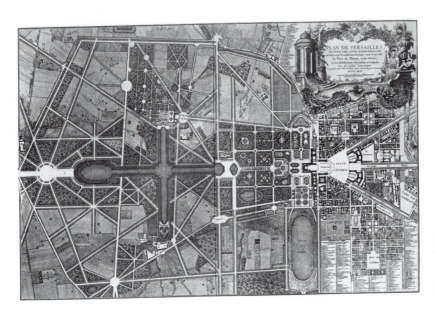

2.12
Andre Le Notre's plan for Versailles from the 1660s. The map is by the Abbé Delagrive from 1746.

through the long vistas of the gardens at suburban Versailles, but he left Paris itself relatively unchanged. If Wren's plan had been adopted, it would have had a far stronger effect on an actual city than the works of Louis XIV and Sixtus V. However, the merchants of the city of London owed their allegiance to their own businesses and trade associations. There was little reason for them to be sympathetic to design concepts that would give grandeur to London itself, when implementation of these designs might prolong the rebuilding process and endanger their economic recovery. Wren did provide many rectangular blocks, an ancient device but an innovation in England at the time, which had the advantage of permitting incremental development; but he placed little emphasis on another Renaissance city-planning device, which had already become established in London's mercantile society—the city square surrounded by individual row houses linked by uniform facades.

The city square

Robert Hooke had attempted an alternative to Wren's plan, based on city squares and a rectangular street grid. This plan also required a new alignment of properties and did not succeed, but the square had a good claim to be the appropriate expression of bourgeois society, based as it was on a grouping of individual houses, joined to form a more palatial whole.

In 1631, during the reign of Charles I, Inigo Jones, then the head of the Royal Office of Works, had drawn the plans of such a square for the subdivision of land at Covent Garden belonging to the Earl of Bedford.[8] According to documentary research carried out by John Summerson, the earl received royal permission to subdivide, at a time when there were strong restrictions on new house construction, by making a payment of £2,000 and agreeing to use Jones as the master planner for the development.[9] Jones had been to Italy and had seen Italian city squares like the one at Leghorn (Figure 2.13). He would also have been familiar with patterns of streets and squares in ideal city designs, such as the city in Vincenzo Scamozzi's *L'Idea della Architettura Universale*. Jones actually met Scamozzi during a trip to Italy in 1614. Jones was also familiar with French examples like the Place Ducale in Charleville and the Place Royale (now the Place des Vosges) in Paris completed in 1612 (Figure 2.14), which were closer to his immediate requirements, and he knew the large number of English palaces and colleges grouped around courtyards. Jones's design created rows of houses on the north and east sides of the square, with arcades along the ground floor. Regularly spaced pilasters were aligned with the piers supporting the ground-floor arches, giving the upper two floors a regular, repeating rhythm. The roofs were continuous and the spacing of the attic windows regular, unlike the Place Royale or Charleville, where the separate nature of the constituent houses was expressed by individual hipped roofs. The west side of the square centered on a church designed by Inigo Jones, which was surrounded by more modest houses that were also part of the plan. The south side of the square

2.13
This sketch is by Elbert Peets of the city square in Leghorn (Livorno), a place known to Inigo Jones, the designer of the square at Covent Garden.

2.14
The Place des Vosges in Paris,
also a possible model for
Covent Garden.

was originally the garden fence of the Earl of Bedford's own house. The decision
to build a church reflected the precinctual nature of London at that time; a parish
church was necessary to give a neighborhood an identity (Figure 2.15).

Covent Garden, and the less formal arrangement of Lincoln's Inn Fields, where
Jones had at least some supervisory role, were models of a more incremental form
of urban organization than the great avenue. The westward expansion of London,
which accelerated as a result of the fire, was to make much use of the square, but
relationships from square to square are informal, even ad hoc, dictated by the
property lines of the estates that were being subdivided.

2.15
The design by Inigo Jones for
the square at Covent Garden,
the first such public place in
England. In this drawing a
market has already been set
up in the Square. Eventually
the whole development would
become commercial.

Traditional city design and the modern city

Up until the mid-eighteenth century, the city square seems to have been understood essentially as an incident in the urban framework, a form of relief from the pattern of streets, rather than as a systematic ordering device in its own right. Squares were usually defined only as a site plan, as at Lincoln's Inn Fields, not as a fully developed architectural concept like Covent Garden.

The square continued to be a design element of mercantile cities. Squares were used in the plan for Philadelphia that Thomas Holme laid out for William Penn in 1682. A public square marked the intersection of the two main streets in the center, and there was a square park or garden in each of the four quadrants. Squares were used more systematically in the plan for Savannah of 1733 by James Oglethorpe, but still as a relief from the street grid.

It was in the design of the new parts of Bath by John Wood and his son, also named John Wood, starting in 1727, that the row house–town square became in itself an instrument of coordinated city design conceived and developed in three dimensions.

The square as an instrument of city design

Bath was a resort; houses were often not occupied all year. Social distinctions in the architecture were blurred by the fact that few families felt they needed a really large house for a visit. On the other hand, almost everyone needed about the same number of entertaining spaces and bedrooms. Thus houses of similar size were available as building blocks for architectural compositions.

Despite their importance to the history of architecture and city planning, not much is known about the Woods. The detective work in piecing together the best available documentary evidence was originally done by John Summerson.[10] John Wood senior seems to have practiced as both a landscape architect and an architect. He was involved for several years in the development of the West End of London, both as a designer and as a speculative builder. The development pattern in London since Covent Garden had been for a master plan to be drawn for a square or street, and for individual builder-developers to undertake the construction of a relatively small number of houses—one side of a square, for example. Sometimes the developer was the owner of the property, but the property owners seldom attempted to be the developers for all of their land. The capitalization and the risk were thus divided among several entrepreneurs, a pattern that continues to exist in subdivision development today.

John Summerson calls attention to the design by Edward Shepherd for part of one frontage of Grosvenor Square in London, dating from the mid-1720s. Instead of each house being a similar, repeating unit, in the way that Inigo Jones had designed Covent Garden, and instead of a random pattern of different groups of houses, which had become the London norm, Shepherd took a row of individual houses and treated it as if it were a single palatial building with a central colonnade and pediment. The concept was not a completely successful design because Shepherd did not control the full frontage of the square, but Summerson points to it as a step towards the fully realized squares that the Woods were to develop in Bath, and that were to influence subsequent development.

Wood had realized that Bath was on the verge of a major development boom and actively sought to become its architect. From the beginning he had a concept that Bath, once the site of a Roman city, should have Roman features like a forum and a circus.[11] The site planning for the houses that John Wood built at Bath from 1727 to the 1750s followed the pattern already established in London: a street and a square. At Queen Square, however, Wood was able to build a row of eight houses unified behind a single palatial facade with central pediment and end pavilions, showing that he was thinking in terms of a three-dimensional architectural realization, and not just following a typical site plan. The Circus, which was begun just before John Wood senior's death in 1754, is a complete architectural concept and something new in the history of city design.

The Circus at Bath is a group of thirty-three houses arranged in a circle at the intersection of three streets. In plan it is similar to the rond-points familiar from garden design, to Mansart's Place des Victoires in Paris, and to several unexecuted circular plazas from the 1750s that appear on Pierre Patte's composite map of Paris published in 1765, and not unlike the circular plazas Wren showed in his London plan. However, it was not clear what kind of architecture Wren imagined for his circular plazas. The Woods chose a simple, uniform three-story elevation with engaged columns. The columns are Doric on the ground floor, then Ionic above and Corinthian at the top story, an allusion to the Colosseum in Rome, which employs this architectural sequence on its exterior. The Circus Maximus at Rome is an elongated oval, not a circle; the Colosseum is elliptical. Perhaps Wood didn't care that he was only loosely following the Roman originals he cites (Figure 2.16).

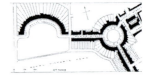

2.16
The Circus at Bath, a group of thirty-three houses arranged in a circle at the intersection of three streets, gives the public square a new form as the hinge in a larger city design.

John Wood the younger completed an even more interesting and influential group of houses off a street that leads away from the Circus: the Royal Crescent. Here a much clearer architectural elevation of basement and two-story columns produces a strongly modeled and unified building. On the site, the reason for the amphitheater shape for this group of houses is immediately apparent, as the topography permits each house to enjoy a spectacular view (Figure 2.17).

The Woods' circus and crescent became the middle-class equivalent to the royal avenue and vista, a means of designing cities that was in keeping with a

2.17
The Royal Crescent at Bath, individual houses organized to form a grand architectural composition.

Traditional city design and the modern city

2.18
Squares and crescents are the
basic elements of design for
early nineteenth-century
Edinburgh.

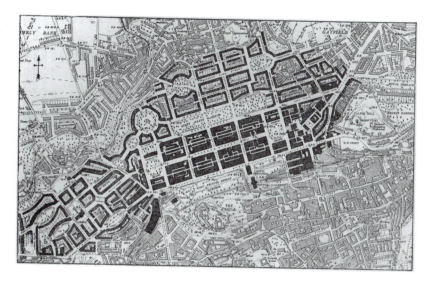

free-market economy and did not require the control of an autocrat. Circus and crescent were to be widely used for the rest of the eighteenth century and most of the nineteenth, notably at English seaside resorts, in the West End of London and in the new part of Edinburgh, where a succession of circuses and crescents were added in the early nineteenth century to James Craig's 1767 design, which has squares placed as formal ordering elements at each end of George Street (Figure 2.18).

The plan for Washington, DC, a city-design synthesis

A far more sophisticated synthesis of avenue and block, vista and square, was Major Pierre Charles L'Enfant's plan for Washington, DC. L'Enfant came to America from France in 1777, when he was twenty-three, to enlist in Washington's army, offering his services as a military engineer although his actual training was as an artist. L'Enfant's father was a painter, principally of battle scenes, and a member of the French Academy. After the Revolutionary War was over, L'Enfant settled in New York to practice architecture. George Washington, who had always gotten along well with the younger officer, chose L'Enfant to prepare the plans for the new capital city.

L'Enfant was responsible to three commissioners, but also received advice from the President, who had been trained as a surveyor, and from Thomas Jefferson, the Secretary of State, who was one of the great architectural intellects of the age.

Washington had played a major role in selecting the site for the city, and had himself negotiated the deal with the property owners that made the city possible: they would give up half of their land, plus whatever land was needed for the new streets and public buildings, in return for the added value that these streets and the new development would confer upon their remaining property. (Compensation was to be paid for land required for parks.)[12] There was strong opposition in Congress to the site on the Potomac, and Washington hoped to be able to finance the development of the city through lot sales, bypassing the need for major government support.

Washington met with L'Enfant on the site at the end of March 1791, and soon after sent him a letter enclosing his own ideas about the city. L'Enfant also received a sketch by Thomas Jefferson which set up a simple grid plan similar to Williamsburg, then the capital of Virginia (Figure 2.19). When L'Enfant showed Washington his much more ambitious plan, ultimately covering some 6,000 acres, it appealed to Washington because the plan included all the major land owners in the region. It would stop them from maneuvering to get the Federal City built on one or another individual property. Washington also seems to have understood L'Enfant's intentions and agreed with him about the scope and grandeur of the future city.

But L'Enfant's vision was not matched by his political skills; he was still only thirty-seven, although his ability to deal with people only became worse as he grew older. L'Enfant opposed the immediate sale of lots and instead proposed that money be borrowed against the value of the properties to finance building streets and parks that would enhance the value of the lots when they were put up for sale. L'Enfant may well have had the better idea, but when Washington and the commissioners decided to go ahead with the lot sale, L'Enfant was slow to cooperate by turning over his survey drawings. In his anxiety to secure the architectural commissions for the capitol and the President's house, he also opened himself to criticism by spending too much of his time on preliminary architectural drawings. By the end of the year all his drawings had been confiscated by the commissioners (the drawings have since been lost) and the commissioners had dismissed him with Washington's reluctant agreement.[13]

Despite L'Enfant's personal failure, his city design, taken out of his hands and drafted in final form by his associate, Andrew Ellicott, has been an enduring success (Figure 2.20). There is no direct documentary evidence of the sources that L'Enfant drew upon, but Elbert Peets, the city planner and city-design theorist, published an analysis in which he drew a genealogical table showing how L'Enfant's design derived from the Rome of Sixtus V, from Versailles and from plans for the reconstruction of London[14] (Figure 2.21). Peets demonstrated how L'Enfant almost certainly used Versailles as a reference in organizing his plan's principal features. As his father was a painter who relied on patronage from the court and wanted to train his son to follow him, L'Enfant had many opportunities to visit Versailles from childhood and would have known the gardens well.

Respecting topography, as he had explained to Washington, L'Enfant placed the capitol on the highest piece of land, and the President's house at the only other elevated location. The triangle formed by the White House, the Capitol and the intersection of their two axes turns out to be almost exactly one and one half times

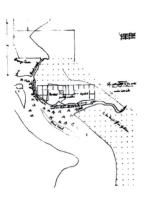

2.19
Jefferson's suggestion to L'Enfant for the plan of Washington, DC, a simple grid plan with a main street like Williamsburg, Virginia, where Jefferson had been governor when it was the state capital.

Traditional city design and the modern city

2.20

L'Enfant's plan for
Washington as presented by
his colleague Andrew Ellicott
after L'Enfant was fired by the
Commissioners.

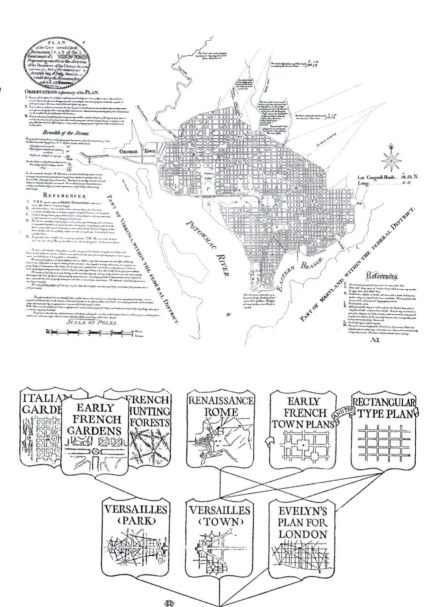

2.21

Elbert Peets' geneology of the
L'Enfant plan.

the distance shown on Blondel's plan of Versailles between the Grand Trianon, the
palace itself and the intersection of the two axes in the central basin of the canal.
The width of L'Enfant's mall is almost exactly that of the canal at Versailles, while
Pennsylvania Avenue is approximately the width of the Avenue de Trianon. Peets
also shows how the shape of the square that L'Enfant planned to surround the

President's house is derived from the two forecourts on the town side of the Palace of Versailles.

Peets also postulates that L'Enfant was heavily influenced by John Evelyn's third plan for the rebuilding of London. Evelyn kept tinkering with his plan in the hope that he could come up with a comprehensive reconstruction scheme that would be acceptable to the city merchants. In this version, Evelyn found a way to keep most of the parish churches in their traditional locations, although he was still proposing a new street system. While the resemblance of Washington to Evelyn's plan is undeniable, there is also a resemblance to Wren's London plan, which L'Enfant would equally probably have known, as the Evelyn and Wren plans were published together in the version that L'Enfant is most likely to have seen.

L'Enfant might well have found Wren's design more architecturally sympathetic because of its greater emphasis on vistas and spaces. It is also possible, of course, that L'Enfant arrived at his design without reference to either London plan, as the logical result of trying to reconcile topography and dominant axes with a street grid that had strong political support as the most practical method of land subdivision.

L'Enfant's eye for topography could have changed Jefferson's ideas about how to organize large architectural compositions. There is an anticipation of Jefferson's design for the University of Virginia in the way the axis from the Capitol goes straight along the open space of the Mall and across the river to the hills beyond, while the axis from the President's house is directed straight down the Potomac.[15]

Jefferson accepted L'Enfant's plan and promoted its development, but his own continued preference for the grid can be seen in the mile-square pattern surveyed all over the western territories acquired from France during his administration.[16] This grid in turn has had a pervasive effect on the cities and towns that have grown up in much of the United States, where the surveyor's square or rectangular blocks have set the basic city design.

John Nash and the realization of large-scale plans for London

The first effects of industrialization on cities, at the beginning of the nineteenth century, were very largely positive, the result of the tremendous increase in wealth, reflected in large numbers of new houses for the middle and upper classes as seen in London, Bath, and other cities. The pollution, overcrowding and other negative effects of industry were to come to the cities later, after the development of railway networks in the 1830s. The first factories were located near sources of water power. As the cities of the time were almost always built near navigable waterways, and waterfalls block navigation, industry almost always began well away from existing cities.

Cities began to grow, following the pattern already visible at Covent Garden in the 1630s: estates on the fashionable side of the city were subdivided, and the houses sold to rich people whose social standing was one notch below that of the estate owners and who wished to enjoy the prestige of the address. Later, commerce followed the carriage trade; and shops, also looking for prestige, invaded fashionable residential districts. Often, as at Covent Garden, the rich moved on, and the whole district became commercial. In Great Britain and North America this pattern emerged earlier than in Europe, where urban growth was inhibited by fortifications. The expansion of fashionable areas in American cities usually took the form of a street of mansions leading out of the city center up a hill or toward some other desirable location: Beacon Hill in Boston, Hillhouse Avenue in New Haven, Broadway in New York City, Charles Street in Baltimore. England, where the new industrial development was strongest, enjoyed the most marked increase in wealth, and the whole West End of London grew rapidly as a series of streets and squares of stylish houses.

John Nash was the architect who did the most to give this new expansion a designed form, and he managed to synthesize the incremental growth that characterized London real-estate development with the long vistas which had long been part of the theory of city design but had not previously been achieved in London. Nash became an official royal architect in 1806 and his most important opportunity followed in 1811, when the Prince Regent (whose father, George III, was still alive, but had become a lunatic and lived in seclusion at Windsor) asked Nash to prepare a plan for a large tract of undeveloped Crown land which was then on the edge of London's rapid westward expansion.

The royal lands were north of the existing fashionable district and could not be developed successfully without a new street that would connect them southward to the important parts of London. The only practical route was through the edge of a poor neighborhood adjoining fashionable areas that had already been built up to the west. The irregular route did not permit the long, straight street that in theory had become the standard vocabulary of city design, and the amount of land involved was far too large to be undertaken by a single developer.

Nash's design for Regent Street is a brilliant work of invention and coordination. Lower Regent Street begins at what was originally the site of Carlton House, the Prince Regent's residence, and a new square just to the north, Waterloo Place. From Waterloo Place the street runs north to a series of intersections at Piccadilly Circus, this circus an application of the Woods' innovation at Bath. Regent Street then switches westward in a reverse curve, the Quadrant, runs not quite straight northward and crosses Oxford Street at another circus. Just to the north, the succession of streets turns westward again, where the transition is marked by the spire of All Souls, Langham Place, and meets Great Portland Street, which leads north to a crescent that is the gateway to the new quarter that Nash designed, Regent's Park (Figure 2.22).

Regent's Park is another significant design formulation. Nash planned this district in a way that anticipated the development of garden-city-design principles, which we will come back to in the next chapter. Instead of a repeating pattern of street and square, Nash created a large park, like the grounds of a country estate,

2.22
John Nash's design for
Regent Street, a grand plan
threaded through an intricate
network of properties.

which was to serve as a green belt between the rows of houses around the outer edge and a circular cluster of development near the center. Around the northern perimeter of the park there was a canal, which served a market district in the southeast portion of the Regent's property (Figure 2.23).

The development of Regent's Park was never fully achieved, but Nash was able to oversee the completion of the whole length of Regent Street. This success helped prompt the Regent, now King George IV, to move to Buckingham Palace and tear down Carlton House, opening a prime development frontage on St. James's Park, which was then also designed by Nash.

2.23

Nash's plan for Regent's Park, originally planned as a complex, mixed-use development, shown as built by 1833.

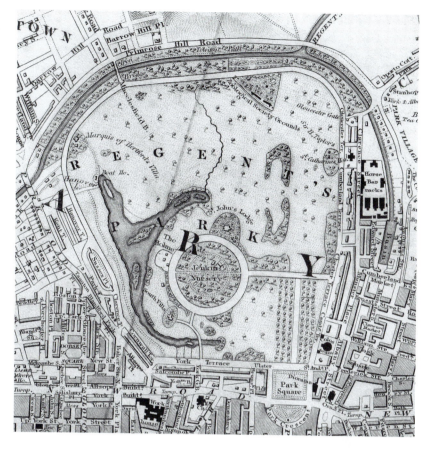

Nash as an architect has been accused of unrolling his facades like wallpaper to cover his large-scale architectural compositions, and because most of the work was executed in stucco, it has often been considered inferior to buildings constructed of stone. The buildings along Regent Street may have lacked studied refinement of detail, but in many cases Nash, as the entrepreneur who was putting the development of the whole street together, achieved the coordination of these buildings through diplomacy and did not design them directly himself. Nash managed to keep the control of the critical facades that close vistas or are important accents when the street system changes direction; and he was able to coordinate the architectural elements, like cornices and porches, needed to ensure the continuity of the whole composition.

As a piece of three-dimensional city design, Regent Street was unprecedented and has seldom been equaled. Trystan Edwards was one of the earliest commentators to appreciate Nash's contribution to London. In an essay written in 1923, while most of Nash's Regent Street was being demolished to make way for larger buildings, Edwards sought to answer Nash's critics with a defense of stucco as an admirably unifying building material which also reflects light beautifully; and followed his defense of stucco by an analysis of the devices, such as the spacing between windows and the ratios of window to wall, that Nash used to maintain unity among his facades.[17] Today, Nash's abilities are understood and appreciated; and most of his London buildings that have survived redevelopment and war damage have been restored; but Nash's Regent Street is gone. The street layout remains, but the new architecture lacks the original unity that came from the careful relationships of part to part and building to street.

Paris, prototype of a designed city

In the 1790s, L'Enfant's plans for Washington were exhibited in Paris, where they would have been seen as innovative and on an impressive scale. There is no evidence that L'Enfant's design for Washington had a direct influence on events in his home country, but large-scale city-design issues were a very relevant concern in France at the time. After the execution of Louis XVI in 1793, the Revolutionary Commune confiscated all royal land and appointed a Commission of Artists to replan Paris. The commission made the first detailed proposals for creating grand avenues and cutting long, straight streets through the densely inhabited parts of the city.

When Napoleon took power in 1799, he began implementing these proposals, notably the Rue de Rivoli, designed by Charles Percier and Pierre Fontaine in 1801, which created the street frontage facing the Tuileries Gardens. This design conformed to height limits related to the width of the streets which had been in force in Paris since the 1783.[18] The ground floor of the buildings facing the street was given over to an arcade and shops. The houses above had two principal floors, then a top story and an attic. The elevation was designed to be a series of simple, repeating elements with no center or end pavilions. Despite the hints available from painting, stage scenery, and individual buildings, it had never been clear just how the long, straight avenues that Fontana, Wren, and L'Enfant drew would be designed in three dimensions. An elevation drawing was signed by public officials to make it the official design guideline (Figure 2.24).

In the 1840s, Louis Napoleon, exiled to London, admired Regent Street and Nash's long rows of palatial house facades fronting on parks and gardens; when he returned to Paris and took power as Emperor Napoleon III, he hoped to be able to create equivalents there. The long, straight streets of the 1793 commission plan were said to have appealed to the first Napoleon as a means of keeping down the unruly Paris mob, and the same motive has been attributed to Napoleon III, who handed a map of priority street improvements to Georges Eugene Haussmann, the energetic administrator he had just appointed prefect of the Seine (Figure 2.25).

Haussmann did cite riot control as one of the advantages of the proposed new street system in a presentation to the Paris city council soon after he took office, but other major aims were slum clearance and traffic improvement, particularly connecting the newly constructed railway stations to each other and to the

2.24
The original design guideline
for the Rue de Rivoli, dated
year 12 of the Revolutionary
calendar, that is, 1805.

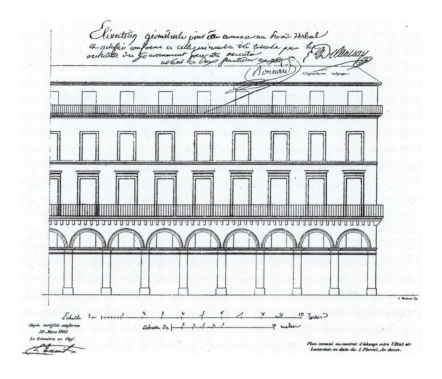

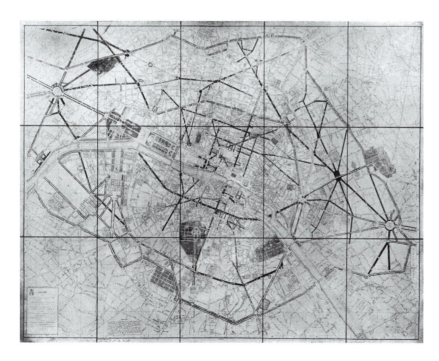

2.25
A progress report prepared
for Emperor Napoleon III by
Baron Haussmann in 1867
showing new streets
completed or in construction
up to that time.

important central destinations. Whatever military advantages the new street system possessed did not prevent the rising of the Paris Commune in 1871.

Haussmann turned out to have seventeen years to carry out the transformation of Paris, including not only new streets and buildings but a comprehensive reconstruction of the water supply, a new sewer system, and extensive park improvements. It was Haussmann who took the concept of the long, straight urban street—whose history by this time went back more than three centuries—and applied it for the first time in a systematic way to the redesign of an existing city. He made use of what we would today call excess condemnation, taking enough land not only for the right-of-way of the new street but for property development on either side. This property was sold to developers with restrictions that ensured a uniform series of facades[19] (Figure 2.26).

The basic building type for these new streets had shops on the ground floor, following the precedent of the Napoleonic Rue de Rivoli, and shops and offices on a mezzanine, if there was one. Instead of dividing the frontage vertically into individual houses, as was done in London or in Parisian squares like the Place des Vosges and the Place Vendôme, Haussmann used a large block divided horizontally. There would be three floors of spacious apartments, with smaller dwellings at the attic level, and even smaller rooms in a second attic, seven flights up. The facades were designed to express these horizontal divisions, with belt courses, balconies, and cornices, while rows of regularly spaced French windows imparted their rhythm to the street.

The new streets were broad boulevards with ample sidewalks that left room for rows of trees—an aspect of Haussmann's formulation learned, perhaps, from Versailles, but more probably from Nash and the gardens maintained in English squares since the end of the eighteenth century. An urban street lined with trees was a concept that would have been foreign to Sixtus V or Christopher Wren. Sometimes there was a garden with trees in the center of the Parisian boulevard as well. Haussmann would often arrange for full-grown trees to be transplanted to the new boulevards, giving a sense of completeness to raw, new districts. The parks designed by Haussmann's landscape engineer, Jean-Charles Adolphe Alphand, were important parts of the overall plan for Paris. Alphand took the kidney-shaped paths and artfully informal vistas of English gardening and applied them in a systematic way that was more French than English. The Bois de Boulogne and the Bois de Vincennes were to have been joined by a green belt that would have surrounded the whole city after the walls were taken down, but Haussmann was unable to muster the political support for this aspect of his plan (Figure 2.27).

Haussmann's methods were high-handed, but he did operate in an environment of law. The courts set the compensation that had to be paid to owners of properties that were expropriated, and that compensation was at least fair, and has been criticized for being too generous, allowing unreasonable profits to real-estate speculators. The money for property acquisition and construction was borrowed against future revenues that would result from the increased property values created by the planned improvements, a principle similar to modern theories

2.26
A Haussmann boulevard: enough property was condemned to permit new buildings on both sides of the new street following strict guidelines enforced through the sales agreement.

2.27
Haussmann and Alphand's plans for Paris included the redesign of the Bois de Boulogne and the Bois de Vincennes as picturesque parks in the English style.

about value recapture and tax-increment financing. Robert Moses, the manager of New York City's slum clearance and its park and highway construction for more than four decades, who perhaps considered himself a successor to Haussmann and a kindred spirit, reviewed Haussmann's career in an article published in 1942.[20] Moses' conclusion was that Haussmann's methods were perfectly applicable in a modern democratic society, and that Haussmann's personal debacle could have been avoided if he had paid more attention to public opinion and legislative fence-mending, and if his loans had had longer maturities.

As the work progressed, Haussmann began to borrow the money first and leave the legalities to be worked out later, and his attempts to evade legislative oversight led him to borrow on a dangerously short timescale. Haussmann's plans were also so comprehensive that he eventually made too many political enemies, particularly when his new streets began to invade the fashionable western district of Paris. As Napoleon III's political control began to weaken, Haussmann's record of mounting debts and unauthorized public expenditures put him in a more and more exposed position, until he was forced out of office in 1870. Haussmann thought he was working for an emperor. He failed to understand the transition to more democratic institutions that was taking place behind the facade of absolutist rule.

Haussmann has been criticized as a vandal who destroyed the historic urban texture of Paris, but the Paris beloved by tourists is very much Haussmann's city. Haussmann has also been praised for making one last heroic effort to impart a rational order to the process of nineteenth-century urbanization, which was rapidly moving out of control. Haussmann's redesign of Paris was a summation of the city-design principles that had been evolving since the Renaissance. It was their first comprehensive application to a major existing city. Despite Haussmann's dismissal and the end of Louis Napoleon's reign because of his disastrous war with Germany, the plans for Paris continued to be implemented.

The influence of Paris on city design

Other cities were making major changes at the same time as Paris. In Vienna the city walls were removed in the 1850s and replaced by the Ringstrasse, grand streets which provided a setting for civic buildings and opulent private mansions and opened up the connections between the old central city and newly annexed districts that had been outside the walls (Figure 2.28). In Barcelona also in the 1850s the walls came down, opening up expansion of the city according to the block plan of Ildefons Cerdà (Figure 2.29). But it was the image of the Parisian boulevard that was emulated in most European cities: a landscaped street lined with buildings, mostly middle-class apartments, of a uniform five or so stories, leading to civic buildings or a public space at the end of the view corridor. It was an adaptable concept that could be applied to a single street or a whole quarter. Haussmann and his collaborators had also created a vocabulary of street lights and street furniture, park designs, and tree

2.28
The Ringstrasse in Vienna formed a new district that replaced the fortifications.

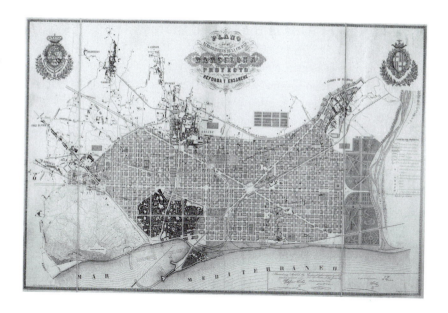

2.29
Block plan of Ildefons Cerdà for the expansion of Barcelona, map of 1859. The original city is at the lower left.

2.30
Street light designs from Alphand's *Promenades de Paris*.

planting methods. An interested visitor could study complete built examples in many different urban situations (Figure 2.30).

The importance of the Ecole des Beaux Arts in Paris to architectural education also contributed to the primacy of Paris as a template for city design. In the nineteenth century many entered the profession by working for established architects. But the French academy controlled prestigious government commissions in France and was considered the leader in architectural education even in countries that had their own academies. While the curriculum had been reformulated in the Napoleonic era, the Beaux Arts system of instruction went back to the classical vocabulary and typologies developed in the seventeenth century and to the unchallenged acceptance of traditional wisdom that Wren and his Royal Society colleagues had helped to overturn in the sciences. Students had to solve architectural design problems of graduated difficulty. At the beginning of the time set aside for solving the problem, the student had twelve hours to come up with the basic concept for the building, working in isolation *en loge*. The student's performance as a designer was assessed largely by how well the final design fulfilled the earlier sketch. This method required acceptance of an existing body of design principles and tested how well the student could use them.[21] It was the antithesis of the experimental methods of modernism, where every design was seen as an opportunity to conceive a building as if it had never been designed before. Beaux Arts instruction refused to adapt to elevator buildings and steel-frame structures. It became a stultifying influence on architecture—but its predictability continued to have advantages for designing cities. Haussmann could rely on a consensus about building design created by the Ecole des Beaux Arts system of instruction. This consensus continued to shape the boulevards of Europe during the early twentieth century, while the first tall buildings were going up in the United States.

The influence of Paris in the United States

During the nineteenth century, American architectural schools were founded to teach the Beaux Arts curriculum and many of the best students went on to study in Paris. There they not only were confirmed in the rightness of their instruction but they were able to observe the new Paris going up all around them. The coalescence of Beaux Arts architecture and Haussmannesque planning principles into the City Beautiful movement in the United States began with the great public success of the design for the central group of buildings at the World's Columbian Exposition, held in Chicago in 1893. The architects for the buildings in the Court of Honor around the central lagoon agreed, under the chairmanship of Daniel Burnham, to follow an arrangement designed by the landscape architect Frederick Law Olmsted and his young associate, Henry Codman; to employ a similar architectural vocabulary, based on French academic classicism; and to coordinate such elements as axes of symmetry and cornice lines. During the design process two of the architectural firms also voluntarily omitted central domed elements from their buildings because they competed with the dominance of Richard Morris Hunt's administration building at the head of the lagoon (Figure 2.31).

Burnham did not have a Beaux Arts diploma but most of the principal architects of the Exposition, including the relatively iconoclastic Louis Sullivan, had studied in Paris. This exhibition, with its colossal architectural and civic spaces quickly built in

2.31
The Court of Honor at the Chicago World's Fair of 1893.

Traditional city design and the modern city

lath and plaster, was intended by its designers to demonstrate both what city design could and should be like and to show the American public what an appropriate civic character could do for their cities. A traditional role for architects has been to assist arriviste clients in creating a background and setting appropriate to their newly achieved status. The United States was a newly rich nation, and the architects of the 1893 fair wished to help it achieve an instant cultural heritage. The fair made Daniel Burnham, its coordinating architect, into a national figure. He was elected president of the American Institute of Architects, which led to an involvement in the politics of governmental architecture, and eventually to the chairmanship of the Senate Park Commission, set up in 1901 at the initiative of Senator James McMillan, chairman of the Senate's District of Columbia Committee.

The other members of the commission were Frederick Law Olmsted, Jr., who had taken over the direction of the family firm when his father retired in 1895, and Charles F. McKim of McKim, Mead and White, who had probably the most subtle architectural intelligence involved in the design of the Chicago fair and who had become a strong friend of Burnham's.[22]

The Park Commission's plan, usually called the McMillan plan, restored and elaborated upon L'Enfant's original design, and became the basis for planning most of the monumental government buildings in Washington during the next forty years, notably the Federal Triangle and the Lincoln and Jefferson memorials. Burnham succeeded in negotiating the railway tracks and station out of the Mall in front of the Capitol, the railroads agreeing to create Union Station north of Capitol Hill as a replacement, and the government agreeing to finance a tunnel to take the tracks under the Mall. The Mall itself was replanned in harmony with the French garden design that must have been L'Enfant's intention, removing various accretions, including Andrew Jackson Downing's picturesque English garden in front of the Smithsonian, and bending the Mall slightly, to place the Washington Monument—which, because of foundation problems, was built off both the Capitol and the White House axes—in the center of the Mall (Figure 2.32).

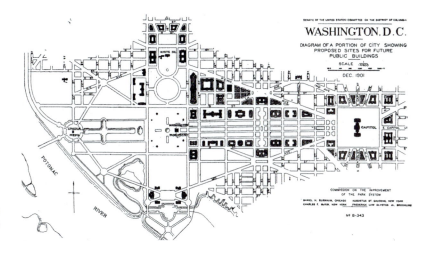

2.32
The McMillan Plan for Washington, which restored the primacy of L'Enfant's plan but closed the vistas from the White House and the Capitol.

Traditional city design and the modern city   **83**

McKim drew elaborate plans, which have never been implemented, to create a setting for the Washington Monument that would also recognize the axis from the White House. McKim's design for the placement of the Lincoln Memorial and the Tidal Basin closed the vistas from the White House and the Capitol that L'Enfant had daringly left open, making the overall composition of monumental Washington much more self-contained and static, in the same way that McKim's partner Stanford White had closed the axis of Jefferson's University of Virginia with a group of three additional buildings.

However, the most important action to ensure the preservation of the L'Enfant plan and the design continuity of monumental Washington was taken in 1898, by Senator McMillan's District of Columbia Committee, when it recommended and Congress enacted height limits of 60 feet for non-fireproof construction, 90 feet for any building on a residential street, and 110 feet for buildings on the widest streets.[23] It is not at all clear that Burnham understood the critical importance of this enactment in preserving the validity of a monumental city-design concept for Washington. The height limit issue would have been settled by the time the commission began work, and there was not that much demand for tall buildings in Washington at the time or up to World War II. Since then there have been many proposals to break the Washington height limit, but so far, the limit has been retained, with only minor modifications.

The height issue was also critical to the success or failure of Burnham's Chicago plan, which was published in 1909. It was the most famous plan of the City Beautiful movement and a pivotal document in the history of city design. By the time Burnham was asked to prepare a plan for his home city, he had designed a civic center for Cleveland, plans for Manila and its summer capital at Baguio, and, with Edward Bennett, a plan for San Francisco that was completed and accepted just the day before the great earthquake and fire of 1906. The San Francisco plan was a comprehensive design in which a group of civic buildings on Market Street became the focal point for Haussmannesque avenues radiating across the city. The earthquake and fire made it more difficult to implement a comprehensive plan. As in London in 1666, the top priority was to get the city in operation again, not to reorganize it. However, the civic center group was later constructed much as proposed in the plan, although in a slightly different location, and some elements of the park plan were also carried out.

Although the purpose of Burnham and Bennett's Chicago plan was civic beautification, the underlying traffic and transportation issues were carefully studied. The plan placed an overlay of Parisian boulevards on Chicago's existing gridiron street system and, by reorganizing the railroad lines, cleared the lakefront for a series of monumental parks (Figures 2.33–2.35).

Chicago owes its landscaped lakefront and the boulevard character of Michigan Avenue to this plan, which was well promoted through an extensive public relations campaign. However, there was no mechanism like the Washington height limit that would supplement the persuasive power of the plan itself and require

2.33
The central civic group from the 1909 Burnham Plan for Chicago, which placed an overlay of Parisian boulevards on Chicago's existing gridiron street system and, by reorganizing the railroad lines, cleared the lakefront for a series of monumental parks.

2.34
Burnham assumed a height limit of thirteen stories but there was no enforcement mechanism.

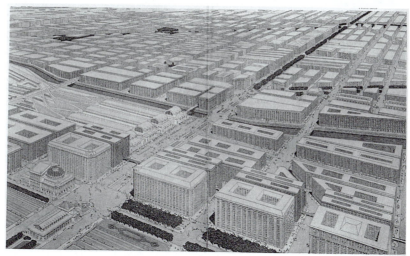

private investors to follow its directions. The legal opinion that forms the final chapter of the Chicago plan, written by Walter I. Fisher, saw no legal obstacles to the construction of the parks, public buildings, and new streets, other than a need for legislation that would greatly increase the city's powers to borrow money. Walter Fisher was doubtful about the applicability of the excess condemnation system that Haussmann had used in Paris, wondering whether such land takings could be justified as a public purpose. The opinion concludes that the problem could be solved if enabling legislation would be passed by the State of Illinois, although with some equivocation about whether the federal courts would find the state action constitutional.

2.35
The Chicago Plan proposed a
Parisian cityscape at the
Chicago River.

Zoning ordinances had already been enacted in Europe, and studies toward the New York City zoning ordinance were to begin only four years later, but neither Fisher nor anyone else seems to have thought of zoning as an implementation mechanism for monumental plans. Burnham had to know that the tall building posed a problem to his design for the city. His own office was continuously producing tall buildings during all the years that he worked on his city plans. The Chicago plan attempts to deal with this issue by setting uniform heights for elevator buildings, but there is no enforcement mechanism, and uniform height regulations run counter to the great variations in real-estate values to be found in Chicago's business districts.

The origins of modern city planning in the Parisian consensus

The Chicago Plan looked for a while as if it had translated Parisian concepts for use in the new industrial metropolis. In 1910 the Royal Institute of British Architects sponsored an international conference on Town Planning at which Daniel Burnham was a major speaker and the drawings for both the Chicago Plan and the Washington Plan were exhibited. To the conference participants it looked as if monumental city centers, railway-based industrial districts, and lower-density residential areas linked by rail lines and designed as garden suburbs—which we will come back to in the next chapter—provided a complete system for city design and development.

The design of Canberra, the new capital of Australia, is a good illustration of what was expected of city design at the time of the London conference and the first conference on city planning in the United States which took place in 1909. The designers, who won an international competition in 1912, were Walter Burley Griffin and Marion Mahony Griffin, architects and landscape architects from Chicago (and former employees of Frank Lloyd Wright). Eliel Saarinen's design was placed second, and that of Frenchman, Donat-alfred Agache, third. Much of the winning design was essentially a garden city, but there was a monumental center to the plan, which is as powerful in its way as the design structure of Burnham and Bennett's Chicago plan.

Like L'Enfant, the Griffins used topography as the basis for geometric organization. Three hills denoted the locations for the capitol, the civic center, and the market center. They are connected by long, straight streets to form an equilateral triangle. The capitol is treated as the vertex, and a straight line, the land axis, runs from the capitol, bisecting the triangle, crosses the municipal axis, which is the base of the triangle, and extends to Mount Ainslie, a prominent landscape feature at the boundary of the city. Halfway between the vertex and the base of the triangle is the water axis, running through a basin, which was intended to be symmetrically disposed about the land axis. The water fills the valley between the three hills and then continues in both directions along the dammed-up Molonglo River valley. The part of the triangle nearest the vertex was the site for the government buildings, grouped symmetrically around the land axis (Figure 2.36).[24]

New Delhi, the planned British capital of India, is also a garden city with a monumental center. The Griffins' design plus seven more premiated entries in the Canberra competition were available to Edwin Lutyens, Herbert Baker, and the other members of the Delhi Town Planning Committee during the formative stages of their work, which was completed at the end of March 1913.[25] This original Delhi plan, which was later modified to permit the addition of a parliament house not at first contemplated in the imperial program, has some strong resemblances to the geometric organization of the Griffins' design, although there are many important differences. The main axis of New Delhi lies approximately east–west, centering on the viceroy's palace and the administrative secretariat, which are placed atop the highest land mass in the immediate area. A line drawn north–south through the secretariat buildings forms the base of two equilateral triangles. The western triangle encloses the viceroy's palace and gardens; at the vertex of the eastern triangle is a memorial arch that lies at the end of a monumental avenue that runs up the hill, passes between the secretariat buildings and terminates at the viceroy's palace. A cross axis halfway down the main avenue runs northward to a circular commercial center, Connaught Place—which is in many ways analogous to Canberra's civic center—and forms the vertex of a larger equilateral triangle which encloses the entire monumental government complex. There is another important line of sight at sixty degrees to the main avenue, which connects the secretariats through Connaught Place to the Jama Masjid, the great mosque in the center of old Delhi. When the parliament building was added, it was placed on this Jama Masjid axis, just to the north-east of the secretariat buildings (Figure 2.37).

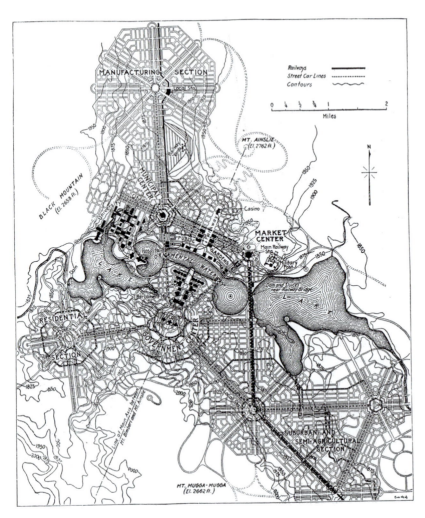

The palace and secretariat at New Delhi are now recognized as one of the great architectural achievements of the twentieth century. Lutyens and Baker were able to attain a vitality in their monumental architecture that has eluded most other modern practitioners, perhaps because their program was a thoroughly traditional one, although for an autocracy that was already an anachronism when construction began.

The Parisian consensus had its opponents among advocates of traditional city design. Sitte's critique of Haussmannesque planning, *City Building According to Artistic Principles,* was first published in Vienna in 1889.[26] Sitte was the head of government schools for artisans in Salzburg and then Vienna, and a champion of the craft tradition. He sought by analysis of the great civic spaces of the past to deduce the principles on which they were designed. While his book includes many medieval town squares, Sitte was equally interested in the great Renaissance plazas. For Sitte, the emphasis placed on the long avenue, which had dominated city design

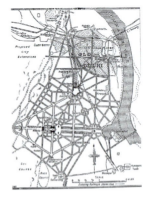

2.37
The plan for New Delhi by
Edwin Lutyens and Herbert
Baker, completed in 1913.

since Sixtus V and would seem to be the essence of most City Beautiful plans, was nowhere near as important as the enclosure of spaces at appropriate scales. The point of conflict occurs at spaces that terminate avenues. Sitte believed that the appropriate enclosure of the space took precedence over the views of important buildings seen down radiating avenues. He particularly objected to the siting of a building like the Paris Opera, which is an island in the middle of intersecting streets. Sitte argued that important buildings of this kind deserved their own enclosed precinct, and his book contains diagrams of the way in which the Votivkirche and other significant buildings in Vienna could be improved by being given what he believed would be an appropriate context of smaller surrounding structures (Figure 2.38).

Because Sitte's book helped bring about a revival of interest in medieval city forms, he is sometimes classified as a romantic and a champion of winding streets and irregular spaces. In his own work as a planning practitioner, however, Sitte showed himself to be interested both in orderly traffic flow and in minimizing practical problems like land assembly. He used straight streets and rectangular city blocks where they suited his purpose. Sitte's greatest influence, nevertheless, was over the picturesque architectural compositions created for garden cities and garden suburbs.

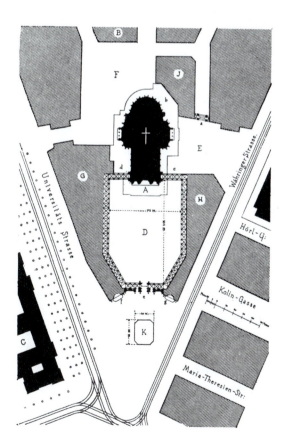

2.38
Camillo Sitte's proposal for enclosing the precinct around the Votivkirche in Vienna. Sitte placed spatial enclosure ahead of using monumental buildings to terminate vistas.

Traditional city design and the modern city

The decline of Parisian city design

Sitte had no more to say about the tall building than Haussmann. Le Corbusier and his modernist colleagues understood that tall buildings made possible by the steel frame and the passenger elevator would undermine traditional city designs based on the unspoken assumption that no building will be taller than the maximum distance people will walk up stairs. The tall building, which permitted growth to take place in large increments, also undermined the assumption that districts would develop gradually at a relatively uniform density. The elevator permitted a direct expression of underlying land values; building owners could choose almost any height they wanted.

For many years the existence of the elevator did not seem to pose an immediate city-planning issue in most countries. During the period between the two world wars, tall buildings were a relative rarity except in North America, and even the modern architecture built in the center of older cities was usually of a type that would fit into the prevailing street frontage with very little disturbance of established patterns.

In North America it would have been possible to maintain building heights and densities by means of codes, as was done in Paris, but codes become harder to enforce the more they run contrary to economic realities. None of the numerous plans for cities produced under the influence of the City Beautiful movement between the 1893 fair and the economic depression after 1929 found a successful means to incorporate the tall building and other types of private investment into the design. As a result these plans have left as legacies park systems and groups of monumental government buildings, but only Washington was given a single, coherent image, because of the height limit and because the monumental center sets so much of its character.

New York City's first zoning ordinance, adopted in 1916, made a simplified version of traditional city design into a legal necessity. Buildings were required to be set back from the building line when they attained a height that was mathematically related to the width of the street, a greatly enlarged version of the kinds of design controls that had been in force in Paris since the eighteenth century. The consistency of the lower portions of apartment buildings facing Central Park, Riverside Park or Park Avenue that were built under the 1916 ordinance (it was revised completely in 1961) created something akin to the Parisian boulevard, although nowhere near as uniform and on a much larger scale. In Manhattan's midtown and Wall Street districts, zoning was less successful in creating design continuity. The framers of the ordinance had recognized that the logical result of setback requirements was that all buildings would have to taper to floor sizes that made less and less economic sense. Using Cass Gilbert's 1913 Woolworth Building as a model, the zoning was written so that once a tower had set back to a point where it filled 25 percent of the lot area or less, it could continue straight up without further modification.

2.39
This 1932 sketch of
Rockefeller Center shows how
the symmetry of the two
pavilions on Fifth Avenue
frame the central office
building and relate the tower
to the scale of the street.

Rockefeller Center, designed in its current form in 1931, used some traditional city-design concepts in an attempt to organize a group of tall buildings. The design, led by Raymond Hood of the associated offices of Reinhard & Hofmeister; Corbett, Harrison and MacMurray; and Hood and Fouilhoux placed two pairs of six-story buildings on Fifth Avenue to frame the axis of the RCA (now General Electric) and Associated Press buildings (Figure 2.39). The concept of a tall tower related by an axis to a forecourt is close to the Beaux Arts tradition, even when the tower is seventy stories high, but there is no comparable logic in the relationship between the dominant RCA building and the other tall structures in the complex.

Rockefeller Center, begun before the worldwide economic depression and kept going by a great private fortune, was an exception in the shifting focus of city design from private investment to the activities of governments. Monumental architectural groups continued to be the preferred expression for governmental buildings, although this was the period of experimentation with modernist ideas of city design in subsidized housing and other government projects.

Traditional city design and totalitarian power

Nazi ideology considered modern architecture decadent, and also questioned the tall building and even steel-frame construction. Adolf Hitler, who had been turned down for admission to the School of Architecture at Vienna's Academy of Fine Arts, frequently stopped in at the studio of Albert Speer, his official architect, to check on the progress of the 1939 plan for Berlin and to make suggestions of his own. Hitler greatly admired Haussmann's Paris and the monumental buildings of Vienna's Ringstrasse, and he sought to surpass them in his own capital.

The Berlin plan resembled other city plans of the period. Its monumental sequence of boulevards lined with governmental and corporate administration buildings was to be achieved without otherwise changing the fabric of the city. Land was assembled by the government, and then individual parcels were assigned to different official agencies or sold to private industries interested in a showcase location for their corporate headquarters. There was a functional purpose to the boulevard design, as it was linked to a plan for rationalizing the railroad system, and there was a major railroad terminal at each end of the new boulevard sequence[27] (Figure 2.40).

Speer's New State Chancellery of 1937 was not radically different from the architecture of other capital cities in the 1930s, including Washington, DC; and much of the government-architecture planned for the new boulevards was similarly conventional, as were private buildings, such as Peter Behrens's projected headquarters building for AEG. Only the gigantic scale of the whole project, and the great hall and triumphal arch, betray underlying megalomania. Speer asserted that the arch and great hall were to be paid for by private donations, which can be read as a sinister statement in view of the expropriation of the property of Jews that was

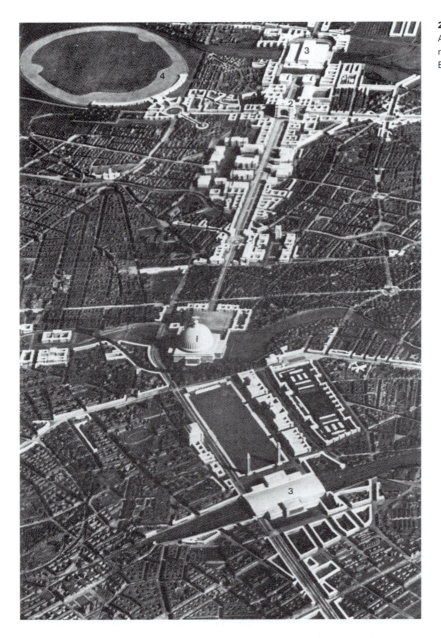

2.40
Albert Speer's plan for a
monumental boulevard in
Berlin.

going on at the time the plan was being drawn, along with grand plans for foreign
conquests.

The Soviet Union, at first receptive to the most advanced projects of radical
modernist architects, was redirected towards traditional city design under Stalin, with
building facades holding the street line in the Parisian manner using neo-classical
architectural motifs such as triumphal arches to emphasize important locations. In
Rome, Mussolini continued modernizing the city in ways analogous to Haussmann's
Paris, a process which had begun with the unification of Italy in 1870. Mussolini

placed strong emphasis on stabilizing and restoring Roman ruins as a way of emphasizing a glorious past, and also on creating long, straight streets, notably the Via della Concilazione, which implemented a long-standing proposal to create a new boulevard leading to Bernini's forecourt in front of St. Peter's.[28]

The identification of monumental architecture with Nazi, Soviet, and fascist ideology and with authoritarianism in general helps explain the widespread revulsion against traditional city-planning ideas after World War II, although the major reasons for the change were the emergence of the tall building as a major ingredient in almost all cities, and the increasing influence of the automobile in dispersing the uniform densities that once prevailed in city centers.

Traditional proportions as an antidote to modernism

In the late 1930s and 1940s art historian Rudolf Wittkower published a series of articles in the Journal of the Warburg and Courtauld Institutes which he collected and published in 1949 as *Architectural Principles in the Age of Humanism*.[29] Wittkower explained the geometry and proportional systems used by Renaissance architects with enough detail that a modern architect could figure out how to use them. This work of scholarship created so much interest among architects that the owner of a London architectural bookstore, Alec Tiranti, republished it for his customers.[30]

Wittkower reminded readers that Pythagoras, the sixth-century BC Greek mathematician, was credited with discovering that:

> musical consonances corresponded to the length of the strings that produced them according to the ratios of small whole numbers ... If two strings are made to vibrate under the same conditions, one being half the length of the other, the pitch of the shorter string will be one octave above that of the longer one. If the lengths of the strings are in the relation of two to three, the difference in pitch will be a fifth, and if they are in a relation of three to four, the difference in pitch will be a fourth. Thus the consonances on which the Greek musical system was based—octave, fifth and fourth—can be expressed by the progression 1:2:3:4. And this progression contains ... also the two composite consonances the Greeks recognized, namely octave plus fifth (1:2:3) and two octaves (1:2:4).

One can understand, Wittkower concludes, "that this staggering discovery made people believe that they had seized upon the mysterious harmony which pervades the universe."[31] Wittkower went on to summarize Plato's explanation in *Timaeus* of the numbers that underlie the harmony of the world: 1, 2, 3, 4, 8, 9, and 27, and how these Platonic systems were then incorporated into Renaissance architectural thinking, such as the proportions that Palladio sets forth in his treatise *I Quattro Libri dell'Architettura*.

Wittkower's pupil, Colin Rowe, contributed to contemporary discussion about Palladio's design methods by relating them directly to what he asserted were comparable geometric and proportional systems in houses designed by Le Corbusier during the 1920s. Rowe's article appeared in the *Architectural Review* in 1947.[32] Le Corbusier himself, perhaps responding to the interest in geometry and proportion across the Channel, published his own theory of architectural geometry and proportion, *Le Modulor*, the following year.[33] Le Corbusier used metric dimensions, but the root of the system was his estimate of the height of the human figure. Originally Le Corbusier used 1.75 meters but in a revised version he decided upon six feet, "the height of the tallest man" (Le Corbusier was evidently not a basketball fan).[34]

The attraction of proportional systems to the first cohort of modernist architects and planners was that it promised a way of organizing both individual buildings and groups of buildings which was not available from modernist ideology. Perhaps these abstract relationships could give architects an equivalent to the organizational mechanisms provided by classical columns, cornices, pediments, pavilions, and the rest of the apparatus of traditional design. Le Corbusier claims to have used his Modulor system in his own designs. However, proportions by themselves turned out to be an insignificant influence on city design; they were insufficient to impart coherence to groups of modern buildings.

Lincoln Center: a failure of modernism

In the early 1960s six of the leading modernist architects of the time were assigned buildings at the Lincoln Center complex in New York City. The architect for the concert hall was Max Abramovitz; for the opera house, Wallace Harrison. Philip Johnson was the architect for the ballet theater, Gordon Bunshaft for the performing arts library, Eero Saarinen for the repertory theater, and Pietro Belluschi was the design architect for the Julliard school of music and its concert hall. The Lincoln Square Urban Renewal District was one of the many projects of Robert Moses, but the performing arts center within it was a project of the Rockefeller family, still looking to create a new setting for the Metropolitan Opera which had once been planned as the centerpiece of Rockefeller Center. John D. Rockefeller III was the Chairman of Lincoln Center. His brother Nelson had just been elected Governor of New York State. Harrison had a long connection with projects backed by the Rockefeller family. He had been one of the directing architects for Rockefeller Center, had been the coordinating architect for the UN Headquarters complex in New York City, where the land had been purchased for the UN by John D. Rockefeller Jr., and was working on what became the Empire State Plaza in Albany, New York, for Governor Nelson Rockefeller. Harrison's partner Max Abramovitz had worked with him on Rockefeller Center and the UN, and their partnership had also designed many corporate office buildings including the Alcoa tower in Pittsburgh. Abramovitz also had an independent reputation as the designer of college and university buildings. Philip Johnson had moved on from being the curator of modern architecture at the Museum of Modern Art to becoming an architect, designing a famous house for himself in New Canaan, Connecticut, plus other well-known houses, and had recently designed a museum in Utica and was working on another one in Fort Worth. He had also collaborated with Ludwig Mies van der Rohe on the design of the Seagram Building in New York City. Gordon Bunshaft was the design partner for Skidmore, Owings & Merrill's hugely successful New York office. Eero Saarinen was gaining attention with his highly sculptural buildings, each one creating a different significant form, from the Kresge auditorium at MIT (see p. 46) to the swooping shapes of the TWA terminal at what was then called Idlewild Airport, which Saarinen was working on at the time of the Lincoln Center design meetings. Pietro Belluschi had been a pioneer of modernist architecture, including his art museum in Portland, Oregon, completed in 1932 and the Equitable Building, also in Portland, completed in 1948, a rigorously designed structure with an expressed structural frame and large panes of glass. At the time of the design sessions for Lincoln Center, Belluschi was the dean of architecture and planning at MIT.

This high-powered group, each member with his own staff of assistants, agreed in principle that Lincoln Center should have its own design identity, and not just be a collection of individual buildings. They were able to agree that most of the buildings should occupy a raised platform, over parking, forming a superblock extending from 62nd Street to 65th Street between Columbus and Amsterdam Avenues. The Julliard School would be built across 65th Street and connected to the raised platform by a bridge. The superblock and the raised plaza were both modernist orthodoxy. But how should the buildings be placed on the platform, how should they relate to each other, what should be their design relationship? The group was not prepared to have any one member set the character of the design for the others, and they could not reach an agreement.[35]

Finally, Philip Johnson found the means for an acceptable compromise by going back to one of the points of origin of traditional city design, Michelangelo's Capitoline Hill in Rome (Figure 2.11, p. 63). From Michelangelo, Johnson took the placement of three buildings with their central axes meeting at a central focal point, and the idea of facing the buildings with a colonnade of regularly spaced columns extending from the ground to the top of each building, a way of organizing multi-story facades believed to be Michelangelo's invention. The three buildings are Harrison's opera house, in the central position, flanked by Abramovitz's concert hall and Johnson's dance theater. Johnson persuaded Harrison and Abramovitz to design their main lobby floors at the same level above the plaza as the main lobby floor of the dance theater. The architects also agreed to use the same travertine facing. In the center of the central plaza, which Johnson ended up designing, is a circular fountain instead of the equestrian statue in Rome, but Johnson's pavement pattern is based on Michelangelo's (Figure 2.41).

2.41
The Plaza at Lincoln Center.
Philip Johnson persuaded the
other participating architects
to use traditional city design
ideas to unify modern
buildings at Lincoln Center.

Of course, there are huge differences between the summit of Capitoline Hill and Lincoln Center's level plaza. Michelangelo was reorganizing an existing site and working with the specifics of what was already there. He used the angles of the two flanking buildings to create exaggerated perspective views, while Lincoln Center's three core buildings form the simplest and most straightforward of arrangements. Lincoln Center's thin steel columns have very different proportions from the stone columns and pilasters of the Capitoline Hill, there are large glass windows, and many other significant differences. All the same, Johnson was reaching back outside of the modernist ideology that he had been so instrumental in promoting in order to find a way of composing a group of buildings. At one point he had even proposed an ornamental colonnade to close the fourth side of the plaza.

It is hard to believe that Saarinen, Bunshaft, and Belluschi were won over by the logic of Johnson's design. The hidden ingredient in its acceptance was the patronage of the Rockefeller family. Johnson had Rockefeller connections through the Museum of Modern Art. Abby Aldrich Rockefeller, Nelson and John's mother, was one of the founders of the Museum of Modern Art. Johnson had designed a guest house commissioned by John D. Rockefeller III's wife Blanchette, a trustee of the Museum of Modern Art. So while the six architects were theoretically equal, once Johnson had brought Harrison and Abramovitz to his side, it was possible to relegate Saarinen's and Bunshaft's buildings to subsidiary positions beside the opera house. Belluschi's Julliard was across 65th Street.

At much the same time as Johnson was working on Lincoln Center he had also been experimenting with a more modest colonnade for the facade of the Amon Carter Museum in Fort Worth, which had a commanding position facing a park that seemed to call for more than the vocabulary of modernism could offer. Johnson's diagnosis of the problem was incisive, even if his solutions were far from definitive. Johnson's extensive knowledge of architectural history was matched by his sense of irony. He was comfortable showing that modernism, for which he had been one of the most important advocates, was incapable of organizing a diverse group of buildings.[36]

Landmarks and historic districts: a critique of modernist planning

In August of 1962 a group of architects and preservationists, including Philip Johnson, set up a picket line in front of New York City's monumental Pennsylvania Station to protest its impending demolition to make way for an office building and a sports arena. The buildings had been completed in 1910 to the designs of McKim Mead and White at a time when traditional city design called for monumental building groups to mark important locations. The protest attracted some press coverage, but did not change the minds of the City Planning Commission or the most prominent supporters of historic preservation, who accepted the demolition as inevitable. While some architects recognized the building's extraordinary merit as a major element of city design, most others at the time felt that it was an outmoded relic that no longer had a place in the modern city. I sat at a table with Max Abramovitz at an Architectural League dinner that fall and mentioned that I had taken part in the protest. "At your age," he said, "I would have been picketing to have the building torn down." Pennsylvania Station was demolished the following year. The shocked public reaction to the loss of a structure that had seemed an integral part of everyday life helped lead to the establishment of the New York City Landmarks Preservation Commission in 1965. Its first full-time chairman, Harmon Goldstone, had been one of the members of the New York City Planning Commission when it unanimously approved the zoning change that led to the demolition of the station.[37]

The Old and Historic District in Charleston, South Carolina was first enacted in 1931, the Vieux Carre in New Orleans became a historic district in 1937, the historic district in Alexandria, Virginia, dates from 1946, and the preservation of Beacon Hill in Boston from 1955. However, the mid-1960s marked a turning point in the preservation of traditional city districts and landmark buildings like Pennsylvania Station. The Federal Historic Preservation Act of 1966 included guidelines for the establishment of local historic districts and the preservation of individual buildings. This act also established the National Register of Historic Places. Much of the political force behind this act and the local actions that went with it came from disillusion with modernist city design which placed no value on the work of the past. People no longer trusted architects and planners to replace what was demolished with something as good or better.

In the traditional city "life takes place on foot"

Another influential critique of modernist city planning was *The Death and Life of Great American Cities* by Jane Jacobs, originally published in 1961 and still selling at a substantial rate some fifty years later. Jacobs drew on examples of the way people lived in her own neighborhood in the Greenwich Village section of New York City to demonstrate the superiority of traditional city design to modernist housing towers set in parks or the desolation created by cutting expressways through older neighborhoods. The way people can meet and communicate when walking to their destinations was a central part of her argument. Streets should promote walking; and short blocks offer a much more flexible choice of routes than the modernist superblock or large, empty park spaces. Another important argument: development should be incremental, with uses changing and evolving along with people's needs. Neighborhoods could "unslum" over time, and the worst possible policy was the wholesale demolition of whole districts, and their replacement with superblocks and towers, the standard modernist prescription. Jacobs also strongly criticized wasteful patterns of urban growth and the resulting destruction of the natural landscape. So many of Jacobs' statements have now been accepted as axiomatic that it is hard to remember that her book was once considered a radical tract. She was by no means the only person saying such things at the time, but the passion and clarity of her writing gave her a wide readership. Both the strength and the weakness of her book was that it was argued from common sense and direct observation. Herbert Gans' *The Urban Villagers,* first published the following year, helped substantiate Jacobs' arguments about the complexity of traditional urban neighborhoods and their ability to "unslum," based on Gans' experience living in Boston's West End, just prior to its demolition for urban renewal, presented as a piece of sociological fieldwork.[38]

Jacobs' friend William H. Whyte was the author of a famous critique of business culture, *The Organization Man,* first published in 1956. Generations of job applicants profited from the book's appendix on how to answer personality tests in ways acceptable to corporate employers. Whyte was also very interested in what was happening to cities, editing a book *The Exploding Metropolis* published in 1958, which included an essay by Jane Jacobs, "Downtown is for People," and an essay by Whyte advocating controlling urban sprawl by conserving the natural landscape. In 1959, Whyte published an article on conservation easements, following this with a book, *Cluster Development,* on development regulations based on transferring development rights away from landscapes worth saving, and then a more general set of warnings and prescriptions, *The Last Landscape* in 1966.[39] Whyte then turned to substantiating some of the statements that Jacobs and others were making about the different ways people responded to traditional and modernist cities, using time-lapse photography and mapping the locations of people in public spaces at busy times of the day. His conclusions were presented in his 1980 book *The Social Life of Small Urban Spaces* and then in 1988: *City: Rediscovering the Center.*[40] Whyte documented behavior. He could show that people would sit in plazas where they could watch other people walking by or where the microclimate was pleasant; that they would walk on streets with interesting store fronts and shun sidewalks flanked by modernist blank walls. He documented how the spare surfaces of the typical modernist public space made them virtually unusable, and suggested prescriptions, such as movable chairs, that allowed people to shape their own public space experience. Whyte's research was the basis for a total revision of New York City's public open space regulations, and has been influential in many other cities.

Whyte's work in New York was paralleled by the research of Danish architect, Jan Gehl, who has successfully advocated giving primacy to pedestrians as a way to safeguard Copenhagen and other traditional cities from high-speed traffic and the demolition of buildings for parking lots. It was Gehl who formulated the most succinct summary of the advantages of the traditional city: "life takes place on foot," the antithesis of Le Corbusier's vision of the urban dweller driving from tower to tower on elevated motor ways at 100 miles an hour.

New York City's neighborhood planning policies and urban design codes

In the mid-1960s New York City adopted new policies intended to be correctives to the problems that had been created by modernist city-design methods. The first was a change in the way urban renewal was implemented: from designating whole neighborhoods for demolition to a neighborhood renewal policy where planners worked with a committee of local leaders to identify sites for new infill housing, while leaving the basic structure of the neighborhood intact. This infill strategy was also applied to commercial renewal projects in downtown Brooklyn, downtown Jamaica in Queens, and the Fordham Road district in the Bronx. Federal guidelines for urban renewal were later changed to make neighborhood-based infill renewal the standard, but this did not happen until Federal funds for urban renewal were being phased out.

New York City had adopted a new zoning code in 1961 which encouraged separate towers surrounded by open space in higher density residential and commercial districts. The first of these new buildings were seen to be so disruptive that the urban design group of the Planning Commission immediately looked for ways to safeguard the existing, traditional fabric of the city. One method used was the special district which overlaid the new zoning with a corrective set of regulations. The first special district was designed to protect Broadway theaters because large office buildings, permitted by the new zoning, were invading the traditional theater district. A second district protected shopping frontages along Fifth Avenue. A third, the Lincoln Square Special District was created to manage the redevelopment induced by Lincoln Center. One of the purposes of the urban renewal that had cleared the site for Lincoln Center had been to induce private investment, but there was no blueprint for managing the private investment when it did take place. The Lincoln Square special zoning district used build-to lines, the opposite of the more familiar setback line, to hold the street frontage of Broadway as a foil for the Renaissance symmetries of the opera house, dance theater, and concert hall. Above a designated height the building towers were required to be set back, separating them from the building mass that defined the street front (Figure 2.42).

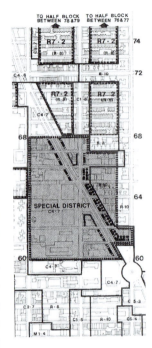

2.42
The Lincoln Square Special Zoning District, an early example of form-based coding.

This vocabulary of build-to lines to define streets and setbacks to control tower placements was ultimately used in the 1979 plan for Battery Park City on the lower Manhattan waterfront, where a modernist tower-in-park plan was replaced by a traditional street and park system with build-to and setback guidelines, designed by Alexander Cooper and Stanton Eckstut, two alumni of the New York City Planning Department's urban design group (Figure 2.43).

A third major corrective for modernism in New York City was the active pursuit of landmark and historic district designation. The city moved to save New York's other Beaux Arts monumental station, Grand Central Terminal, not only through landmarks designation but also by a special zoning district that allowed the transfer of the development permitted by zoning from the station to adjacent properties. This special district was a factor in the 1978 Supreme Court Decision, after ten years of litigation, upholding the landmarks designation of the Terminal, as well as the refusal of the Landmarks Preservation Commission to approve a modernist tower directly above it.[41]

I participated in many of these events in New York City during the 1960s and early 1970s and wrote an account of them, *Urban Design as Public Policy*, published in 1974.

Colin Rowe and "Roma Interrotta"

As a professor at Cornell University from 1963 to 1990 Colin Rowe taught generations of architects not to ignore the importance of the street, the axis, and the role of building mass as the definer of urban space. Rowe was an articulate critic of the strong utopian component in modernism, which caused many of its adherents to believe that older cities could and should be swept away. Rowe and Fred Koetter published a critique of modernist city design, entitled *Collage City*, first in the August 1975 *Architectural Review* and then, in a somewhat more complex version, as a book

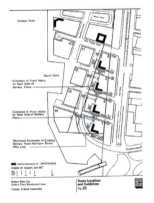

2.43
Guidelines for buildings at Battery Park City are based on traditional relationships between buildings and streets. The location of the towers is regulated to secure open vistas.

in 1978.[42] Rowe and Koetter's basic point is that city design is more like collage than like drawing on a clean sheet of paper, and the city designer should use the materials at hand, including the existing development of the city to date, and transform them into a new design. There was a bias in favor of examples of traditional city design in the illustrations chosen. The figure-ground map was one of Colin Rowe's favorite didactic techniques. Giambattista Nolli's 1748 map of Rome was often used by Rowe as a prototype. Nolli showed all buildings in plan as solid masses except for courtyards and major interior spaces. The texture of the map makes space read as a positive quality, the obverse of the building mass. Of course, this effect comes not just from the map technique but from the nature of Rome in the mid-eighteenth century, with its closely spaced buildings of essentially uniform height.

In 1978 Michael Graves, then architect-in-residence at the American Academy in Rome, invited twelve architects, including Colin Rowe, to take one of the twelve segments of the Nolli map and redesign that segment of Rome in any way they chose. Indicating that what was implied was the kind of interpolation or collage technique advocated by Rowe, the event was called "Roma Interrotta," which might be interpreted as "Interventions in Rome after a lapse of time." The results, not surprisingly, were extremely diverse. James Stirling used variants of his own buildings to compose his sector. Rowe and his associates made a drawing that might have been the Nolli map itself, except for the regularity and repetitive quality of the new elements. Perhaps the most unexpected interpolations were those designed by Leon Krier, who modified St. Peter's Square, the Via Corso, the Campidoglio, and the Piazza Navona with different versions of the same structure: a long-span hipped roof supported on columns that were actually individual buildings, each about seven or eight stories high but with a floor plan only large enough for one artist's studio per floor.[43]

Leon Krier's drawings for Roma Interrotta seem to mark a transition in his work from the design of projects for monumental, symmetrical megastructures ("megastructures" in the sense in which they will be discussed in Chapter 4) to traditional city design of a somewhat more conventional kind. Krier's projects are both more and less antiquarian than his early-nineteenth-century presentation style would lead one to expect. He favors plans in which monumental boulevards section off districts into strongly articulated precincts, more regular than in a medieval city but just as distinct. In this way his plans resemble the texture of Paris, where Haussmann's boulevards cut through the pre-existing fabric of the city, and do not resemble L'Enfant's plan for Washington, or Burnham's plan for Chicago, where the boulevards are an overlay on a continuous, regular grid pattern (Figure 2.44).

Leon Krier also seems to accept Camillo Sitte's critique of Haussmann and, by extension, of earlier Baroque plans, in considering the enclosure of space more important than the vista. He often made the intersection of two major boulevards in his drawings take place in a monumental, covered outdoor space where the roof is supported by a group of buildings, a totally non-traditional concept that was not even technically possible until the late nineteenth century.

2.44
Plan by Leon Krier for redesigning Washington, DC. Krier suggests making the Mall even more open by turning it into a lake, but by contrast makes the street blocks much smaller and more densely urbanized.

Ricardo Bofill

Another city designer who came back to traditional city design via an investigation of megastructures is the Barcelona architect Ricardo Bofill. His point of departure might well be Adolph Loos's entry in the *Chicago Tribune* competition of 1922, a tall office building in the form of a gigantic Doric column. This project has long been an embarrassment to historians of modern architecture, who counted Loos as a pioneer of a new sensibility. They hoped that the column was really a joke, but it was all too evident that Loos was perfectly serious. Bofill has taken this architectural dead end and turned it into a medium of expression, creating whole building groups whose component parts are columns and entablatures at an enormously inflated scale. The most extensive of his designs has been a large group of social housing buildings in Montpellier (Figure 2.45). Bofill seems to have abandoned this approach in more recent work for a more conventional modernism that emphasizes the creation of abstract form.

Seaside and the New Urbanism

In the early 1980s Robert Davis began developing an eighty-acre parcel of land along the Florida Gulf Coast into Seaside, a resort. The design of this community was prepared by Andres Duany and Elizabeth Plater-Zyberk who, after a number of false starts, including a modernist megastructure, arrived at a site plan with some advice from Leon Krier that used traditional city-design devices such as avenues radiating

2.45
Ricardo Bofill's social housing in Montpellier, reimagining the vocabulary of traditional architecture for modern-scale buildings.

2.46
Aerial view of Seaside, a resort community designed by Andres Duany and Elizabeth Plater-Zyberk which has helped lead to a revival of traditional site plans for suburban residential development.

from a central square (Figure 2.46).[44] The vernacular of the houses at Seaside, specified in a code that all buildings had to use, was derived from traditional houses in Key West, Florida, with pitched roofs, front porches supported by columns, and white picket fences. As Seaside, adroitly publicized by Robert Davis, became well known, Duany and Plater-Zyberk began receiving calls from other resort developers and also from the developers of planned suburban subdivisions. The Kentlands, a suburban development in Gaithersburg, Maryland, begun in 1988, helped establish a new development pattern for suburbs and a new business pattern for Duany/ Plater-Zyberk. The developer needed zoning approvals to convert a 356-acre farm to suburban houses. The architects conducted a workshop with participation by local residents, a technique that had become well established in planning inner city neighborhoods, and developed a sketch site plan which participants felt embodied a community consensus. The plan helped lead to the necessary government approvals. The site plan had traditional boulevards leading to a circle and to a crescent, but most of the site was more informally organized, more like pre-World War II suburban development than the tight axial organization of Seaside, but very unlike suburban subdivisions where houses are segregated by size and price and grouped around cul-de-sacs rather than a connecting system of landscaped streets. The architecture specified by the Kentlands code was the neo-Georgian vernacular popular with builders in the Washington, DC, region. Duany / Plater-Zyberk have subsequently developed many more plans in participatory workshops for investors developing housing in suburban locations.

In 1993 Andres Duany invited about a hundred planners and designers to a meeting in Alexandria, Virginia to launch what became the Congress for the New Urbanism. The outcome was predetermined, as the six founders of the Congress had already prepared a book on the New Urbanism which was ready for publication. The book showed Seaside, which by this time was more than half completed, the Kentlands, and other examples of projects and built work with a similar philosophy, using traditional street plans and public open space systems, but usually also with buildings designed in the historic styles that had been common architectural currency before modernism.[45] The Congress for the New Urbanism, or CNU, whose structure was originally modeled on the CIAM (see p. 14), has held a meeting every year since its establishment. The fourth Congress, held in Charleston, SC, adopted the Charter of the New Urbanism, divided into twenty-seven statements of principle about: region, metropolis, city, and town; neighborhood, district, and corridor; block, street, and building.

The CNU Charter was created as a response to the charter produced by the CIAM. While silent on the question of architectural style, the CNU Charter was meant to be a corrective to modernist planning and city design. It stressed the metropolitan region as a basic planning unit rather than individual cities, it gave primacy to walkable neighborhoods and districts over places that could be reached only by automobile, and it stressed that buildings should contribute to larger ensembles grouped around streets and public places.[46]

The CNU Charter opposed the modernist superblocks and rigidly zoned districts that had been adopted for much suburban development. The charter said that walkable neighborhoods, and walkable, park-once commercial districts should be the building blocks for all new development, in suburbs as well as cities.

Anti-modernism in architecture

The criticism of modernist city planning that began in the 1960s was paralleled by what is sometimes called post-modern architecture, in which architects began experimenting with the elements of classical design that had been expressly forbidden in modernist doctrine: first as ironical quotations, and then as incorporated elements, then in such evocative scenic styles as the buildings at Seaside, and finally in new attention to architects who had never accepted modernism at all. An exhibition, *The Architecture of the Ecole des Beaux Arts* opened in October, 1975 in the galleries of the Museum of Modern Art itself. The curator was Arthur Drexler, a successor to Philip Johnson as Director of the Museum of Modern Art's Department of Architecture and Design. Drexler assembled some of the most elaborate student drawings of classical facades and ornaments, plus documentation of work by leading architects who had taught at the Beaux Arts, plus a gallery of photographs of precisely the buildings most reviled by the modernists, including Pennsylvania Station. Drexler's exhibition signaled that something was happening, and the Museum of Modern Art did not wish to be left out of the discussion. Robert Stern's *Modern Classicism*, published in 1988, summarized trends that the Museum of Modern Art had detected. Stern began by rewriting the history of modern architecture to emphasize classical tendencies that had been part of modernist work all along, and added the work of other architects that had not been included in Hitchcock and Johnson's *International Style*, Giedion's *Space, Time and Architecture*, or other partisan histories of modernism. He then went on to publish current examples of what he called: Ironic Classicism, where there were exaggerated quotations from classical design; Latent Classicism where modernist building seemed to be organized according to classical principles; Fundamentalist Classicism, where buildings were stripped of ornament but seemed classical in overall massing; Canonic Classicism, which carried on, like Quinlan Terry, as if modernism had never happened; and Modern Traditionalism, which Stern described as a catch-all category for buildings that used, or were inspired by, some elements of pre-modernist architecture. Stern's closing section showed city designs, including Colin Rowe's Roma Interrotta project, Bofill's Montpelier development, drawings by Leon Krier, the plan for Seaside, and work by Rob Krier, Leon Krier's older brother.

Rob Krier, formerly a professor at the Technical University in Vienna and more recently in practice in Berlin, has specialized in fitting new buildings into existing

2.47
"Normal" architecture by Rob Krier that fits into traditional cities, or re-creates them.

European cities. He has completed a series of city designs that carry on development as if the tall building and the modernist revolution in architecture had never happened. More traditional than Leon Krier, he uses a rich variety of urban spaces and gardens, and is also adept at fitting the small rooms of a modern apartment within a palatial building form. He does not call his work classical; he calls traditional city design normal, and the structures he designs normal buildings (Figure 2.47).

The Golden City?

Henry Hope Read wrote a critique of modernist architecture, *The Golden City*, originally published in 1959, which compared photos of the plain, abstract facades of modernist buildings with much more ornate examples of what Reed called classical architecture, such as the entrance elevation of the UN General Assembly Building compared to the facade of the New York Stock Exchange. While Reed was concerned primarily with architectural expression, he did include sketches by John Barrington Bayley of elaborate traditional city designs for Columbus Circle in New York and a National Opera House in Washington. Reed was a co-founder in 1968 of Classical America, an organization dedicated to "advancing the classical tradition in architecture, urbanism and their allied arts," which now also incorporates an Institute of Classical Architecture founded separately in 1991. It offers some courses, but not a complete curriculum. The Architecture School of the University of Notre Dame is the only established architecture school teaching classical and traditional architecture; it abandoned a modernist curriculum in the mid-1990s. Professor Carroll Westfall made a distinction on the school's website between classical architecture and what he calls tradition:

> In a well-designed, livable city, the public realm complements the private realm, and not all buildings are classical. Indeed, most are good traditional buildings contributing to a complementary public realm (think of Rome). We therefore teach our students how to work with the appropriate national, regional, and local traditions of urbanism, architecture, and construction.

Notre Dame also offers the Driehaus Prize which is given to an architect "whose work embodies the principles of traditional and classical architecture in contemporary society," and is currently awarding twice the money given by the better-known Pritzker Prize, which has always gone to modernist architects.

The Congress for the New Urbanism appears to be drifting into the same position on classical architecture as Notre Dame and Classical America, from an initial stance that traditional principles of city design could be independent of architectural expression. CNU founders Elizabeth Plater-Zyberk and Andres Duany were the winners of the Driehaus Prize in 2008. Duany's acceptance speech was a powerful affirmation of adopting and extending classical design principles. His closing lines: "We are almost there. We have only to climb one last Everest."[47] While Andres Duany remained active in the CNU, his wife and partner, Elizabeth Plater-Zyberk, moved over to the board of Classical America. Another architect, Raymond Gindroz, has served on the board of both institutions. Henry Hope Reed closed his book with a vision that the Golden City will be ". . . seen in the vast framework of classical beauty led by visual splendor and the past. . . A nation to be great must build its Golden Cities." This was distinctly a minority opinion in 1959. It is still an unconventional viewpoint, but it has the support of a much better organized minority.

Transit-oriented development

The strongest support for elements of traditional city design is coming from a change in transportation technology. The modernist vision of a city of towers linked by expressways has become in many places a city of traffic jams and difficult searches for parking space. The growth of ridership on local transit systems is surprising the skeptics; and public support for new transit lines is growing. The evolution of urban areas into multi-city regions is making high-speed trains necessary because the destinations are too close together for efficient air travel and the highways are too congested. The countries of the European Union and the government of China are emulating Japan and Korea in creating high-speed rail links, and the United States is beginning to do so also.

Transit and high-speed rail stations are high-access locations that generate real-estate investment. Once the passenger gets off the train, the most efficient way of reaching a destination is to walk. What the walking experience will be like is important to the success of the investment related to the train or transit stop. The modernist design solution is to connect individual buildings to the train station by pedestrian bridges or underground passageways; a more traditional design would be to take people through an outdoor plaza or public space. Using an outdoor space to make connections among buildings creates a traditional design situation where the outdoor space can become an organizing element for the placement of the buildings.

Vancouver

Vancouver, Canada has recently undergone a transformation comparable to the transformation of Paris under Baron Haussmann. The center of the city occupies a peninsula of limited size in the midst of a region where growth is constrained by geography and by the preservation of agricultural land. For most of its existence Vancouver was a typical North American city, but beginning in the 1980s it began to evolve into an extraordinary place where modernist towers have been organized according to traditional design principles. The towers are a response to strong growth pressures, particularly demand for residences, channeled into the relatively constrained city center. A big boost in development came from immigrants and investors from Hong Kong looking for a haven as the British lease on the colony came to an end in 1997.

Through development regulation the City has limited the breadth of towers and preserved view corridors, so that the towers have spaces among them. The lower floors are required to preserve continuity along street frontages up to a height that is in scale with the width of the streets, and the taller elements of the building are then set back. The most effective organization has taken place along waterfronts reclaimed from industrial use, particularly Beach Crescent and Marineside Crescent on the north side of False Creek (Figures 2.48 and 2.49), and Coal Harbour (Figure 2.50) on the opposite side of the peninsula. The organization of the crescents is based on traditional symmetries, the base buildings provide spatial enclosure, and the waterfront parks create a public realm that is protected from traffic and is friendly to bicycles and pedestrians.

The modern architecture that replaced traditional city design almost everywhere had never evolved large-scale design concepts to take the place of the boulevard, the square, or the axis of symmetry; and no system of modulating facades ever completely replaced the regular repetition of columns. In downtown Vancouver all of these traditional elements are employed in the service of completely modern architecture.

2.48
Traditional building organization in the plan for the Quayside Neighborhood in the False Creek North district in Vancouver.

2.49
Development at Quayside,
modern buildings within a
traditional plan.

2.50
Development at Coal Harbour
in Vancouver, another
traditional plan with modern
buildings.

3 Green city design and climate change

The average air temperature of the entire planet is rising because of increasing greenhouse gasses. The burning of fossil fuels has been the most important contributor to this change. The traditional assumption that nature is a stable system modified in small increments over a very long time is turning out to be incorrect. It is now considered inevitable that sea levels will rise during this century at a rate that is dangerous for the many important cities located on low-lying land at coastal river mouths and deltas. The sea is warming as the result of past increases in carbon dioxide and other greenhouse gasses, and warmer water occupies more volume. Melting glaciers around the world and water from Greenland's polar ice cover are contributing more to rising seas than was predicted at first.[1] There is a feedback effect. Land absorbs more heat as the reflective ice cover retreats, and this heat absorption accelerates future melting. A prediction of an average rise in sea level worldwide of .4 meters by 2050 is considered conservative by many scientists. Stefan Rahmstorf suggests that sea-level rise could continue to directly track global mean surface temperature, which could put average sea-level rise as high as .7 meters by 2050.[2] Sea levels could be lower where waters are colder and the land mass is rising, and higher where land is subsiding and waters are warm; but all predictions are much higher than historical average changes. Sea-level rise amplifies the effects of high tides and storm surges, making dangerous flooding both more frequent and more severe.

Rising air temperatures bring about other changes as habitat migrates towards the poles and rainfall patterns shift, eventually turning some places to desert and others to flood zones. These progressions may set off abrupt climate changes where feedback takes over and change accelerates. If the average global air temperature rises by more than 2 degrees Celsius, the world will enter a period without parallel in human history.[3]

Controlling the adverse results of these changes will require global cooperation, and the time available to make significant reductions in the amount of greenhouse gas going into the atmosphere is growing shorter.

Adapting to changes that are already inevitable will transform development along coastlines and alter many coastal cities. Reducing greenhouse gas emissions will mean not just changes in fuel, but changes in settlement patterns and transportation methods, and will require much more conservation of the natural environment in areas not yet urbanized and more accommodation to the natural environment within urban areas.[4]

People have been changing the environment for a long time

When people started farming ten or twelve thousand years ago they began altering the natural environment both by selecting plants and by creating irrigation and water retention systems. Canals uniting bodies of water have been built since ancient times, as have dams creating artificial lakes. People living in the Amazon three thousand years ago learned to enrich the soil with charcoal, an effective technique that has only just been rediscovered. Early religious structures sometimes reached an environmental scale: the pyramids in Egypt, Carnac in northern France, Stonehenge in England. Some nomadic peoples used fire to control their environment. European settlers in North America found forests where the understory of brush had been carefully burned away. The western prairies had also been shaped by fire.

The relationship between actions by people and the responses of natural systems became stronger as populations multiplied, and have now reached the point where there is no longer an unaltered natural environment. Some human actions, particularly mining and tree cutting, have been largely destructive but many have sought to improve human surroundings. The history of these constructive actions offers some guidance for what we need to do today.

The beginnings of landscape design

The history of gardens, constructed environments, goes back at least to scenes portrayed in Egyptian wall paintings from 1500 BCE and the legendary hanging gardens which may have been built in Babylon around 600 BCE, which were said to be a series of elevated, irrigated terraces with the soil supported by masonry vaults.[5] We don't know what the gardens of the Academy where Socrates and Plato conversed might have looked like, but most evidence about gardens in classical and medieval times, and also in the Islamic design tradition, indicates that gardens were enclosed and shaped as an extension of the architecture of buildings. These enclosed gardens recreated nature in a subdued and altered form, where trees and shrubs were trimmed, water was confined to channels, and flowers were planted to form patterns.

An exception might be the grounds surrounding Roman country villas, which may have sometimes taken the form of a naturalistic landscape. However, the great Renaissance and Baroque gardens, which accompanied the revival of Roman architectural ideas, were geometric, as we have seen in the previous chapter, with long straight vistas cutting across the landscape as an assertion of power.

It was in China and later in Japan that gardening became landscape design, with the artifice concealed so that the result appeared to be natural. Some of these gardens were artificial landscapes constructed within courtyards, but some were created at the scale of the landscape itself. Chinese and Japanese landscape gardens were designed to be viewed as if they were a painting, either from a position within a building or teahouse or as a series of views experienced in sequence while walking, rather the way a series of views are seen when unrolling a landscape painting on a long horizontal scroll. Sometimes these gardens truly altered the natural environment. A Chinese imperial garden, begun in the seventh century, covered some 75 square miles and required a million laborers.[6] The western lake in Hangzhou, which still exists, is part of an artificial landscape also created in the seventh century (Figure 3.1).

3.1
The Western Lake in Hangzhou is part of an artificial landscape created in the seventh century.

Transformation of landscapes in eighteenth-century Britain

In Britain in the eighteenth century, and later on in Europe, real landscapes were rebuilt to create scenic views like those shown in landscape paintings, the same course that landscape design had followed in China and Japan. Landscape architects re-graded and stabilized the terrain, created lakes, and planted trees and shrubs to frame the effects they wanted. The successful completion and maintenance of these artificial landscapes shows what can be done to create a new natural equilibrium, an important lesson in technique that will need to be emulated on a large scale within urbanized areas to ameliorate the effects of climate change. Like the Chinese garden, the picturesque garden created a series of carefully designed naturalistic views that changed with the viewpoint of the observer, as opposed to the geometric organization of the landscape as an extension of architecture. This revolution in garden design was part of a larger change in aesthetic sensibility which elevated individual sensations experienced by the viewer over participation in a ceremonial occasion which followed traditional rules.

There are close parallels between what has come to be called picturesque garden design in western Europe and the painting and gardening tradition that originated in China. It is possible that the picturesque garden could have developed independently, but the gardens have such similarities that there may well have been direct influence from China, both on landscape painting and on the design of the gardens themselves.

Paintings where the landscape is the principal subject become important in western art, particularly in the Netherlands, during the sixteenth century. Renaissance artists in northern Europe, unlike the Chinese and Japanese—or the artists of Roman wall paintings—used optical perspective, which they could construct geometrically and also by means of devices that could help the artist plot distant views on a sheet of paper. In landscape paintings the perspective vanishing point is concealed, and recession into the distance is defined by the diminishing size of overlapping natural elements like trees and hillsides. Sebastiano Serlio's "Satyric Scene" from his architectural treatise of 1537 shows that this type of composition was understood in Renaissance Italy contemporaneously with the strict perspective grids that outlined ideal cities. Serlio's drawing also documents the connection between this type of artistic composition and stage scenery, where the landscape shown on a backdrop is given dimensional reality by flats of trees, the largest at the proscenium and diminishing sizes placed to frame the backdrop (see Figure 2.10 p. 63).

The word landscape itself comes from the Dutch language. At the end of the sixteenth century land reclamation began taking place in Holland on a large scale by pumping lakes and wetlands dry using the energy from windmills. This is also the time when Chinese porcelain begins to be known in Europe and imported into the Netherlands. Landscape paintings are often the decoration on Chinese porcelain. The Dutch began putting Chinese scenes on their own pottery in the 1630s. In 1665

Johannes Nieuhof published a book in Amsterdam about an official Dutch delegation's visit to the Chinese emperor. The book included drawings of real Chinese buildings and landscapes brought back by the travelers.[7] In Britain large landholders gradually were able to take over lands that had been held in common for grazing as well as the plots of farmers who were tenants but had tilled the same land for generations. During the eighteenth century in England the invention of machinery to produce woolen cloth in quantity began to make it more profitable for landlords to raise sheep rather than rent land to tenant farmers. The process of enclosure accelerated. Villagers left the land for America or to work in newly established factories. Oliver Goldsmith's poem, *The Deserted Village*, was written in 1770 as a protest:

> ... Sweet smiling village, loveliest of the lawn,
> Thy sports are fled, and all thy charms withdrawn!
> Amidst thy bowers the tyrant's hand is seen,
> And desolation saddens all thy green:
> One only master grasps the whole domain ...

The tyrant, the prosperous landholder, would be likely to collect landscape paintings, and it was also fashionable for gentlemen to learn to make sketches from carefully chosen picturesque vantage points. Perhaps the last English land owner who still does this is Prince Charles.[8] Gentlemen returned from the grand tour with a collection of art objects, their own amateur sketches, and sometimes a desire to create picturesque landscapes out of their own domains, which became more and more the fashion during the eighteenth century. In addition to influence from Chinese painting and gardens that might have come through landscape painting, information about Chinese gardens was available in eighteenth-century England through travelers' reports and drawings. Richard Boyle, Lord Burlington, had a set of thirty-six engravings of the Chinese emperor's palace and gardens in his library.[9] William Kent, who worked with Lord Burlington on the latter stages of his gardens at Chiswick helped turn what had been a geometric garden into a more naturalistic landscape. Did Kent consult the engravings in the library? Knowing how designers work, it is likely.

Kent was also one of the designers of Stowe, the estate of the Temple family, as the grounds of Stowe were transformed from a geometric garden into a naturalistic landscape.[10] Kent and other designers at Stowe added architectural objects, ruins or small buildings, to give the landscape incident, as in the paintings of Poussin and Claude (Figure 3.2).

In the mid-eighteenth century there was also a fad for Chinese decoration in England, which could mean ornamental buildings in Chinese as well as Classic and Gothic styles. A pagoda, which still exists, was used as an incident in the royal gardens at Kew (1762) by Sir William Chambers, but Chambers also included garden buildings in other types of architecture. Chambers, who had been to China as a young

3.2
The plan of the parkland at Stowe begun in its current form by William Kent after 1735, assisted later by Capability Brown, uses concepts comparable to Chinese stroll gardens to create a varied sequence of landscape vistas that appear to be natural.

man, wrote a book on Chinese decoration, published in 1757, and also wrote *A Dissertation on Oriental Gardening*, published in 1772.[11]

Capability Brown[12] was the head gardener at Stowe and went on during the last half of the eighteenth century to become the leading practitioner of picturesque landscape design, eventually reshaping more than 170 estates. Vistas were laid out from the main house, framed by trees in the foreground and by artfully placed clumps of trees in the middle distance, and then carefully graduated plantings framed distant views. Walks were laid out through woods and fields, with prospects designed to be appreciated at intervals, where there would be benches or a garden pavilion to allow leisurely contemplation of the picture created. Brown did not generally use architectural incidents, but made pure landscape compositions. The continuous landscapes that Brown and other designers created made use of concealed fences to keep the picturesque sheep or deer safely in the middle distance and not all over the terrace in front of the drawing room. Retaining walls with the ground sloping down to it on the far side, or a ditch with a fence inside of it, were designed not to be visible from prime viewing locations. This technique is called a ha-ha, from the exclamation of surprise that the viewer was expected to make on discovering it.[13]

Throughout the eighteenth century there was a spirited debate about the nature of personal reactions to landscapes and works of art. By the late eighteenth century this discussion extended to garden design itself. Instead of a disagreement about different modes of appreciation, a theoretical debate took place about the most appropriate means of intervention to create the desired effects. Uvedale Price wrote a series of essays defining the picturesque which included comments on architecture and landscape design.[14] Price's neighbor, Richard Payne Knight, who, like Goldsmith, engaged in that truly eighteenth-century form of discourse the didactic poem, criticized Capability Brown's lawns and fields in *The Landscape*:

Oft when I've seen some lonely mansion stand,
Fresh from th'improver's desolating hand,
Midst shaven lawns, that far around it creep
In one eternal undulating sweep . . .[15]

Humphrey Repton, a contemporary of Knight's and a generation younger than Brown, was a landscape architect whose work was considered to have answered some of Knight's criticisms.[16] Repton created landscapes that, while they are as artificial as Brown's, look far wilder and more like undisturbed nature. Garden designers like Brown and Repton were given more and more opportunities by the continuing trend towards enclosure of the land tilled by tenant farmers. As rural villages became less economic, it was possible to edit them as well, and make them part of the landscape ensemble. There were many late-eighteenth-century and early-nineteenth-century pattern books for rural cottages, which, because they were part of the composition to be seen from the drawing-room window of a great estate, had to have more style than the genuine hovels of a rural laborer.

Landscape design begins to influence building design

The rich began to acquire a taste for elaborate rural simplicity themselves, the most extreme example being the English garden, make-believe farm and rustic village that Marie Antoinette had constructed on the grounds at Versailles (Figure 3.3). The fashion for rural simplicity also extended to the middle class. John Nash, master designer of Regent Street in London, was also an important figure in relating the picturesque design of large estates to a new city-design problem of the early nineteenth century: suburban developments for middle-class merchants who could commute by carriage to their place of business in the city center.[17] Nash's design for Cronkhill in Shropshire, for the steward of a great estate, foreshadowed the houses that would be drawn in architectural pattern books for suburban houses during the nineteenth century, houses that united the picturesque composition of the rural cottage with the large, elegant rooms suitable for the new merchant class, for vicars of rural parishes and for others who wished to sustain an elegant way of life while lacking the resources of the great landowner. In 1810 Nash designed Blaise Hamlet, a group of charity houses on the estate of a wealthy banker. Instead of ranging the houses in neat rows, Nash grouped them around a green, positioned to define a foreground, a middle distance and a background, as in picturesque landscape composition. The design of the individual cottages anticipates the "stockbroker's Tudor" that was to become a staple of later suburbia (Figure 3.4).

3.3
The make-believe farm that Marie Antoinette had built at Versailles beginning in 1783, which she considered to be a garden in the English style.

Garden design becomes city design

Picturesque landscape design came to influence the development of cities in three ways: the creation of picturesque public gardens in cities, the design of garden suburbs, and the design of model towns for factory workers.

The royal parks in London, estates of the royal family gradually opened to the public, became a model for the large urban public parks now to be found in every city. Two royal estates on opposite sides of Paris, the Bois de Boulogne and the Bois de Vincennes, were turned into public parks in the English style during the transformation of Paris beginning in the 1850s under Napoleon III and the administration of Baron Georges Eugene Haussmann, also described in the previous chapter. The landscape designer was Adolphe Alphand (Figure 3.5).[18] Louis Napoleon had lived in exile in England, and knew the London parks well, which may have influenced Alphand's instructions as he prepared his designs. Frederick Law Olmsted and Calvert Vaux's design for Central Park in New York City where construction began in the late 1850s was also a naturalistic landscape. The area selected for the park, while not fully developed, was already subdivided, had many residents, and was filled with urban and semi-rural activities as well as a major reservoir. It also had to accommodate four cross-town street connections. That the park looks like a natural preserve and the cross-town streets are mostly hidden from view is a tribute to the skill of the designers. Olmsted corresponded with Alphand about the technical problems of artificial landscape creation they were both encountering, including the transplanting of mature trees. Central Park, and Olmsted and Vaux's Prospect Park in Brooklyn, became the model for major parks across the United States, many of them designed by Olmsted or the successor firm run by his son. A naturalistic park on the fashionable side of town, with winding drives and carefully contrived vistas, often with an art museum in it, became a distinguishing characteristic of American cities.

Regent's Park in London, as designed by John Nash beginning after 1811, unites town-house development with a picturesque park on the scale of a great

3.5

The Parc des Buttes Chaumont, on the site of a former quarry, was laid out by Adolphe Alphand during the regime of Napoleon III with the winding paths and informal organization of the English style, rather than the traditional geometry of French gardens seen at Versailles. The other parks for Paris planned by Baron Haussmann and Alphand during this period also created landscapes in the English manner, including redesigns of the Bois de Boulogne and the Bois de Vincennes.

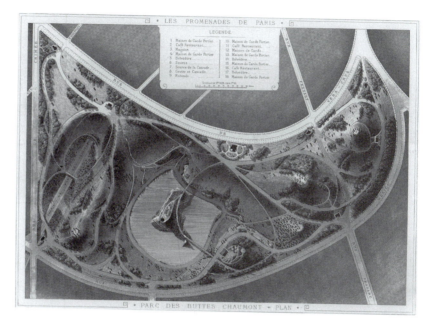

estate, and, had it been developed as originally planned, would have included about fifty picturesque villas integrated into the landscape (see the illustration on p. 75). On the north-eastern edge of the Regent's Park development were Park Village East and West, split by the Regent's Canal. The rows of houses, each house different, were again anticipations of later garden suburbs.

Most of the early picturesque villas in suburbs occupied rectangular plots on conventional streets. Birkenhead Park near Liverpool, designed by Joseph Paxton in 1844, creates a picturesque setting that was meant to provide preferred sites for suburban villas as well as row houses in the Regent's Park manner (Figure 3.6). Paxton, with the architect John Robertson, had been the designer, in the late 1830s, of the picturesque model village Edensor, for the employees of the Duke of Devonshire's Chatsworth estate. Paxton's work was to prove influential in the development of the garden suburb in the United States. Birkenhead Park was visited and praised by Frederick Law Olmsted, and Edensor by Andrew Jackson Downing, who was impressed by both the site plan and the varied architecture of the individual houses.

3.6

Birkenhead Park in Liverpool. The park, opened in 1847, was designed by Joseph Paxton as a setting for row houses as well as a garden open to the public.

The garden suburb

Llewellyn Park in what is now West Orange, New Jersey, seems to be the first complete synthesis of English garden design, and a village-like composition of elegant, but relatively small and convenient, houses into a garden suburb. Laid out by Alexander Jackson Davis in 1853, the streets are like the garden walks of an

English estate. The houses were influenced by Davis's friend Andrew Jackson Downing's *Architecture of Country Houses,* which set down plans for the new type of informally arranged rural gentleman's house that had been developed in England. As at the Park Villages in Regent's Park or at Edensor, each house had a different type of architecture (Figure 3.7). The house lots at Llewellyn Park, or at Riverside, the Chicago suburb laid out by Frederick Law Olmsted in 1869, are small compared with country estates and farms, but large enough that each house is seen to be separate from its neighbors and part of a larger landscape composition. Olmsted in a memorandum to his client explained that there was no way to control the bad taste of individual owners once the lots were sold, except by setting the houses well back from the streets and planting the streets to give them a continuous park-like character.[19] Olmsted's plan, which was to influence many other garden suburbs (Figure 3.8) is a network of winding streets that create kidney-shaped blocks. The vistas change constantly as you traverse the streets.

In the mid-nineteenth century architects became interested in English vernacular architecture of the late seventeenth and eighteenth century as a lower-key alternative to classical or gothic styles. Historians categorize this style of design and decoration as Queen Anne.[20] An important work of town planning during the Queen Anne revival was Bedford Park, a garden suburb of London. A community that attracted upper-middle-class intellectuals, it was developed beginning in 1875 by Jonathan Carr, a member of an artistic and intellectual family, and its basic architectural character was established by Richard Norman Shaw, the architect who was probably most important in creating the vernacular revival. Unlike earlier suburbs, where each separate villa had its own character, Shaw and the other architects who built at Bedford Park tried to create a unified environment, a village; but a village composed of commodious upper-middle-class dwellings. The resulting architectural consistency added a new element to garden suburb design, something that Olmsted had feared would not be possible. Other major concentrations of Queen Anne houses are to be found at Oxford and Cambridge, confirming that the Queen Anne mixture of relative architectural informality with honest expression of materials like brick and wood had a strong appeal to intellectuals.

3.7
The plan for Llewellyn Park in what is now West Orange, New Jersey. Laid out by Alexander Jackson Davis in 1853, the streets are like the garden walks of an English estate.

3.8
Frederick Law Olmsted's plan for Riverside, a railroad suburb of Chicago, which was to influence many other garden suburbs, is a network of winding streets that create kidney-shaped blocks.

Model villages for workers

Another major use of Queen Anne was in houses for the model villages constructed by enlightened manufacturers, such as Bournville for the Cadbury chocolate company and Port Sunlight for Lever Brothers, who named the village for one of their products, Sunlight Soap. Both villages date from the early 1890s. Port Sunlight has an interesting street plan, not unlike a formal garden, with the buildings forming the perimeter of the blocks surrounding allotment gardens for the residents (Figure 3.9). Another chocolate manufacturer, Joseph Rowntree, built a model village for low-income tenants, not just his own employees, near York in northern England. The

3.9
The plan of Port Sunlight, a model village near Liverpool for employees of Lever Brothers.

3.10
Houses for workers built by the philanthropist Joseph Rowntree in New Earswick, near York in England. The buildings, designed by Raymond Unwin and Barry Parker, gave the outward form of a traditional English village to progressive social policies.

designers were Raymond Unwin and his partner—and brother-in-law—Barry Parker. Their buildings show the influence of the simplified cottage architecture of their contemporary, Charles F.A. Voysey, and they had their own strong interest in cottage improvement. They had recently published two books—*The Art of Building a Home* and *Cottage Plans and Common Sense*—which emphasized the traditional values of the English village and advocated getting rid of wasteful snobbish elements, like the front parlor in small houses, in favor of larger rooms and convenient open plans (Figure 3.10).

The Suez and Panama Canals

The Suez and Panama Canals are two of the most significant interventions in the natural landscape ever made: both were advanced by the French engineer, Ferdinand de Lesseps. De Lesseps obtained a franchise to build the canal from the ruler of Egypt, Sa'id Pasha in 1854. The canal began construction in 1859 with the backing of Emperor Napoleon III and was completed ten years later. It is a sea-level canal, without locks, that allows water to flow between the Mediterranean and the canal and the canal and the Red Sea. British Prime Minister Benjamin Disraeli purchased the Egyptian shares in the canal in 1875, although the majority ownership remained French. The British then took control of the operations of the canal in 1882 during a civil war in Egypt. Although the British government had initially opposed the canal, it proved to be a most important link in preserving the control of European nations over their colonial empires in Asia. In 1879 de Lesseps was appointed president of a French company to build a canal across the Isthmus of Panama, but the conditions for building in Panama were much more difficult than at Suez, with unfavorable soil conditions, a need for locks to deal with changes in elevation, and serious problems with malaria and other tropical illnesses. The construction effort failed and the company went bankrupt. The United States eventually bought the assets of the failed company in 1904 when Theodore Roosevelt was president and completed the canal ten years later. The two canals, now owned by the countries where they are located, have been a major influence in furthering the development of global shipping and thus the growth of many port cities.

National parks in North America

The appreciation of the beauties of the natural landscape which began with landscape painting helped generate support for the protection of extraordinary landscapes in the US and Canadian west, some of which had been painted by artists such as Albert Bierstadt and had thus become familiar to influential people who had never actually been to the west. The actual process by which land has been preserved is complicated. Some places, such as the Yosemite Valley,[21] have been designated as national parks for their scenic value, other areas are national forests designated to preserve them as a resource where some logging is permitted. Recreation has been permitted in some parts of both national parks and national forests, other areas are designated wilderness and visiting them is restricted. In general the most significant natural areas in both countries have some form of protection, but the process has been far from systematic, and it remains controversial.

Garden cities and the beginnings of Landscape Urbanism

Landscape Urbanism has been defined by Charles Waldheim in a recent book as a situation where "... landscape replaces architecture as the basic building block of contemporary urbanism."[22] Ebenezer Howard should be considered the great prophet of Landscape Urbanism as Waldheim defines it, although Howard, who was intent on making his views clear to a wide audience, used the term town–country. Howard was the most important person in creating the garden-city movement at the turn of the last century. The garden city united public parks, suburban development, and affordable cottage housing in a green setting, but its real meaning is a device for organizing human settlement as self-contained clusters within the natural landscape and implies a new way of thinking about cities as parts of geographic regions rather then as ever-denser central locations. Town–country had an even deeper meaning for Howard. He believed that bringing the advantages of urban life, with its variety of activities and opportunities, to a setting where people could continue to be in touch with nature would create a more balanced way of life for everyone.

Ebenezer Howard was not an architect, landscape architect or planner but a shorthand reporter in the London courts. In 1898 he published a book originally called *To-morrow a Peaceful Path to Real Reform,* but better known by its later title, *Garden Cities of To-morrow.* This short, simply written volume launched the planning of new towns and the creation of green belts and had a profound effect on regional development up through the middle of the twentieth century. More recently it looked as if Howard's ideas about balancing town and country had been superseded by suburban sprawl, but today the need for energy efficiency and landscape conservation has given Howard a new currency.

Howard's first choice of a career had been to emigrate to the American frontier and become a farmer in Iowa, but he had learned that love of rural life was not enough; farming was not for him. He had also lived in Chicago from 1872 to 1876, while the city was rebuilding after the great fire.[23] There he not only learned to take down speeches in shorthand, a skill which would support him for the rest of his life, but he lived in a place whose social structure was open, where people with innovative ideas could expect to get them accepted and to become successful themselves, a very different atmosphere from the stultifying class structure of England at the time.

Howard returned to London and became a shorthand reporter in the court system. London was in the midst of industrialization, and Victorian, laissez-faire capitalism was at its strongest. Two views of Fleet Street looking up Ludgate Hill give some idea of what was happening. The first scene, drawn in 1827 for *London in the 19th Century* shows a city that is still preindustrial and, allowing for the fact that the artist has left out the horse manure and the flies, possesses real charm. Gustave Doré's drawing of almost the same view in 1872 for *London, A Pilgrimage* shows the pollution and traffic congestion of the modern world (Figures 3.11, 3.12).

Other Doré drawings from the same book document the unspeakable conditions of the poor and the down-and-out; as well as the crowded but opulent life of the rich. While some social reforms had taken place by the 1890s, extreme poverty, unsanitary housing, and overcrowding still characterized much of London. Life was not much better in the countryside, where a prolonged agricultural depression was driving farmers off the land and reducing land prices.

Howard had an inventive mind, and had devised several improvements for typewriters and other machinery used in his office. He began to apply this inventiveness to the problems of society after reading Edward Bellamy's *Looking Backward*, which he obtained soon after it had been published in the United States, in 1888. Bellamy's novel described Boston in the year 2000 as a city where cooperation was the mainspring of society, and told of the stages by which this utopia had been brought about. Howard was so enthusiastic about the book that he immediately arranged to have it published in England, guaranteeing the sale of one hundred copies himself.

As he walked to and from the law courts through the crowds and smoke of London, Howard began to devise a new kind of city that would bring more life to

3.11
Fleet Street in London looking towards Ludgate Hill in 1827. The scene still shows a charming pre-industrial city, although the artist has left out the horse manure and the flies.

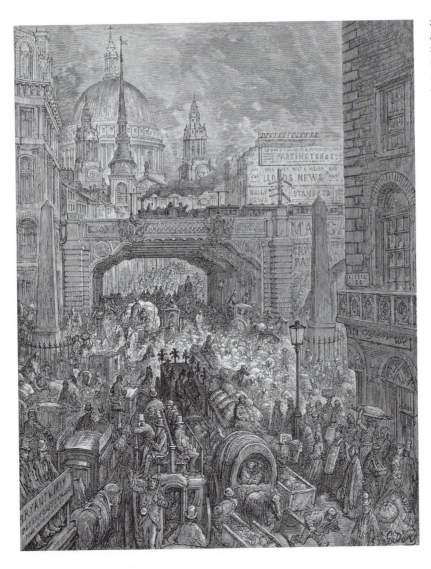

3.12
Almost the same view of Fleet
Street drawn by Gustave Doré
in 1872 shows how the
railroad brought pollution and
congestion into cities.

rural areas, and would combine the beauty and healthfulness of the countryside with
work in a modern office or industry, opportunities which at that time could be found
only in a crowded, unhealthful metropolis. The more Howard thought about *Looking
Backward*, the more authoritarian and mechanistic he found its vision; and the more
concerned he became that Bellamy had not thought enough about how society could
make a gradual transition to a new way of life. He began to read other reformers,
particularly about concepts of colonization, centralization of land ownership, and
model communities, before coming to his own formulation.

The book that explains his proposal is a model of clearheaded exposition.
Howard begins by asking the reader to imagine that a 6,000-acre agricultural estate
has been purchased by issuing bonds secured with a mortgage on the property.
This property is owned by a trust, which builds a community for 30,000 people on

one-sixth of the land, leaving the rest to continue in agriculture. At the center of the new city are the public institutions that serve the whole community: the town hall, the art gallery, theater, library, concert hall, and hospital. These are surrounded by a park, which is flanked by what Howard calls the Crystal Palace and we would call a shopping center. All the shops of the city are contained in this glass-roofed building, which has a winter garden (the equivalent of the enclosed mall) as an added attraction. Around the center are the residential districts of the city, which provide building lots of different sizes for the modest or the opulent. At the perimeter are the factories, served by a circular railway siding. Beyond the factories the whole community is surrounded by rural land, which is to remain that way perpetually (Figure 3.13).

Howard knew that the railroad had made many rural areas immediately accessible to the existing network of cities and had changed the old reasons for city location. Population could be shifted to what had been remote agricultural sites if the right transportation was provided.

One of the most profitable aspects of real-estate development has always been the conversion of land from rural to urban uses. The real-estate developer ordinarily withdraws that profit from the community. Howard, providing a middle-class answer to the theories of Karl Marx, proposed instead to finance the development of his co-operative new city with the proceeds of the factory and house sites, and he drew up trial balance sheets to illustrate the feasibility of this development concept.

But Howard was not content to describe in outline how his proposed community might work. He was determined to include enough detail to convince any skeptic. He discusses the economics of the agricultural land, pointing out that the proximity of the new community would make market gardening and dairies feasible, and give local residents a price advantage because there would be only small shipping and distribution costs. This idea, little-regarded at the time when local farms were still plentiful, looks remarkably pertinent today as the "slow-food movement" is put forward as a response to the international industrialization of agriculture.

Howard makes sure the reader understands that the monthly payments homeowners would have to make for land and city services would be well within their budget. He also discusses how the municipality would be staffed, and how the services could be provided and community debt retired within the amount of income to be expected. Howard was also determined that no one should take him for an impractical utopian. He makes it clear that everything he imagines could "be accomplished by the common business practices" of the time in which he lived. If farmers preferred growing wheat to market gardens, fine; but it was likely that some farmers would plant vegetables because of their proximity to a good market. The factories that took sites in the new community would be ordinary factories, and the garden-city corporation would have no control over them, beyond seeing that they observed some health and building regulations.

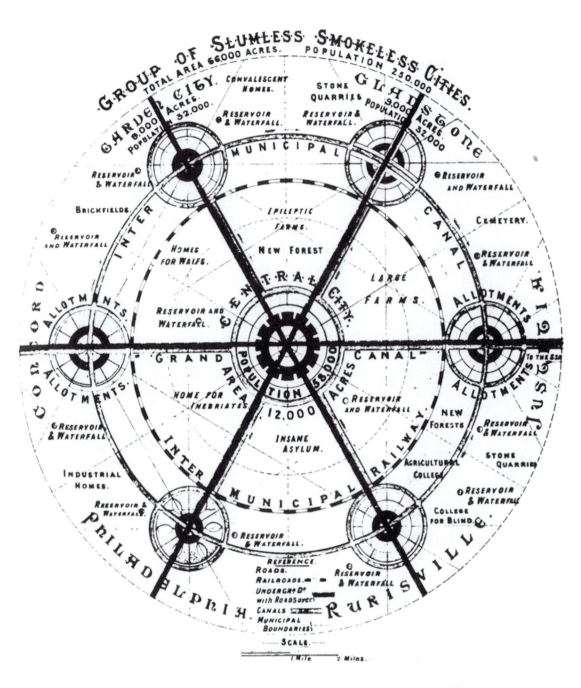

GROUP OF SLUMLESS SMOKELESS CITIES.
TOTAL AREA 66000 ACRES. POPULATION 250.000.

3.13
Ebenezer Howard's famous diagram of the garden city, a cluster of manageable communities set within green space.

Howard then looks beyond the success of the first community to imagine what should happen when growth pressures begin to be felt. Instead of the community expanding, it should hive off a second garden city beyond the agricultural belt. Howard includes an illustration of Colonel William Light's 1836 plan for Adelaide, Australia, to show how this growth should take place. Colonel Light planned a belt of parkland all around the city of Adelaide, separating it from its suburbs, particularly

3.14
Colonel William Light's 1836 plan for Adelaide, Australia showing a suburb separated from the main city by a green belt, as published by Howard in his book, *Tomorrow a Peaceful Path to Real Reform.*

from the original suburb of North Adelaide, which was also surrounded by parkland (Figure 3.14).

But this type of growth could not take place indefinitely without the assistance of the government, and Howard was confident that government would inevitably play a leading role in establishing garden cities. He reasoned by analogy to the establishment of the railroads, whose rights-of-way were at first acquired by negotiation. As the railway network became larger and of vital importance to the country, the government intervened to help railway companies acquire their routes.

In his quiet and matter-of-fact way, Howard was advocating nothing less than the total reorganization of the entire country as something quite feasible and practical, in fact almost inevitable. His belief in the possibility of immediate constructive change was distinctly un-English: it was the confidence born of life on the American frontier.

What would become of London and other existing industrial cities after large numbers of the new garden communities had been built? Howard predicted that the population of the old cities would thin out until eventually they would have to be reorganized because they could no longer pay their debts. Property values would fall and the remaining people would be able to move into the best houses, leaving the slums to be torn down and replaced by gardens. Something very like Howard's prediction has happened to cities, which have become much less dense as people and industry have moved to suburban locations. In the 1970s it looked as if some cities could not survive this process; New York came very close to defaulting on its obligations much as Howard had predicted. Today most cities have come back with more intense downtown development and an influx of new upper-income residents, but many cities still have large under-used areas that need to be rebuilt. Howard understood the mechanisms at work, but underrated the importance of high-intensity centers for finance and trade, and could not predict the big increases in income and mobility that have taken place worldwide.

Howard's book was not greeted with acclaim when it was published. Even the reformist Fabian Society was dismissive, the review in their newspaper stating that Howard's plans might have been adopted "if they had been submitted to the Romans when they conquered Britain."[24]

But Howard was a tireless worker, and, although he was an unpretentious person, he was an effective public speaker. Eight months after his book was published, Howard succeeded in forming a Garden City Association, promoting it by making alliances with other reform groups whose aims would be assisted by garden cities. Many of the earliest members of the association were important figures in the Land Nationalisation Society. Other influential backers were prominent lawyers who knew and respected Howard from his work in the courts. The most effective of these legal friends was Ralph Neville, who became chairman of the Garden City Association and helped Howard bring into it two important philanthropists who had supported model industrial villages, George Cadbury and W.H. Lever.

In 1901 and 1902 the Garden City Association held annual conferences: the first in Bournville, and the second at Port Sunlight. The first conference drew three hundred attendees, the second over a thousand. That year Howard's book was reissued under its new title, *Garden Cities of To-morrow,* and a company was set up to acquire a site for a prototype.

Letchworth, the first garden city

During 1903 over 3,800 acres were assembled at Letchworth, near the railway junction at Hitchin in Hertfordshire, and a company was formed to purchase the land and develop the new community. The groundbreaking was held on October 9, 1903. For the design of the new community the directors selected Raymond Unwin and Barry Parker. Unwin at that time was forty, Parker thirty-six. They were members of the Garden City Association and had just completed their design for New Earswick. Joseph Rowntree, their client at New Earswick, had been influenced by Howard's book, and had made sure that each house had its own garden plot. Now Parker and Unwin had an opportunity to give definitive physical form to the garden city itself.

Howard, of course, had his own ideas about what a garden city should be like, although he was careful to label the illustrations that he drew for his book: "Diagram only, plans can not be drawn until site selected." All Howard's design ideas were based on concepts of cooperative action and ownership, in which he had been influenced by Edward Bellamy. Howard says in his book that his "concept of ideal city size was derived in part from James S. Buckingham's Victoria, a model town for 25,000 described in his *National Evils and Practical Remedies.* Buckingham's designs for Victoria resemble Howard's diagrams, a rigidly symmetrical concentric plan. Buckingham, who envisioned a centrally controlled society, may well have meant his design literally. Howard understood that the workings of topography and free enterprise would produce something a great deal less organized. We also know that Howard was interested in Adelaide as a model for planned city growth, because he includes a map of it in his book, and he has to have been well aware of Nash's Regent's Park in London. The original design for Regent's Park, with its circular central element surrounded by park, has a strong resemblance to Howard's diagrams.

Raymond Unwin and Barry Parker brought to their design of the garden city the already well-established concepts of the garden suburb and the model village, which in turn were a synthesis of two important design and planning concepts: the picturesque English gardening tradition with its artfully artificial landscape that was developed during the eighteenth century, and the conveniently planned cottage or villa with irregular and picturesque massing, also a late-eighteenth-century invention.

Their immediate design context was the revival of vernacular architecture that took place in the latter part of the nineteenth century as seen in Voysey's cottage-style houses and Richard Norman Shaw's Bedford Park, plus the plan for Port Sunlight. As a result, the Parker and Unwin design for Letchworth gave Howard's radical ideas an expression that was totally unthreatening, and that had been artfully designed to evoke traditional English villages.

3.15
Raymond Unwin and Barry Parker's plan for Letchworth, the first garden city to be implemented according to Ebenezer Howard's financial and design principles.

Parker and Unwin placed the community athwart the railroad, rather than tangential to it, as Howard's diagram showed. The plan is divided into four quadrants by the railway, which runs roughly east–west, and a main street, called Norton Way, which runs from south to north. The town square, situated on high and level ground, is located in the south-west quadrant. A monumental boulevard, Broadway, connects the town square to the place in front of the railway station and also forms the centerpiece of the residential district extending away from the town square to the south-west. The south-east quadrant contains many of the industrial sites, grouped around railway sidings, and neighborhoods of relatively modest attached houses. The shopping district lies between the station and Norton Way, on the south side of the railroad. The north-east quadrant has more factory sites along the railroad and development grouped around the previously existing village of Norton. The north-west quadrant, the last to be developed, contains Norton Common, a seventy-acre park preserve, and additional sites for light industry along the railroad (Figure 3.15).

The site plan shows a synthesis of formal and informal design concepts, with the group of straight streets leading to the town square balanced by an overall road network that is informal, but not winding and deliberately picturesque. The groups of houses and cottages, however, are artfully arranged to form architectural spaces, and were planned to create architecturally related groups, not a variety of different styles. Site design decisions were made on the basis of topography, prevailing winds, and existing vegetation. The industrial location on the east side of the town meant that prevailing winds would blow industrial pollution away from most residences. There is no sign of the Crystal Palace that Howard had suggested, but the main shopping street could be interpreted as representing about one-eighth of the shopping district Howard had diagrammed, which was actually all a community the size of Letchworth could be expected to support.

Hampstead and other early twentieth-century garden suburbs

Barry Parker and Raymond Unwin's next commission, in 1905, to develop the site plan for Hampstead Garden Suburb, was to have a far wider influence on the design of expanding urban areas, by creating a powerful image of desirable suburban development. Their client was Henrietta Barnett, a social reformer who was married to Canon Samuel A. Barnett, a pioneer in the settlement-house movement. She had managed to buy control of farm land in the Golders Green section of London north of Hampstead Heath. The area was about to become accessible as a result of the extension of an underground rapid transit line, completed in 1907. The social program was to create a community open to a wide range of different incomes, with the hope that eventually proximity would help break down class barriers; the community was also to be made as close to an ideal environment as possible, embodying, as

Howard had suggested, the advantages of both town and country. However, Hampstead was to be a suburb, an extension of London, and thus contrary to Howard's basic theory that the growth that was going into the extension of the metropolis should be channeled into separate garden cities instead. Unwin and Parker's acceptance of this commission has often been described as something very like an act of disloyalty to the garden-city movement, but the garden suburb was actually a well-established concept combining picturesque landscape and suburban villas, as at Olmsted's plan for Riverside, Illinois.

By the time Parker and Unwin began the design of Hampstead they had become aware of the theories of Camillo Sitte and had begun reading *Der Stadtebau*, the German periodical that published the work of Sitte and like-minded city designers and was a primary force in creating city planning as a professional discipline. Raymond Unwin's *Town Planning in Practice*, published in 1909, contains the first serious treatment of Sitte's theories in English.[25] Sitte's approach was to look not at the logic of plans but at what the viewer would actually see walking near the buildings, and then to codify principles based on comparative experience. The perception of the city as a succession of changing viewpoints is very close to the picturesque aesthetic of English garden design. Sitte believed that many monumental plazas were far too large; and while important public buildings should keep their prominent position, they should be attached to the other buildings that form the wall of a plaza, or be closely related to them. In this way, space would be contained and not merely implied in plan.

Reading Sitte and *Der Stadtebau* led Unwin and Parker to look at some of the examples of city design continually referred to in German practice. The exceptionally well-preserved medieval city of Rothenburg seems to have been of particular interest, judging from the illustrations selected by Unwin for his book.

Another important influence on the design of Hampstead Garden Suburb was the association of Edwin Lutyens with the plan and Lutyens' work as architect of some of the principal buildings. Lutyens was a master of scenographic architectural effects, and far more sophisticated than Parker and Unwin about what was needed to create a strong architectural design. Lutyens, however, was more inclined than Parker and Unwin to put architecture ahead of social objectives. As the architect for the central building group at Hampstead, Lutyens struggled with Henrietta Barnett and the board of directors over the height and scale of the central buildings, Lutyens seeking to give the two churches architectural dominance over the community, the board feeling that such prominence was inappropriate. The board did get Lutyens to modify his designs. From an architectural standpoint, Lutyens was probably right, as the central district is not immediately visible from many parts of Hampstead, so that the overall composition loses legibility. However, dominance of the two central churches would have mis-stated the nature of the community; it was not a medieval village (Figure 3.16).

The site plan of Hampstead is much tighter than that of Letchworth and the architectural grouping far stronger. The key difference is the use at Hampstead of

3.16
The plan for Hampstead Garden Suburb, also by Raymond Unwin and Barry Parker, shows elements of more traditional city design in its central building group, under the influence of Edwin Lutyens, the architect for the two central churches.

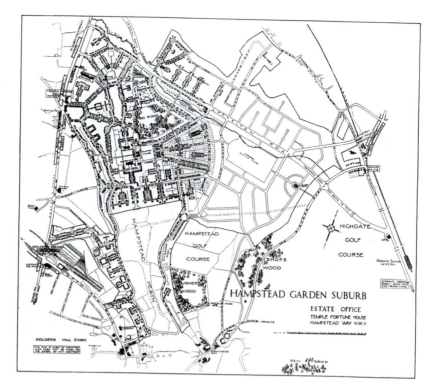

3.17
Plan of cul-de-sac streets at Hampstead, which provide both a street and a garden frontage for the houses.

cul-de-sac streets. The cul-de-sac had been made illegal under English building bylaws because of its abuse in the early urban slum districts. It required an act of Parliament to use the cul-de-sac at Hampstead. The cul-de-sac creates a hierarchy of streets, by distinguishing between streets needed purely for access to individual dwellings and streets that carried traffic. It encouraged the grouping of buildings into courts, alternating streets and gardens so that each house had both a street and a garden view (Figure 3.17). This concept was later to be more fully developed at Radburn by Henry Wright and Clarence Stein.

Ebenezer Howard's writings and tireless promotional efforts made the concept of the garden city internationally known, but the image of the garden city was established by Unwin and Parker, and it is much more the image of Hampstead Garden Suburb than it is of Letchworth. Hampstead was more accessible; it had a superior site plan, which created architecturally defined spaces; and with its greater range of incomes, it had far more distinguished architecture—including the central grouping of buildings by Edwin Lutyens, Waterlow Court by M.H. Baillie Scott, and courtyard groups by Parker and Unwin themselves.

It was the image of Hampstead that had an immediate effect on the design of suburbs almost everywhere, while it would take another generation for Howard's basic planning concepts to begin to receive a comparable degree of acceptance.

Green city design and climate change

Garden suburbs in Europe

While Unwin and Parker were learning from Camillo Sitte and *Der Stadtebau*, their work was becoming influential in the German-speaking world because it was included in the book entitled *Das Englische Haus* (1905), by Hermann Muthesius. Muthesius had been a cultural attaché in the German embassy in London, where part of his assignment was to make a serious study of English domestic architecture.

A German Garden City Association was founded in 1908 to construct a garden suburb at Hellerau, near Dresden. Hellerau was in some ways a company town for the workers in the Dresden Craft Workshops, owned by the enlightened furniture manufacturer Karl Schmidt. The town was run independently, however, and contained a district of relatively large houses as well as the attached cottages for workers, all designed in a picturesque German village style by Richard Riemerschmid. Hellerau, like Hampstead, became a center for advanced social thought, and the site of Emile Jaques Dalcroze's well-known school for teaching music and what he called eurhythmics.

The Falkenberg district of Berlin, designed by Bruno Taut in 1912, was a much more ambitious garden suburb, sponsored by cooperative housing associations. It was designed in a more urbane style than Hellerau, with Hampstead-like cul-de-sacs, row houses and even a crescent. The initial buildings, begun just before World War I, resembled the restrained architectural style of the early nineteenth century.

The planned suburb of Margaretenhohe, near Essen, designed by Georg Metzendorf in 1912, one of a series of model company towns for workers in the Krupp steel and munitions plants, clearly shows the influence of Unwin and Parker's planning. So, interestingly enough, does contemporary work by Camillo Sitte himself, such as his plan for a new district for the city of Marienberg (Figure 3.18).

Other important early examples of garden suburbs created under the influence of Hampstead include Munkkiniemi-Haaga outside Helsinki, designed by Eliel Saarinen in 1916; Ulleval, near Oslo, by Oscar Hoff and Harald Hals, designed in 1918; and the garden suburbs of Stockholm.

3.18
Plan by Camillo Sitte for a garden district in Marienberg.

Garden-city influence in Canberra

In their winning competition design for Canberra, the new capital of Australia in 1912, Walter Burley Griffin and his wife Marion Mahony Griffin used monumental principles of organization; but in its overall density, their plan was that of the garden city, and its use of a railway line to link population subcenters was also related to garden-city theory as well as contemporary practice. Both Griffins had worked in Oak Park for Frank Lloyd Wright, but their plan is closer to Burnham's designs for Chicago than to anything that came out of Wright's office. The three highest points on the contour map were chosen as the political, commercial, and military centers and linked by long, straight avenues forming an equilateral triangle. In the valley between Parliament Hill and the other high points is a chain of lakes, with formal basins within the triangle and adjoining it. A third axis from Parliament Hill crosses the central basin, creating the familiar system of three radial axes seen at the entrance to Rome and at Versailles. While the street system is essentially formal, based on long boulevards and radial streets around subcenters, it is carefully adjusted to the contours, and the neighborhoods are scaled for houses on individual lots (Figure 3.19).

There was strong political opposition to the selection of Griffin, a foreigner, as the planner of Canberra as well as to the whole idea of a new capital, which turned the victory in the competition into a bitter experience. Griffin stuck it out until 1920, doggedly mapping the street system, knowing that once it had been laid out no one would bother to do the work over again. As a result, despite many changes, the essence of the Griffin plan has been implemented, making it in some respects a complete garden city, replete with suburban garden districts.

3.19
Aerial view of Canberra, the capital of Australia, designed by Walter Burley Griffin and Marion Mahony Griffin who won an international design competition. The plan is illustrated as an example of traditional city design in the previous chapter, but in many ways Canberra is also a garden city.

The first garden suburbs in the United States

The influence of Letchworth and Hampstead Garden Suburb was seen almost immediately at Forest Hills Gardens in New York City, developed, beginning in 1909, at the instigation of the Russell Sage Foundation. The landscape architect who designed the parks and curving street system was Frederick Law Olmsted, Jr.; Grosvenor Atterbury established the character of the architecture and designed the important buildings and groups of houses. Although many of the houses at Forest Hills Gardens are of poured reinforced concrete, which was still an experimental building material in 1909, they are covered in brick, stone or stucco in a free interpretation of the Tudor style, more of a single period than the Queen Anne that had characterized Bedford Park. As the informal, comfortable house, suitable for the upper-middle-class life, had been an English invention, an English country-house style often seemed to be the appropriate symbol of these qualities. Forest Hills Gardens, like Hampstead, was designed for a mix of incomes, with apartment houses in the town center and along the railroad tracks, attached houses, and individual houses of various sizes (Figure 3.20).

In designing Forest Hills Gardens the Olmsted firm could also draw on its experience at the planned suburb of Roland Park, north of Baltimore, in the late 1890s; but where Roland Park depended for its design on the arrangement of its streets, Forest Hills Gardens, like Hampstead, created real architectural spaces, particularly in Atterbury's design for the center near the railroad station and for housing groups. Forest Hills Gardens and Hampstead can be seen to have influenced the groups of houses around courtyards constructed in suburbs like Germantown and Chestnut Hill, Pennsylvania, about the time of World War I and the design for the town center of Lake Forest, Illinois, by Howard Van Doren Shaw, dating from 1918. Lake Forest is otherwise a garden suburb of the older type, laid

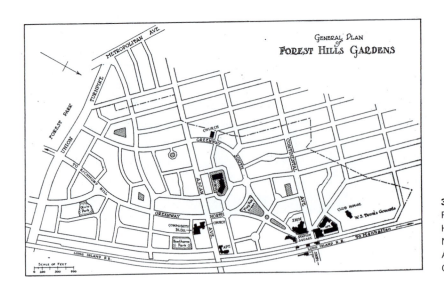

3.20
Plan begun in 1909 for Forest Hills Gardens in Queens, New York, by Grosvenor Atterbury and Frederick Law Olmsted, Jr.

out in the mid-nineteenth century as a loose composition of winding streets and large house lots.

American company towns influenced by English examples include Kohler, Wisconsin, laid out by the Olmsted firm in 1913, and Tyrone, New Mexico. For Tyrone—begun in 1915, never completed, and ultimately demolished in 1967—the architect, Bertram G. Goodhue substituted an architectural vocabulary based upon Spanish colonial and pueblo architecture for the English village images being used in other contemporary planned towns.

Other company towns were built as emergency housing in response to the vast industrial expansion that began during World War I. When the United States entered the war in 1917, it was clear that unprecedented amounts of new housing would be needed to accommodate the large number of workers suddenly brought to industrial sites.

Two federal agencies supported housing construction. The Housing Division of the Emergency Fleet Corporation gave loans to private companies, which built the towns; and the United States Housing Corporation built and operated units. Private companies completed 9,000 family dwellings plus another 7,500 small apartments and boardinghouse rooms; the Housing Corporation completed 6,000 dwellings in twenty-seven projects.

Charles Whitaker, then the editor of the *Journal of the American Institute of Architects*, campaigned to make sure that this wartime housing was designed not as temporary barracks but as permanent communities. He sent the architect Frederick L. Ackerman to England to consult with Raymond Unwin, who was in charge of the British war-housing effort and published a series of articles on British housing standards, which dealt with war housing as a permanent investment. Frederick Law Olmsted, Jr., who had earlier volunteered to help organize the design and building of army bases for the Quartermaster Corps, was put in charge of the planning section of the United States Housing Corporation. Olmsted also wished to make sure that the American wartime housing ended up as permanent communities designed to high standards; and he was in a position to name as designers for this housing some of the best architects and planners in the United States. George B. Post & Sons' design for Eclipse Park, in Beloit, Wisconsin—planned for the employees of Fairbanks, Morse and Company—bears a distinct resemblance to Forest Hills Gardens, although the houses were more modest (Figure 3.21). There is a town center, which acts as a gateway to the community, curving landscaped streets and a large park. Another excellent example is Kingsport, Tennessee, designed by John Nolen, an important planner whose work showed a strong understanding of the principles followed by Unwin and Parker. George B. Post & Sons designed houses and apartments for shipyard workers at Craddock, Virginia (near Hampton Roads), that were as well planned and detailed as contemporary private housing being built in well-to-do suburbs, although building dimensions and lots were smaller.

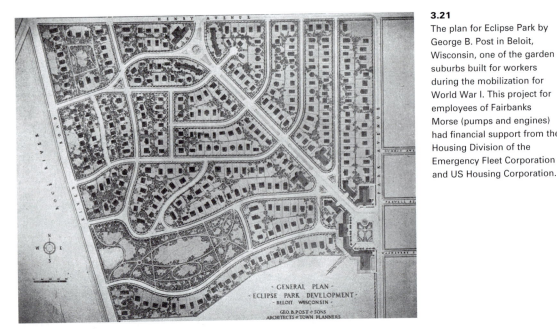

3.21
The plan for Eclipse Park by George B. Post in Beloit, Wisconsin, one of the garden suburbs built for workers during the mobilization for World War I. This project for employees of Fairbanks Morse (pumps and engines) had financial support from the Housing Division of the Emergency Fleet Corporation and US Housing Corporation.

Other company towns built under these programs as garden suburbs include Westinghouse Village in South Philadelphia, Pennsylvania, whose plan by Clarence W. Brazer shows the influence of Hampstead adapted to an American vernacular; Yorkship Village, West Collingswood, New Jersey, by Electus D. Litchfield, also clearly influenced by Hampstead Garden Suburb; and Seaside and Black Rock in Bridgeport, Connecticut, planned by Arthur Shurtleff, with R. Clipston Sturgis and A.H. Hepburn as architects.

The government subsidy for workers' housing was viewed at the time as a necessary, but temporary, expedient, and the laws setting up the programs required that the housing be sold as soon as the war was over. In an introduction to a book describing these wartime housing projects, William B. Wilson, then secretary of labor commented:

> I have found that the man who owns his own home is the least susceptible to the so-called Bolshevist doctrines and is about the last man to join in the industrial disturbances fomented by the radical agitators. Owning a home gives a man an added sense of responsibility to the national and local government that makes for the best type of citizenship.[26]

Garden cities and suburbs after World War I

Belief in the importance of the owner-occupied house was not shared in Europe, where governments began to subsidize housing on a large scale after World

War I. In England large amounts of subsidized housing for workers were designed to similar standards to those created at Letchworth, helped by the 1912 publication of Raymond Unwin's pamphlet *Nothing Gained by Overcrowding* and Unwin's own activities as a government official. Unwin's argument was that the conventional by-law streets required for densities of twenty houses per acre or higher cost so much more to develop that they more than canceled the higher price of land per house at densities of twelve houses per acre.

The absorption of the Garden City Association into the more broadly based Town and Country Planning Association was symptomatic of what seemed to be happening to Ebenezer Howard's ideas in the years after World War I. Howard, with his cheerfully optimistic temperament, remained undeterred in his belief in a future radical transformation of society, and refused to accept that the major result of his efforts to date seemed to be better-designed suburbs, not a new type of city. After all, he had turned out to be correct in predicting that a planned garden city under community ownership would be economically feasible. Howard's only miscalculation, which was serious but not fatal, was that it took much longer than he had estimated to bring the community up to a size that generated sufficient income to pay off its debts. Pleased but not satisfied by the modest success of Letchworth, Howard began looking out for places to build a second prototype. A site near Hatfield that he had marked down as ideal before the end of the war came on the market in 1919 and Howard persuaded his backers to buy it, although many of his colleagues urged him to put his energies into getting the government to incorporate new-town policies into post-war housing development, as proposed by Frederick J. Osborn in his 1918 book *New Towns After the War*. Howard did not wish to wait idly for governmental support; he preferred to continue demonstrating the virtues of garden cities by direct action. The result was Welwyn Garden City, which also was to become an established community. Welwyn would not have succeeded, however, without government money, made available as part of the post-war housing programs, which included a clause that permitted loans to associations created for developing garden cities.

The design concept for Welwyn, by Louis de Soissons, is close to that of Letchworth. The monumental boulevard has more importance, and the overall site plan is somewhat more tightly organized, but the industrial district is positioned analogously to the one at Letchworth and there is a similarly informal network of winding streets. The design of housing groups is more architectural, reflecting design advances made at Hampstead, and the prevailing architectural character is a somewhat anemic neo-Georgian.

Additional planned communities were created in Britain during the interwar period on Howard-like principles, but they were constructed by major cities as part of public policies dealing with housing and overcrowding, and were not developed by an autonomous private group, as Welwyn was. Wythenshawe, near Manchester, was constructed by the city of Manchester and designed by Barry Parker (Unwin had remained in government service after the war and the partnership had been dissolved). While it was far more a one-class community of subsidized housing than Howard had advocated, and it lacked its own employment base, Wythenshawe continued the development of the garden-city concept by creating new types of housing groups and cul-de-sacs, and made extensive use of natural landscape features. Wythenshaw continued to be developed after World War II with the later conventional modernist work obscuring some of the original green intent.

The London County Council began a series of what it called cottage housing estates after World War I, the largest of which were definitely on a new-town scale, but they were suburbs rather than complete communities. Beacontree, east of London, was designed by C. Topham Forrest, architect to the London County Council, in 1920. It was planned for a population of 115,000, making it far larger than other LCC cottage housing groups planned at the same period around the fringes of London. Some of these housing projects were nevertheless at new-town size, such as Downham, designed to house 30,000 people, or the St. Helier estate, for 45,000. Altogether, dwellings for some 300,000 people were developed, all designed under the direction of Forrest or his successor, E.P. Wheeler. Densities were almost always at twelve households to the acre, the magic threshold identified by Unwin, there were ample reservations for open space, and the buildings were well designed. Care was taken to create architectural groups along curving streets or around cul-de-sacs, but the uniformity of income level, density and building type inevitably produced a certain monotony (Figure 3.22).

The new-town ideal also influenced some of the subsidized housing development on the continent of Europe during the interwar period, although most of this housing, as we saw in the chapter on Modernist City Design, was constructed in a more urban pattern. Ernst May, the city architect of Frankfurt, had worked for Unwin and Parker before World War I and was thus thoroughly familiar with the theories of Ebenezer Howard and with the completed English garden cities and suburbs. While May and his colleagues used a modernist architectural vernacular,

3.22
A street in Beacontree, east of London, designed by C. Topham Forrest, architect to the London County Council, in 1920. Beacontree was planned for a population of 115,000, making it far larger than other LCC cottage housing groups planned at the same period around the fringes of London.

3.23
An aerial view from the late 1920s of the satellite community at Romerstadt, near Frankfurt, designed by Ernst May, then Frankfurt's city architect. May had worked for Unwin and Parker, but his version of a garden suburb used a modernist design vocabulary.

3.24
The plan for Radburn in Fairlawn, New Jersey, designed by Clarence Stein and Henry Wright as a garden suburb for car-owning middle-class residents. The central segment of the plan was implemented, but the full concept was a victim of the economic downturn in the 1930s.

they gave their work a humane quality that was missing from the mechanistic efforts of many other modernists of the time. May prepared a comprehensive plan for Frankfurt, which was the context for his housing projects. He also developed new satellite communities at Romerstadt, Praunheim, and Westhausen, which combined English garden-city-planning principles, like curving streets and green belts, with German ideas about simplified architectural expression and the importance of orientation as an architectural determinant (Figure 3.23).

In the United States after World War I, some of the best new housing took the form of model garden communities built by private companies seeking a sound, long-term investment, as well as a worthwhile social purpose. Mariemont, east of Cincinnati, was built on land assembled by Mrs. Mary M. Emery starting in 1923. Mrs. Emery donated a park, a church, and the first school buildings, but the aim of the company was to make a suitable profit while providing good-quality housing for skilled workmen and salaried office workers who would not otherwise be able to afford it. The planner was John Nolen, one of the pioneers of effective city planning in the United States, and the layout followed the now familiar garden-suburb pattern.

Sunnyside, in the New York City borough of Queens, was begun in 1924 as a model community by the limited-profit City Housing Corporation. The planners, Clarence Stein and Henry Wright, had to accept a pre-existing street grid pattern, but were able to create open spaces in the interior of the blocks and, later, through-block common spaces between groups of buildings. The result was far better than the rows of identical houses on narrow lots that were the normal form of competing development. Also, through its limited-profit structure, Sunnyside, like Mariemont, was able to reach people of somewhat lower incomes than the buyers of conventional houses. There were also apartment houses, both rental and cooperative.

Sunnyside was a dress rehearsal for the City Housing Corporation's more ambitious Radburn, New Jersey, planned as the American equivalent of Letchworth or Welwyn, after consultation with Unwin and Parker, and begun in 1928. Because of the Depression, only a portion of the community was completed in accordance with the original plan; but that plan, also provided by Clarence Stein and Henry Wright, has proved tremendously influential. Its most publicized feature was its greenway system, which allowed children to walk to the primary school by pathways that never crossed a street—except for one underpass below a main road. Clarence Stein used to say that the greenway and underpass system was suggested by the separation between pedestrians and vehicles in Manhattan's Central Park, but the design can also be interpreted as deriving from some very similar arrangements at Hampstead Garden Suburb and from the traditional alternation of streets and service alleys. At Radburn, all services are on cul-de-sac streets leading to clusters of houses, and what in other projects might have been an alley has become the greenway (Figure 3.24).

The concept of a neighborhood unit like the one at Radburn as a group of houses and apartments large enough to require a primary school was part of Clarence

Perry's definition of a neighborhood in a 1929 essay published as part of the First Regional Plan for New York City. This plan, which was issued in installments starting in 1926, was supported by the Russell Sage Foundation, which had developed Forest Hills Gardens, where Perry, the foundation's director, lived. Not surprisingly, the theoretical drawing of a neighborhood given in the plan bears a strong resemblance to Forest Hills Gardens (Figure 3.25). The idea of neighborhoods has become such an axiomatic part of planning that one tends to forget that it was formulated by a few individuals, such as Perry, Stein, and Wright, as part of the design of isolated model developments that housed only a few thousand families. In time the ideas were to feed back into the English garden-city movement and into the CIAM Charter, and would ultimately be adopted in many countries. Barry Parker was particularly impressed by Radburn, and incorporated its redefinition of the cul-de-sac into his designs for Wythenshawe.

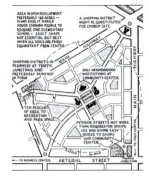

3.25
Clarence Perry's famous diagram of the Neighborhood Unit, published in the 1929 *Regional Plan for New York City.*

The green belt communities

The coming of the New Deal in the United States seemed to create the opportunities to apply all the city-planning ideas that had been created as prototypes by privately supported developments. The Tennessee Valley Authority would offer the opportunity to do real regional planning on an unprecedented scale. New federal programs accepted the principle already established in Europe that it was up to government to supply good-quality low-income housing if the private market could not do it.

Many of these programs were federal subsidies to local housing authorities, but the government also went into the housing development business itself. The Resettlement Administration, one of the many agencies established during the early days of the New Deal, was under the direction of Rexford Tugwell, a believer in Ebenezer Howard's garden-city theories. The Resettlement Administration proposed four green belt communities and actually constructed three of them: Greenbelt, Maryland, located about ten miles north-east of Washington; Greendale, Wisconsin, seven miles from Milwaukee; and Greenhills, Ohio, five miles north of Cincinnati (Figure 3.26).

While planned to be self-contained satellite communities on Howard's model, these towns actually ended up becoming garden suburbs. The one green belt town site that might successfully have attracted industry would have been Greenbrook, near New Brunswick, New Jersey, which was not built because of political opposition. Despite the actual construction of these green belt communities, the model had little effect on American real-estate development practice, perhaps because construction by the federal government, and the income restrictions on tenancies, made the whole green belt idea seem remote from normal development practice.

3.26
An aerial view of Greenbelt, Maryland under construction in 1941. It was one of three garden communities built by the Works Progress Administration during the New Deal.

The Tennessee Valley Authority

The most interesting aspect of the Tennessee Valley Authority, looking back at it today, is that it is a public authority whose boundaries encompass an entire ecological region of some 42,000 square miles that includes parts of seven states (Figure 3.27). The Authority was created by Congress in 1933, at the height of New Deal innovation, to aid some of the most economically depressed areas in the whole country. The mechanism for economic development was primarily hydro-electric power generation to bring electrification to rural areas, although the constitutional justification was flood control and the improvement of navigable waterways. While TVA's system of dams was more interventionist than would be recommended now, it has been an important demonstration that environmental design can take place at a regional scale. The economic success of the project was fully realized during a huge spurt of dam construction in the TVA area during World War II, where the availability of relatively inexpensive power was necessary for aluminum plants and other wartime manufacturing. TVA also engaged in other regional management activities, including coordinating the planning needed to rehouse people displaced by the dams, reforesting cut-over areas, and helping farmers make their holdings more productive.

The first dam built by TVA, named for Senator George Norris of Nebraska, the author of the TVA legislation, is 265 feet high and created a lake 73 miles long.

3.27
Map of the area under the jurisdiction of the Tennessee Valley Authority.

Four miles downstream from the dam is Norris, TN, originally constructed by the TVA for the dam's construction workers. TVA's planner, Earle S. Draper, did not want to build typical minimal barracks for construction workers but a permanent settlement that could later house the employees who would operate the dam and others who would live and work in the area. Norris is a low-density rural community of individual houses, with roads planned in response to the topography and vegetation, with a civic center and a block of stores (Figure 3.28). Sold to a private investor after World War II, the houses were then sold to their residents. Not far from Interstate 75, Norris has become a northern suburb of Knoxville.[27]

3.28
Plan of Norris, Tennessee, designed by TVA staff architects and begun in 1933, was built originally as workers' housing for the TVA.

The Norris dam is just one of many hydroelectric, water supply, and irrigation projects built by the US government in the mid-twentieth century, such as the Boulder (now Hoover) Dam on the Colorado River begun in 1931 and the Grand Coulee Dam in the Columbia River Gorge begun in 1933. The hydroelectric function of the Grand Coulee Dam was completed in 1942, in time to help power war production in the area. The irrigation element was added in the 1950s. Both dams have benefited development but have also had serious adverse environmental impacts. Lake Mead, the enormous reservoir behind Hoover Dam, has helped make Las Vegas possible, but recently the Lake has been drawn down to levels from which it may never recover while endangering the flow of the river downstream. Grand Coulee completely altered the way of life for Native Americans who lived in areas that have now been flooded and who depended on the annual run of salmon which can no longer swim up the river. The dam has also had clearly negative effects on the world's salmon population. In retrospect it is amazing how confidently these dams were built, despite little understanding of what their long-term effects would be on the complex natural systems of their river environments. The most massive and controversial of all dams is the Three Gorges Dam on the Yangtze River in China. One of the original proposals for this dam was drawn up by engineers from the US Bureau of Reclamation in the mid-1940s.

Broadacre City

During the exciting early days of the New Deal, when almost any radical idea could be given a serious hearing, no one talked seriously to Frank Lloyd Wright, who was understood to be a great architect, but was also well known to be a controversial and difficult personality. Wright's remedy was to prepare designs for his ideal development prototype: Broadacre City, exhibited in 1935 at Rockefeller Center in New York City, and then used by Wright as illustrations for various books and polemics, as well as sources for actual building designs. Wright had already predicted, in his book *The Disappearing City*, published in 1932, that the automobile would cause a fundamental change in city design, with urbanization spreading out over the landscape. Wright welcomed this change, rejecting the modern central city as an unnatural and inhumane environment.

For Broadacre City, Wright went back to a design for a typical mid-western mile-square land segment that he had prepared in 1913, and enlarged his prototype area to four square miles. Wright rejected the curving streets of English and American garden-suburb design, and proposed a much lower density: in some sections of his plan, each family would have an acre of land. The social intentions behind Broadacre City have puzzled a number of commentators, and its ideological contradictions have been the subject of a long essay by Giorgio Ciucci.[28] Unlike Ebenezer Howard, or Clarence Stein, Wright had no serious social agenda. If you look closely at the floor plans for Broadacre City houses, you find that many of them have one or more maid's rooms. Wright accepted society as he found it. He just wished to shape its buildings. Broadacre City is probably best understood as an advertisement. It is also, at a secondary level, an answer to Le Corbusier's Ville Contemporaine and the more mechanistic architectural ideas of European modernism (Figure 3.29).

Wright wanted to show Americans a modern city that was closely related to the American way of life. Broadacre City is a fairly accurate prediction of post-World War II suburban sprawl, particularly areas with large-lot zoning, showing that Wright understood the American public well. What he was unable to do, however, was invent

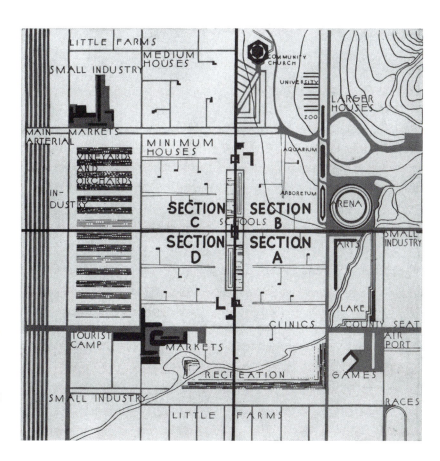

3.29
The plan for prototype quadrants of Broadacre City designed during the 1930s by Frank Lloyd Wright. Wright understood what Americans wanted, and devised what would now be considered a plan for urban sprawl. Sprawl might have been far more satisfactory if it had followed Wright's prototype.

a mechanism that would ensure that this type of suburban and exurban growth would follow any overall design. Thus Broadacre City itself has had very little influence. Where Wright has been influential has been through the house types that he was developing for individual owners at the same time that he was working on Broadacre City. The influence of these "Usonian" houses did much to transform the typical suburban house from a miniature version of the English gentleman's residence into a dwelling that was far more open, functional, and in tune with modern life.

New towns after World War II

Ebenezer Howard died in 1928. The two garden cities Letchworth and Welwyn had reached a combined population of 40,000 by World War II. While this is success, the population of Great Britain increased enough between 1898 and 1945 to have created 300 garden cities without changing the population of the cities that already existed. Economic viability for a planned community is more difficult to achieve than Howard anticipated, requiring a long-term investment strategy that is possible for governments but is beyond the time horizons of most real-estate developers. Howard had foreseen a role for government in creating new towns, but realized that governments have more limited social objectives than he did. In his quietly subversive way, Howard had hoped to bring about a total transformation of society, not marginal improvements.

It was not until after World War II that Howard's satellite city formulation was widely adopted in Great Britain and Europe, and more recently in Asia. The process of acceptance, however, also involved a transformation. It is not clear that Howard would have approved the planning that has been done in his name, or even have recognized the results as garden cities. Where Howard sought to disperse all social classes from cities into networks of autonomous communities, the new town has been used as a satellite for big cities, and has often become a community made up predominantly of factory workers.

Patrick Abercrombie's Greater London Plan for post-war reconstruction, published in 1944, used green belts and satellite towns as a way of limiting the growth of London. Government new-town policy then extended the concept to all of Britain; and some forty of these communities were created. Decentralization of industry laws made it possible to give each new town an economic base, in keeping with Howard's ideas; but because the new towns did not constitute the whole of urban development, they became primarily working-class communities.

In Sweden, where foresighted land acquisition policies had enabled the city of Stockholm to control its growth, much of the suburban development was channeled into planned communities like Vallingby, designed by Sven Markelius, and Farsta. The map of the Stockholm metropolitan region has a cellular appearance, with shopping centers along regional railroad corridors and higher-density growth around the stations, with feeder roads leading out to lower-density areas.

Helsinki, Finland, has also successfully channeled growth into satellite communities, some of which, like Tapiola, have attracted international attention for the high quality of the buildings.

French national planning policies have directed the growth of the Paris metropolitan region into planned satellite communities along two axes roughly parallel to the Seine north and south of Paris, with this development pattern supported by a new regional rail system.

Satellite new towns have also been created in Korea and are being used in China to help manage rapid urbanization.

The original garden-city image has been altered in these newer planned communities by the introduction of elevator buildings, but curving streets and informal building arrangements are still sometimes used. While most European cities have planned garden suburbs of this newer high-density type, anything like a self-contained community is rare, except in Great Britain.

In the United States there have been a few economically successful planned communities built since World War II. These include Reston, Virginia, near Washington; Columbia, Maryland, between Washington and Baltimore; the Woodlands north of Houston, Texas; and the Irvine Ranch development between Los Angeles and San Diego. While there were more apartments in these new towns than were found in typical suburban development, there were many more individual houses than would be found in new towns in Europe. The original plan for Reston assumed it would be connected to Washington by the access highway that leads to Dulles Airport. When access to that highway was denied, development at Reston was slowed down. Later, a toll road was built on both sides of the access highway, enabling the growth of what is now the Northern Virginia office corridor with its attendant residential development. Reston is now just a part of this much larger corridor.

In the 1970s there was also a brief official flirtation with new towns as a federal policy, with government-subsidized loans provided to developers of approved planned communities. While a few of these communities, notably the Woodlands, have proved to be sound investments, most were financial failures. The program no longer exists.

Suburban sprawl

Chatham Village in Pittsburgh, by Clarence Stein and Henry Wright with the Pittsburgh architects Ingham and Boyd, begun in the early 1930s and completed in the 1950s, could have been the model for post-World War II development in the United States with its cost efficiency for both buildings and land, but that is not how things turned out. Chatham Village was intended to be a prototype that would turn the American public away from the single-family house on an individual lot to a planned village environment similar to Letchworth, Welwyn, and Hampstead Garden Suburb.

Developed by the Buehl Foundation as a limited-profit investment, Chatham Village builds on the experience of Sunnyside and Radburn but possesses an architectural and landscaping distinction not achieved in the earlier projects (Figure 3.30).

It was not the new town or the common green areas of Chatham Village that captured the admiration of the American public, but the private houses in garden suburbs for upper-income people that could be found on the fashionable side of almost every American city by the end of the interwar period. One of the major changes that took place in Middletown (Muncie, Indiana) between Robert and Helen Merrell Lynd's original study in 1928 and their *Middletown in Transition* study of 1937 was the growth of a fashionable suburban district and the consequent segregation of well-off citizens in their own enclave, away from the center of the community. Whatever the negative social effects of the new garden suburbs, they frequently included elements that made them desirable environments, such as parks, curving streets, and secluded cul-de-sacs. The Country Club district of Kansas City, River Oaks in Houston, and Palos Verdes and Beverly Hills in Los Angeles are well-known examples.

The individual house on an individual lot, similar except in size and landscaping to those found in the garden suburb, was supported by mortgage subsidy programs of the Federal Housing Administration, originally created in 1934, and the special mortgage programs for veterans created at the end of World War II. The best account of the influence of these government programs on suburban development remains Kenneth T. Jackson's *Crabgrass Frontier*, which also makes it clear how racial segregation was reinforced by these government programs.[29]

Levittown, Long Island, begun in 1947, made use of the rationalized building techniques, such as pre-cut lumber to fit standard room dimensions, pioneered by Clarence Stein and Henry Wright and used by the military during World War II; but each house was built on an individual quarter-acre lot, not as an ensemble of attached town houses as at Chatham Village, or the mix of town houses and garden apartments used in the green belt towns. Abraham Levitt and Sons was a firm established before World War II. William Levitt became the executive and his brother

3.30
Chatham Village in Pittsburgh by Clarence Stein and Henry Wright with Ingham and Boyd. Begun before World War II, and completed in 1956, Chatham Village was considered a prototype for moderate income housing for the US, but Levittown became the prototype instead.

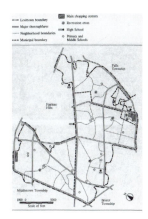

3.31
A diagram of the plan for Levittown, Pennsylvania, begun in 1952, which followed the Long Island Levittown, begun in 1947. Both were designed by Albert Levitt, brother of the developer William Levitt. Although houses on quarter-acre lots were the most prominent feature of the design, the plans had a strong neighborhood structure organized around parks and schools.

Albert was the architect and planner. The site plan for Levittown Long Island is a loose assemblage of garden-suburb streets, contained within arterials that enclose a series of neighborhoods each with schools and parks. A later Levittown in Pennsylvania north of Philadelphia is also planned around neighborhood schools and parks, but here the neighborhoods are also connected by a greenway system. The original houses were affordable by entry level home buyers who qualified for mortgage insurance under US government FHA or VA programs. Because there was plenty of extra room on the lots, individual home owners could later remodel and expand their houses to meet their own needs, so that two generations later there are few of the original houses to be seen and the initial cookie-cutter, one-class environment has almost disappeared. The Levittowns have to be considered as successful in their way as Chatham Village or the green belt towns (Figure 3.31). Evaluation of success as housing policy has to be tempered by the knowledge that African Americans were excluded from the Levittowns; segregation was also US housing policy when the Levittowns were first offered for sale.[30] Greenbelt, Maryland was intended to include a segregated section for African Americans, which was not completed.

The housing market learned economies of scale and rationalized construction from the Levittowns, but not neighborhoods with parks and schools. The predominant post-World War II housing type in the United States, and also in Canada and Australia, was the single-family house, constructed as tracts of similar houses with similar sales prices, by builders using the large parcels of land that were available on the fringe of cities and suburbs. The growth was managed by local towns and villages using newly enacted zoning codes which separated individual houses from attached houses and apartments, and employment or shopping from residences. These codes mandated large areas of housing built for the same sized lots, and required that stores, services, and offices be constructed in narrow strips along highways. Access to this new development was almost always by car, as car ownership became almost universal. In the United States, the rapid increase of individual houses was supported by Federally subsidized mortgages and an income-tax deduction for mortgage interest. More houses and cars meant more traffic, which meant road widening and new highway construction. After the Interstate Highway Act was passed in the United States in 1956, the highway system became the means of transforming cities, suburbs, and close-in rural areas into a new kind of multi-centered urban metropolis where jobs followed the population out of old urban locations to new suburban office and industrial parks, and shopping and office centers grew up at highway interchanges. The self-reinforcing cycles of mortgage subsidy, tract development, road and highway construction, followed by the migration of jobs and shopping centers to suburban locations have been well described by many writers, almost always using the term urban sprawl.[31]

Howard's diagram of self-contained communities separated by green belts was perfectly adapted to the railroad as a means of transportation; but there is no reason to confine development to areas around station stops and along railway sidings when cars and trucks are available. Howard's concept of town–country embedded urbanized areas within green belts and preserved the continuity of the natural landscape. The newly urbanized regions supported by cars and trucks became engineered environments instead of natural environments, and that began to create serious problems.

Earth Day and environmental legislation

Rachel Carson's *Silent Spring* appeared in three parts in the *New Yorker* magazine in the summer of 1962 and was published that fall. Spring would be silent, Carson predicted, because DDT moved up the food chain from insects to birds, causing deformities and failures to reproduce. Her book began with what she called a Fable for Tomorrow: the story of a fictional community where every living thing sickened and died and the residents had brought this calamity on themselves. Carson concluded this opening chapter by saying she knew of no actual community where every one of the disasters she described had happened, but they had each happened somewhere. The same thing that was happening to birds was also beginning to happen to human beings, as chemicals that got into the body would stay there for a lifetime, causing illness and genetic effects as well. The book was fiercely attacked by spokesmen for the chemical industry but its message got across to the public and, not only was the use of DDT and some other chemical poisons generally discontinued, but both the fragility and the interconnectedness of life began to be understood.

By the end of the 1960s the future of the whole environment had become a major public issue. Paul Erlich's *The Population Bomb* was published in 1968 and became a best-seller. It warned of unsustainable population growth and worldwide food shortages in the decades to come. The Club of Rome, concerned with the limits of the Earth's natural resources, was founded in 1968. Its report, *The Limits to Growth*, predicting the increasing scarcity of the world's resources, was published in 1972, just before the first oil crisis. The first Earth Day, a nation-wide call to stop and consider environmental issues, was an initiative of Senator Gaylord Nelson of Wisconsin and took place on April 22, 1970. The Natural Resources Defense Council was founded in 1970, joining the much older Sierra Club, founded in 1892, as environmental advocates.

Advocacy and public discussion had significant policy consequences. The National Environmental Policy Act of 1969, The Clean Air Act of 1972, The Federal Water Pollution Control Act of 1972, The Noise Control Act of 1972, and The Endangered Species Act of 1973 are the foundations of modern environmental regulation in the United States, all passed while Richard Nixon was president.[32] A United Nations Environment Program was set up in 1972. By 1983 the UN had created the World Commission on Environment and Development, which in its 1987 report produced the famous definition of sustainable development as meeting the needs of the present without compromising the ability of future generations to meet their own needs.

Design with Nature; environmental zoning

But how do you meet the needs of the present without compromising the future?

Ian McHarg, a professor of landscape architecture at the University of Pennsylvania, published *Design with Nature* in 1969.[33] McHarg was one of the first to make a connection between planning and design and the science of ecology.[34] The science in his book was very basic: McHarg's point was how remarkable it was that major works of civil engineering, planning, and development went forward seemingly oblivious to precisely these most basic issues: the causes of erosion and flooding, and the reasons for the loss of tree cover and habitat when a landscape is developed. McHarg's answer was to map the areas where new construction was planned to assess their suitability for development. Areas with the least suitability included dunes along shorelines, hillsides with steep slopes, and wetlands or floodplains. Mature woodlands would be somewhat more suitable, well-drained uplands would be the best. By overlaying maps of areas with the least suitability for building, the parts of the land where development would cause the fewest environmental problems would become visible. McHarg and his assistants mapped these areas by hand on tracing paper; today the same analysis can be done on computers, and part of the impetus for developing the necessary computer programs came from McHarg's research.

Local zoning codes mapped large areas for development without regard to their ecology or terrain. Property lines cut across the landscape, often with no relation to natural features. Often portions of a property mapped for development would include areas that by McHargian analysis were not appropriate for building. Planned development chapters of many zoning codes permit transferring development rights within the property on the basis of an approved plan for the whole development. To do this, these special procedures accept smaller lots and setbacks than would ordinarily be permitted. William H. Whyte called this procedure cluster development, and advocated it in a report for the Conservation Foundation in 1964 and in his 1968 book, *The Last Landscape*, which refers to McHarg's mapping procedures in plans for a suburban area north of Baltimore and McHarg's analysis of alternative highway routes in New Jersey. Whyte also mentions the work of Philip Lewis, a professor at the University of Wisconsin, and another pioneer in relating natural systems to development proposals.

Cluster development has not turned out to be an effective way to implement McHarg's prescriptions. Planned development chapters of zoning codes usually make it an optional procedure, and, as it generally requires a separate public hearing, many developers pass this option up and simply re-grade the property. Property lines usually don't coincide with the boundaries of natural features, so even when a developer respects the environment on one parcel of land, it may well cause disjunction with adjacent properties. There can also be a problem with decanting development rights from one side of a property to another, creating a combined density that the market, or the neighbors, may not want.

McHarg made it clear that his aim was to reconcile development rights with the natural landscape. While he undoubtedly felt that there were many properties that should not be developed, he must have thought he would not be taken seriously if he asserted this. Today, some of his design suggestions seem too accommodating, such as the sketches in *Design with Nature* of equally spaced houses in the midst of woodlands.

Lane Kendig was among the first to raise the question of whether development rights should be associated with land that ought not to be built on. In a 1980 book, *Performance Zoning*,[35] he proposed a system of discounts for the amount of environmentally sensitive land that should not be counted for zoning purposes, such as no credit at all for beaches, bluffs, lakes, ponds or water courses, wetlands, flood plains, or erosion hazard areas. Only 2 percent of land in the form of dunes or ravines could be counted for zoning purposes, and only 5 percent of slopes steeper than 30 degrees, 15 percent of mature woodlands, 30 percent of slopes between 18 and 30 degrees, and so on. There would be few development rights from such areas that would need to be transferred to the more buildable parts of a property.

Here is a precise method of translating the kind of analysis that McHarg had proposed into a zoning calculation that would directly affect what it was legally possible to build. In addition, in a different portion of Kendig's model zoning ordinance, he proposed restrictions on the percentage of sensitive land that could be built upon at all. Erosion hazard areas had to remain as permanent open space; only 15 percent of mature woodlands could be built upon. In an agricultural district, only 15 percent of an area of prime soils could be developed.

These were revolutionary ideas, unfortunately buried within the entirely different concept of performance zoning, so that only a relatively few places have recognized their importance. All that performance zoning means is that instead of definite prescriptions written into the code there should be performance specifications defining the desired results. Kendig's environmental zoning requirements are in fact prescriptive; an example of a performance specification for erosion would be to say that there should be no more erosion after development than there had been before. When Kendig chose to describe as performance zoning his environmental zoning prescriptions—no zoning credit for land where there is an erosion hazard, all such areas must be permanent open space—he fatally confused the nature of his proposals.

Some of Kendig's environmental zoning ideas have been written into ordinances in Bucks County, Pennsylvania and Lake County, Illinois, places where Kendig worked as a planner. I have worked on ordinances that made use of these ideas in the town of Irvington, in Westchester County, New York, and in the city of Wildwood, in suburban St. Louis County, Missouri, both ordinances written to meet the laws of the state where they were located. There has not been a definitive court decision as to whether the kinds of discounts against zoning rights and restrictions against development proposed by Kendig in his model ordinance meet all constitutional restrictions on the regulation of private property. Kendig's proposals are both comprehensive and based on objective criteria, but that may not be sufficient.

Land trusts, development rights transfers and urban growth boundaries

The safest way to implement restrictions on environmentally sensitive private land is to buy it for that purpose. An alternative is to buy the development rights, leaving the land permanently as, say, productive agriculture.

There is a World Land Trust headquartered in London which provides funds to help purchase permanent wildlife preserves. The Nature Conservancy is another international organization that has helped protect more than 119 million acres of land and 5,000 miles of rivers worldwide and operates more than a hundred marine conservation projects. In the United States there are Federal programs to provide funds for conservation land acquisition, for example, a program in the Environmental Protection Administration to help acquire lands needed to protect supplies of safe drinking water. The State of Florida has protected some two and half million acres of land by purchase of the land outright or by buying development rights. Other states have their own conservation funds. There are also many state and local land conservation trusts that can buy land or easements to keep land in its natural state or in use as agriculture.

An alternative to purchase is to permit the transfer of development rights from a landmark building or environmentally sensitive site to a more appropriate location for development. While development rights transfers have been used effectively, the process is not as simple as it may sound. The receiving site has to be environmentally appropriate and politically acceptable, and the property owner may not be able to sell all the development rights at one time, so that realization of value is deferred, sometimes indefinitely.

A better alternative to buying or transferring development rights is to preclude the creation of excessive development rights by the use of urban growth boundaries. An important prototype in the United States has been the growth boundary system enacted in the State of Oregon in 1973 under the leadership of then governor, Tom McCall. The legislation requires all cities in the state to draw growth boundaries. Within the boundaries, urban services will be provided and development regulations will permit relatively dense development. Outside the boundary, development is to remain rural. The boundaries are intended to permit a reasonable amount of conversion of land from rural to urban and are meant to be redrawn when the supply of developable land is exhausted. Understandably, the process of drawing these boundaries has had many political complications, and the concept has been subject to frequent attempts to repeal or dilute it.

The Portland metropolitan region's 2040 plan combines urban growth boundaries with a rapid transit system to help concentrate development within the areas where growth is permitted. The regulations have been in place long enough that it is possible to see the physical effects. The suburban areas are not notably different from other US suburbs, except where there are transit stations. In these locations, there is more concentrated development than would be the norm elsewhere. The effect of the urban growth boundary is much more visible in the city of Portland itself, where the downtown is more residential and more intensely developed than would be expected in other US cities of the same size, and the close-in urban neighborhoods are noticeably more healthy, with strong local shopping and new infill construction in all parts of the city, not just a favored quarter.

An important adjunct to growth management policies that have directed growth inward to the older city areas has been a strong effort to make Portland greener, through tree planting on streets and the development of urban parks, creating an environment that rivals the attractions of more rural areas (Figures 3.32, 3.33).

3.32
View of the park system designed in the late 1960s by Lawrence Halprin for an urban renewal district in south-west Portland, Oregon.

3.33
A landscaped pedestrian walkway, also designed by Lawrence Halprin, in Portland, Oregon.

Environmental evaluation for buildings

The US Green Building Council, a non-profit private organization, was formed in April, 1993 at a meeting held in the boardroom of the American Institute of Architects by about sixty representatives from non-profit environmental organizations and from the building industry. The meeting was organized by S. Richard Fedrizzi, David Gottfried, and Michael Italiano, considered the founders of the USGBC. The intent of the organization was to make the entire construction industry far more environmentally responsible, as buildings account for about 40 percent of energy use in the United States, and many construction practices are wasteful of materials or create pollution. Today the USGBC has more than 15,000 member organizations, as well as an existing system of certified professionals and a more recently formed Institute to issue more strictly administered credentials to design professionals. The organization also holds annual regional conferences, and a well-attended annual national meeting and trade show. The World Green Building Council, an organization of similar councils in other countries founded in 1998, is growing rapidly.

The LEED (Leadership in Energy and Environmental Design) Green Building Rating System was begun 1994 by Robert K. Watson, then a scientist with the Natural Resources Defense Council, who continued to chair the rating system's development until 2005. The rating system's initial preparation was supported by two grants from the US Department of Energy, and later versions have been supported by other grants, but LEED, like the USGBC, is private and non-profit. The rating system confers points for the successful completion of specific requirements, leading to ranking in four grades: Certified, Silver, Gold, and Platinum. Currently for new construction of an individual building 69 points are possible. To reach the Certified level requires 26–32 points; Silver: 33–38 points; Gold: 39–51 points, and Platinum: 52–69 points. The points are given within subcategories, such as Sustainable Sites, Water Efficiency, and Materials & Resources. Up to 5 points are awarded for design innovations proposed by the applicant. There are usually threshold requirements in each category that do not confer points, but must be complied with before any points can be awarded. Each threshold and point requires specific submission requirements to show compliance, and the evaluation is done by the USGBC itself, supported by fees paid by the applicants. Currently building projects reaching the Platinum level have their certification fees refunded.

The point system has proven to be a brilliant motivating device, conferring rank and status on building projects; and reaching a minimum LEED standard is becoming typical of government and non-profit building today. Commercial buildings sometimes use a LEED rating as a marketing tool. The LEED system taps into deeply ingrained human desires for advancement and recognition by peers, reminiscent of the point and badge systems used by the Boy Scouts of America. The LEED point system for buildings has been expanded to allow for a multiple building campus and for neighborhood residential developments.

The LEED system aims for objectivity, which has permitted various governments to incorporate LEED ratings into ordinances. There has never been any suggestion that the LEED system in the US is not objectively administered. However, the recent failure of the rating system for bonds, particularly collateralized mortgage securities, shows the weakness of a rating system supported by fees from the applicants whose products are being evaluated. As the LEED system becomes more and more accepted, and its ratings are required by law, or translated into competitive advantages for more highly ranked projects, it may be that it would be better if the rating system were paid for and administered by government.

There are other standards for environmentally responsible building. The Building Research Establishment (BRE), originally a government organization but private since 1997, created the BRE Environmental Assessment Method (BREEAM) for buildings beginning in 1990. Since a 2008 revision, this method is now being promoted as the basis for international standards in Europe and the Middle East. There is an International Institute for a Sustainable Built Environment with its own evaluation system, SBTool. Canada has Green Globe; Japan has the Comprehensive Assessment System for Built Environment Efficiency (CASBEE). There are also national standards in Australia, Hong Kong, China, Brazil, and many other countries. In the United States there are the Enterprise Green Communities Criteria created by the Green Communities program of Enterprise Communities, which is similar to the LEED point systems for buildings and neighborhoods and also the NAHB Green Building Guidelines developed by the National Association of Home Builders. This is also a point system with four attainment levels: Bronze, Silver, Gold, and Emerald.[36]

Unfortunately much more is known about measuring the environmental impacts of buildings than about the environmental impact of different design alternatives for groups of buildings or whole communities, as such assessments require a systematic understanding of many interrelated variables. As a consequence, communities tend to be assessed for their policies rather than the performance of what is being built. There is also a basic problem with point systems: they have to provide more opportunities to attain points than the number of points required. Otherwise they are enforcing a rigid template and do not allow for the variety of situations being assessed. That flexibility offers the opportunity to accept glaring environmental inadequacies, attain points in other categories, and emerge with the desired badge of attainment. Including some mandatory requirements helps solve this problem, but not completely.

Green building also requires green regional design

Point systems creating incentives for more sustainable buildings can help solve major policy issues of energy conservation by harnessing individual initiatives. But green buildings will not solve basic environmental problems created by the location of development. Effective environmental protection has to be regional because the environment is regional: river valleys, ridgelines, shorelines, and estuaries seldom coincide with property lines or jurisdictional boundaries.

The design of a region should begin with the characteristics of the natural environment and their suitability for development. Ian McHarg's mapping methodology, now translated into Geographic Information Systems programs, remains the best way to begin. It is possible to overlay the criteria for land that should be preserved and use the computer to produce a map of the areas that score the highest on all of the overlaid criteria. Having determined the environmental context, the next step is to design the distribution of urbanization within the natural setting, which needs to be based on the design of transportation and other infrastructure systems. These illustrations of the Orlando region in Florida from the University of

3.34
Potential urbanization in the Seven County Orlando region in Florida by 2050 according to population projections if development follows current trends, from the University of Pennsylvania's CPLN 702 Studio report of 2005.

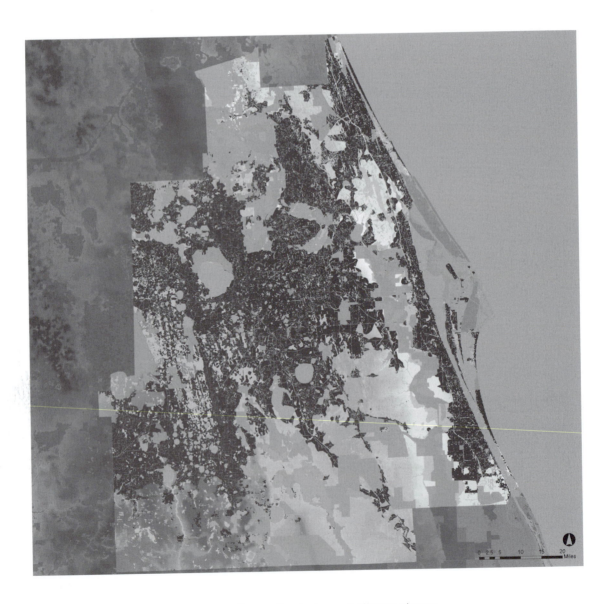

Green city design and climate change

3.35
An alternative projection
for future urbanization in
the Seven County Orlando
region assuming proactive
environmental conservation
and effective use of new
high-speed rail and local
transit systems, also
from the University of
Pennsylvania's CPLN 702
Studio report of 2005.

Pennsylvania School of Design show an alternative distribution of population in 2050 within the ideal conservation network with the population distributed in accordance with assumptions about improved transportation infrastructure, contrasted with a map in which current trends were projected into the future without either conservation measures or changes in infrastructures systems (Figures 3.34 and 3.35). These computer simulations show the power of systems to shape the design of a whole region: in this case, systems of conservation and systems of transportation, which would be allied with environmental zoning codes and urban growth boundaries, both of which are also design systems. Systems city design will be discussed in depth in the next chapter.[37]

McHarg was working at a time when an undisturbed natural environment could be assumed to be a constant, except in the case of shorelines, where he

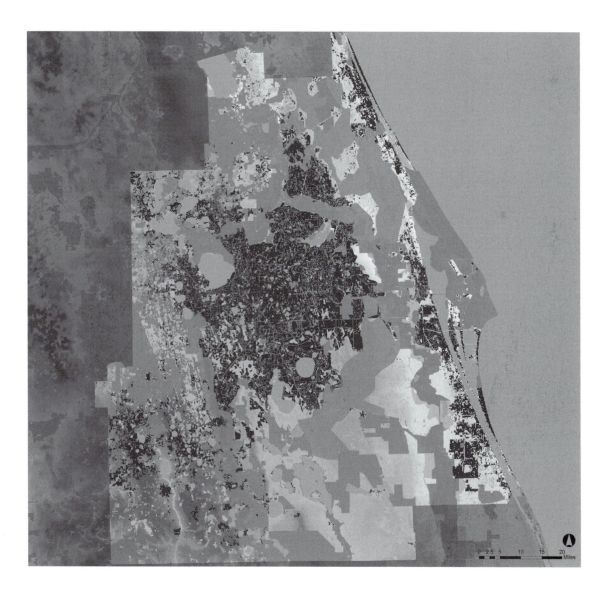

documented that a changing equilibrium was part of nature. Today, predictions of climate change have transformed our understanding of nature from a constant that should be preserved to unpredictable sets of future conditions which require flexible means of accommodation.

Hurricane Katrina, which caused the disastrous flooding of New Orleans in 2005, has functioned as a warning to other coastal cities of the future dangers that could come from rising sea levels and more frequent and severe flood surges, both of which could be the consequences of climate change. Paradoxically, New Orleans actually had levees and pumps that provided systematic protection from flood surges, but the protection failed because of design and construction flaws. Biloxi, Gulfport, and other coastal cities east of New Orleans that took the full force of the hurricane had no such systematic protection. There is no collective protection system for rebuilding in these cities; each owner has to make a decision whether to rebuild with an individual system of flood protection sufficient to qualify for insurance, or to move further inland.

The urbanized parts of the Thames Estuary in England and the coast of the Netherlands at the delta of the Scheldt River and at the entrance to the harbor at Rotterdam have been protected by special coastal installations completed in the 1980s in response to a devastating storm in 1953 (Figures 3.36, 3.37). In the future many more coastal cities are likely to require engineering systems to protect against storm surges.

3.36
Coastal protection barriers along the eastern Scheldt Estuary in the Netherlands, installed in the 1980s as a response to devastating floods in 1953.

3.37
The gate that protects the
Port of Rotterdam from
storm surges.

4 Systems city design

Sim City, the computer game first released by its creator Will Wright in 1989, permits a single player, the Mayor, to build a simulated city, making decisions according to a system of rules built into the program. The simulation may turn out well or badly in terms of the budget and the provision of services, depending on the decisions. The rules are comparable to a modernist urban zoning code. There are three different zones: residential, commercial, and industrial, and three intensities of development. Later versions of the game introduced elements normally found in a subdivision code: grading of the site, and rules governing the building and extension of utilities. Sim City demonstrates that zoning and subdivision codes have a strong formative influence on cities: they are a system. Taxes and services are systems also.

The decisions made playing Sim City are simpler than the real decisions that mayors and city officials need to make, and the connection between cause and effect is much more simplistic. But the game is a strong indicator that the design problems of modern, complex urban areas are capable of resolution through understanding systems, and it makes a case for the feasibility of using systems to create new city designs.

Problems of organized complexity

Jane Jacobs proposed understanding cities as systems in her 1961 book, *The Death and Life of Great American Cities*. Following Warren Weaver's terminology[1] she identified the city as a problem in organized complexity, as opposed to problems with only a small number of related variables, which Weaver called problems in simplicity, and problems in disorganized complexity which have so many variables that they need to be dealt with through estimates of probabilities. Jacobs' diagnosis: many of the big errors in urban renewal and traffic planning were caused by treating cities as problems in disorganized complexity, and relying on statistical generalizations that could be refuted by observing systems of urban activities easily understood by people who are not experts and are not filtering their view of what is going on through inappropriate mathematical models.[2] A good example of what Jacobs was writing about is provided by Herbert Gans's study, *The Urban Villagers*, originally published in 1962, about the complex and useful social functions of Boston's West End neighborhood, just before it was torn down because it met the statistical profile for slum housing.[3]

At the time Jacobs was writing, it was hard to conceptualize problems of organized complexity in which a simple set of rules governs agents that act independently to create a complex interdependent system. Since then, as Warren Weaver predicted, there has been great progress in understanding such problems using vastly improved computation capabilities and the work of inter-disciplinary teams.

Steven Johnson's *Emergence: The Connected Lives of Ants, Brains, Cities, and Software*[4] published in 2002 is a well-written overview of research that may one day be applicable to cities. Johnson uses the term Emergence to describe how an ant colony, a complex system, is created by individual ants, going about their own genetically predetermined behaviors without any other directing mechanism. He writes of a visit to a research laboratory where ant colonies are studied and where he is shown that the ants invariably place their rubbish heap at the greatest possible distance from the main part of the colony and the bodies of dead ants are taken to a place that is equally distant from both the colony and the rubbish heap. From such observations it should be possible to work out the rules of the system that has evolved to produce the ant colony.

Johnson also writes about the slime mold, a cellular organism that can sometimes function as a group or colony. The mechanism of collective action has been decoded and it is now possible to write computer programs that simulate the behavior of colonies of slime molds. Programs can also be written to simulate the flocking of birds, which are now understood to flock through the collective actions of individual members, and not by the direction of a lead bird, or group of birds.

In a recent article entitled "Swarm Urbanism" Neal Leach discusses the potential for writing computer programs that would model the actions of individual actors in city development and their interactions with the city as it had developed so far, following principles of emergence. His conclusion: "Quite how such a relationship could be modeled digitally remains an interesting challenge for urban designers."[5]

One way to study the emergence of complex behavior from agents acting independently is to create computer programs that set simple rules from which patterns emerge of increasing complexity. An encyclopedic description of such research is contained in Stephen Wolfram's *A New Kind of Science*, originally published in 2001.[6] Cellular automata are programs where simple rules can produce patterns, some of them complex. Some automata quickly resolve into patterns, some take many iterations of the program to resolve into patterns, and some become random and never resolve into patterns. A rule which starts from a single black square, or cell, on a background of square graph paper, makes the next cell black if either of its neighbors was black on the step before, and makes the cell white if both its neighbors were white. This rule produces a simple checkerboard pattern of black and white squares. Wolfram then revises the rule so that a cell should be black when either its left neighbor or its right neighbor—but not both—were black on the step before. Five hundred steps according to this rule produce a pattern of nested triangles (Figures 4.1–4.3). Wolfram describes a third rule as follows:

> First, look at each cell and its right-hand neighbor. If both of these were white on the previous step, then take the new color of the cell to be whatever the previous color of its left-hand neighbor was. Otherwise, take the new color to be the opposite of that.

Starting with a single black cell and repeating this rule over and over produces an irregular and complex pattern.[7] Wolfram's primary focus is experimenting with mathematical formulas and the patterns they produce, of which cellular automata are just one example, and cataloguing the results. He is confident that these discoveries will have far-reaching ramifications for those aspects of science which require an understanding of how complexity is produced, but he only hints at possible applications.

Michael Batty's *Cities and Complexity: Understanding Cities with Cellular Automata, Agent-Based Models and Fractals*[8] is a description of computation procedures selected because Batty believes they may one day inform thinking about cities.

> ... cities should be treated as emergent structures, built from the bottom up whose processes are intrinsic to the form and structure that ultimately develops. Yet at many points we have hinted that there are deeper theories to be discovered about the forms and structures that develop, universalities that could integrate the variety that has been displayed throughout these chapters. We have not been able to present such coherent theory although we have presented glimpses of coherence in the making.[9]

Batty goes on to say that it is unlikely there can ever be an all-embracing theory, because of the complexity of cities and the multiplicity of agents.

Where Batty has applied computational procedures to real-life situations in this book, the experiment could have been improved by closer observation of existing urban systems. For example, the emergence of a suburban retail strip in the preferred growth sector east of Buffalo, New York can perhaps be explained, as Batty does,

4.1, 4.2, 4.3

A few of Stephen Wolfram's illustrations of cellular automata: In the first example, starting with a single black cell, with each row of cells representing the next step, any cell adjacent to a cell that was black in the step before becomes black. This system yields a pyramid of black cells. In the second example, the rule makes a cell black if either of its neighbors was black on the step before and makes the cell white if both its neighbors were white. This system yields a checker-board pyramid. In the third example, the rule is that a cell should be black whenever one or the other, but not both, of its neighbors were black on the step before. This rule yields a system of nesting pyramids.

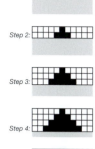

Step 1:

Step 2:

Step 3:

Step 4:

Step 5:

A visual representation of the behavior of a cellular automation, with each row of cells corresponding to one step. At the first step the cell in the centre is black and all other cells are white. Then on each successive step, a particular cell is made black whenever it or either of its neighbors were black on the step before. As the picture shows, this leads to a simple expanding pattern uniformly filled with black.

Step 1:
Step 2:
Step 3:
Step 4:
Step 5:
Step 6:
Step 7:
Step 8:
Step 9:
Step 10:

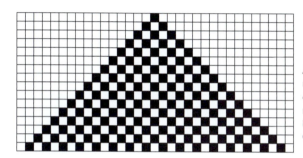

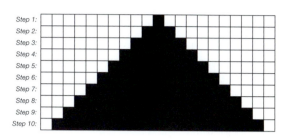

A cellular automation with a slightly different rule. The rule makes a particular cell black if either of its neighbors was black on the step before, and makes the cell white if both its neighbors were white. Starting from a single black cell, this rule leads to a checkerboard pattern. In the numbering scheme of Chapter 3, this is cellular automation rule 250.

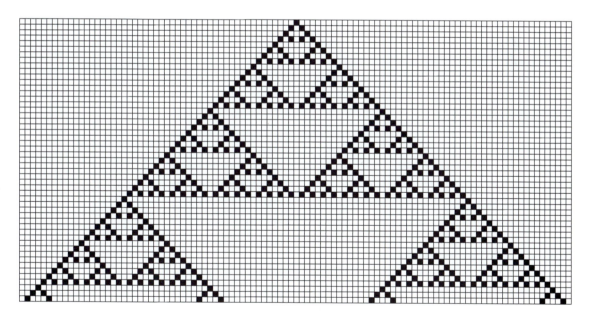

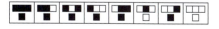

A cellular automation that produces intricate nested pattern. The rule in this case is that a cell should be black whenever one or the other, but not both, of its neighbors were black on the step before. Even though the rule is very simple, the picture shows that the overall pattern obtained over the course of 50 steps starting from a single black cell is not so simple (. . .)

as urban growth based on fractal dimensions. But it can also be understood as a result of the local transportation system, particularly the way the arterial road on which the commercial land has developed is connected to highways and radial arterials from the city center, as well as zoning codes that mandate commercial development as narrow strips along main roads, a pattern originally devised for main streets but extended far into the countryside by legislation. While Batty in his introduction generously acknowledges Jane Jacobs as the source of his interest in self-organizing systems, he could perhaps pay more attention to her strictures about using direct observation to understand what is happening in cities.

More recently Michael Batty has published an article entitled "A Digital Breeder for Designing Cities" using cellular automata that start from a rule system that:

> people aggregate in cities to realise scale economies of agglomeration, which means that people should always be connected to one another; and second, that people should be able to live with as much space around them as possible.

The digital system starts with one cell. New cells are introduced. When one reaches a position adjacent to the initial cell, it becomes stationary. The next cell can attach to the two already adjacent, itself becoming stationary, and so on. The eventual order emerges as a result of a sequence of incremental, random events. In the automata used by Batty, the resulting pattern is dendritic, a series of branches. Additional rules can be added to the system, excluding some cell locations or favoring certain attachment patterns; these modifications can stand for climate or topographic influences (Figure 4.4). Batty's conclusion is that much more experimentation is needed following the same type of investigation. Like Stephen Wolfram he is looking to establish a large inventory of patterns that can emerge from various rule systems, expecting that the real applications will be found from recognizing significant patterns and then relating the rule system that produced the pattern to the urban conditions it appears to mimic.[10]

Ultimately the understanding of cities as systems and the creation of systematic ways of producing new cities will require a fusion of sophisticated mathematics with accurate understanding of the systemic behavior that has always characterized cities.

4.4
Experiments by Michael Batty using cellular automata to simulate city growth patterns where the overall development takes its form from a series of local decisions.

Prehistoric cities as systems

Cities emerged before any recorded history that is still available. All we know is from interpretation of archaeological evidence. The domestication of plants and animals and the development of agriculture took place as the last ice age ended, around eleven thousand years ago. Agriculture enabled bands of nomadic hunter-gatherers to create permanent villages. The village is still the basic unit of human habitation in many parts of the world. The first places where cities, a larger and more complex social unit than a village, grew up are believed to be Mesopotamia and Egypt around six thousand years ago, but parallel processes took place in India and China, and then later in Meso-America. The earliest remains of cities that have been uncovered by archaeologists reveal dependence on some basic systems of cooperation and control. There is likely to be a walled citadel that includes storerooms for a communal food supply, an important religious shrine, and quarters for the ruling group. Streets and a market place are other likely components.[11] How this archaeological record relates to theories about emergence depends on the interpretation of these common features that developed in different cities, at different times, and under diverse sets of conditions.

Eleven thousand years ago and six thousand years ago are not long periods of time in the evolution of human beings. We can assume that the people who constructed the first villages and the first cities were not very different from us, except that they lacked the accumulated information that we now have.

There are only a few possibilities for arranging habitations in a village: variations on a main street or a circle when people live together and walk to their fields or a dispersed pattern where people live on their own farmland. There would need to be some kind of common meeting place, a reliable water supply, and latrines best located at a distance from houses. The village should be in a place where climate conditions are favorable. It is easy to imagine that there were many different configurations of villages, but that some met the needs of the inhabitants much better than others. Some villages failed, others prospered, and people learned from the differences. The question is how this knowledge was transmitted. Did it live in the collective consciousness of the villagers, who all knew how to locate and put together a good village; or were there some specialists whose memories were longer and experience was broader, who took the lead when a new village was being planned, or an old village was being renovated?

The same questions apply to prehistoric cities. Archaeological evidence shows that most cities had walls and gates. It may be that one way to define a city was a population group large enough to be able to afford a collective defense system, in some cases big enough to enclose the city, but at least a citadel where everyone could go in an emergency. Within the walls, cities had streets—shared spaces— that gave access to individual buildings. The presence of a market is another defining element: a place where people from the surrounding villages could trade. While each village probably had a specialized religious building or area, cities could support larger and more elaborate religious establishments. Cities could support individual occupations, like baking bread, or making weapons. These people might not have time to grow their own food. Full-time rulers might have their troop of full-time soldiers, and full-time religious figures would also need to be supported by the agricultural efforts of others. These needs would produce the collective granaries, as opposed to food storage by individual families. Collective food storage was also needed for emergencies.

Systems city design

Did these common features of cities evolve as the consequence of the social systems that required them, or were they shaped by specialists in fortifications, street layouts, religious buildings, and grain storage? Either way, the designs for prehistoric villages and cities were essentially problems in the design of interrelated systems.

Pre-industrial city-design systems

Cities from the beginning of recorded history to the industrial revolution some two hundred and fifty years ago continued to share many similarities, just as they had in prehistoric times. Successful cities almost always grew up on rivers and harbors, because large quantities of goods were moved most effectively by water. Many cities evolved gradually from villages, their growth spurred by an especially good location, energetic leadership, or abundant resources. The demands of defense required walls; the costliness of fortifications gave cities a compact shape. A circular wall system enclosed the largest amount of town for a given amount of stone or brick, a fact that was more important for cities run by citizens who had to raise the money among themselves than for cities built by military commanders or emperors. Within the walls there was usually a citadel, a last resort if the outer defenses failed. Inside a city, the major thoroughfares were likely to lead from the necessarily limited number of gates to a central market square, where the important religious and public buildings were often located. The main streets subdivided the city into neighborhoods, crossed by smaller lanes, including functional districts that would serve the whole city, such as a street of armorers or a warehouse district by the waterfront. A specialist may have been employed to design the fortifications, the street systems, or important buildings; but many cities may have evolved slowly with little overt direction, a product of the interaction of the defense perimeter, the subdivision and development of individual properties, and the needs of collective institutions.

By contrast, preconceived designs were likely to be imposed when cities were rebuilt after a war or when new cities were founded as colonies or military outposts. Grids of rectangular streets were the most common device in such circumstances. The concept of dividing a city into square or rectangular blocks with long, straight streets is often attributed to Hippodamus of Miletus. The principal source for information about Hippodamus is the account of him in Aristotle's *Politics* where Hippodamus is described as both a theorist of ideal city organization and a practical planner. He is said to have designed the Greek colony of Thurii in southern Italy and redesigned Piraeus, the harbor city of Athens, during the age of Pericles. Hippodamus may have brought the grid plan to Greece but was unlikely to have been its inventor. His own home town of Miletus, on the Asian mainland in what is now Turkey, was destroyed by the Persians and rebuilt on a right-angle plan after the Persians were expelled in 479 BC, when Hippodamus is thought to have been either two years old or no older than nineteen. In fact, grid plans had been in use in the Ionian cities of Asia Minor since the seventh century B.C. and have been used in many other cultures, including Babylon, China, and India, without there being any demonstrated link among them.

Vitruvius, the Roman architect of the early imperial period who wrote the only text on architecture to survive from Greece or Rome (although we know from Vitruvius's own internal references that his was one of many), includes a few short chapters on selecting a healthful location for a city, the construction of fortifications, the best orientation of city streets, and the placement of the central forum and important public buildings in the first book of his *Ten Books on Architecture*: "First comes the choice of a healthy site. Such a site will be high, neither misty nor frosty, and in a climate neither hot nor cold, but temperate; further, without marshes in the neighborhood."[12]

Good advice. Vitruvius also advises that the location of the main public space should be in the center of the city, unless the city fronts on a river or harbor; in that case the central space should be close to the water. The section on street design begins with instructions on how to use a sundial on the site of the city to locate eight different wind directions and thus fix the layout of the streets to avoid unhealthy climate conditions. Unfortunately, the text is ambiguous about how you do this. Most people have read the passage as instructions on how to orient a rectangular street grid so the wrong kinds of wind won't blow down the streets. However, it could be understood to prescribe avenues radiating from a central point, which produces the polygonal cities shown in some Renaissance treatises on architecture, and sometimes actually built, for example the new city of Palmanova begun by the Venetian Republic in 1593.

Vitruvius was giving advice about building new cities, which the Romans frequently did as they established control over their colonies. These cities were based on the pattern of the Roman military camp, which often preceded the city, typically a walled compound in the shape of a square or rectangle divided by two main, straight streets crossing at right angles, with other streets parallel to them to form a rectangular grid, and a central forum near the major intersection. Pompeii originally had a plan of this kind, as did hundreds of other cities founded or rebuilt by the Romans, such as those on the sites of what are today Florence and Turin, as well as cities like Damascus in Syria and Trier in Germany, or Djemela and Timgad in what is now Algeria. The Roman colonial city was a system which could be applied in many places. The perimeter fortifications would be adapted to the location and the topography, and the main streets would be located based on the roads leading up to the city. The main streets would then become the armature for a succession of public buildings.[13]

German architect and city planner, Karl Gruber, published a series of drawings in 1914 describing the evolution of a hypothetical German city from the twelfth century to the eighteenth.[14] These drawings show the interplay of location with city organization and fortification systems, and the persistence of this configuration through six centuries of growth and change. The series begins in 1180 at the time when cities in Europe were beginning to grow after a long period of shrinkage and stagnation. The drawing shows a walled city on a river with gates that lead to a street that traverses the city from east to west, and a gate, reached by a bridge, on the south side that leads to another straight street heading north. These two main streets meet in a market square where there is a cathedral and a town hall. This basic organization is comparable to the planned colonial Roman city. However, on the north side, instead of another gate, there is a walled citadel. The water from the river is drawn into a moat around the walls. Across the river is an unfortified monastery identified by Gruber as built by the Benedictines. Outside the walls on the east and the west are some farms and inns for travelers. The forest is drawn as coming close to the city on all sides (Figure 4.5).

By 1350, in the next Gruber illustration, the same city has grown to enclose the Benedictine monastery and a newer Dominican monastery across the river with a wall and moat, and this new district has become densely developed. In the main part of the city the waterfront has become more industrial, with warehouses and a water mill; the citadel has become more elaborately developed, and there is yet another monastery, identified by Gruber as Franciscan, in the unfortified area to the east. An inn for travelers is now in the unfortified area just outside the south gate; there is more farmland, and the forest has retreated to the edges of the drawing. However, the basic organization of the city has not changed in the 170 years between the two drawings: it is still the same system of walls and main streets. The citadel, market, town hall, and cathedral are still in their same places (Figure 4.6).

Fast forward to 1580, four hundred years from the original view. The biggest change is an outer ring of fortifications, a response to the invention of cannons, which can be seen in place on the ramparts. The original walls around the city were

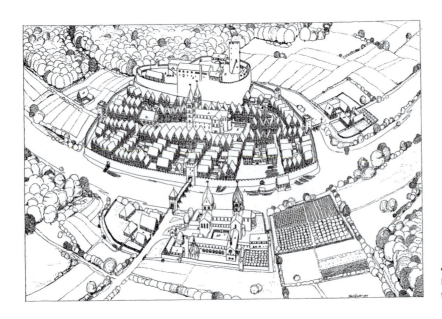

4.5
Karl Gruber's rendering of a typical German city in 1180.

Systems city design

4.6

Karl Gruber's rendering of the same hypothetical German city in 1350.

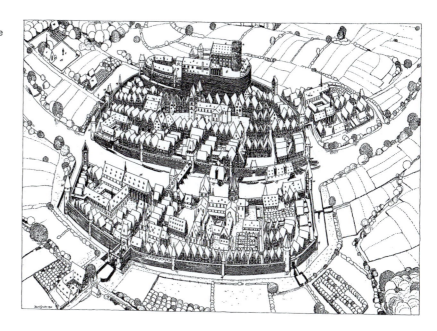

vulnerable to cannon fire, but the new ramparts could absorb the impact. Development, confined by the walls, is now denser, the citadel has become a palace, indicating that the needs of defense have imposed a new social system. The cathedral has been remodeled so that the nave is now in a late Gothic style, there is more farmland, and almost no forest. Nevertheless, the basic organization of the city is still the same (Figure 4.7).

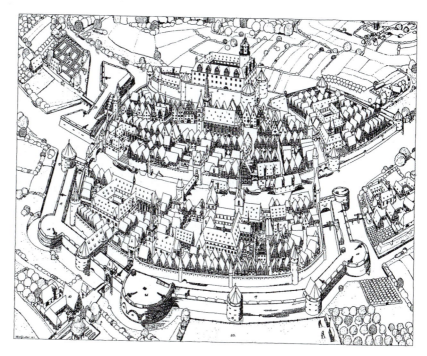

4.7

The third drawing in Karl Gruber's sequence illustrates the relatively slow development of cities. Four hundred years have passed, the city has grown on the south bank of the river, the fortifications have been improved and the castle and cathedral rebuilt but it is still recognizably the same place.

Systems city design

However when you go forward another 170 years, to 1750, you see a startling change. The devastating Thirty Years War (1618–1648) and subsequent conflicts have caused the city to invest heavily in defensive technology. A complete system of star-shaped ramparts surrounds the city and has taken over the adjacent countryside. Inside the walls there is an equally significant change, particularly on the south bank of the city, which has been redesigned according to Renaissance principles of order and symmetry. The two monasteries are gone, replaced by a Jesuit church on one side of a symmetrical square and a new palace on the other. Across the river, the town hall on the market square is now a symmetrical structure with a new square behind it. Elsewhere, in the city many of the spiky roofs of medieval houses have been replaced by the balanced masses of Renaissance-style courtyard buildings. New social and design systems overlay the old organization, but the underlying systems visible in 1180 are still there. It is still recognizably the same city, and has a strong kinship with other pre-industrial cities that were also surrounded by fortifications, have a central market square, important religious buildings, and a citadel (Figure 4.8).

Law of the Indies

The essentials of the city were codified by the Spanish government during the sixteenth century as part of the management system for their colonies in the West Indies and the Americas. The portion dealing with cities is part of a subset of some 148 regulations. There are clear influences from Vitruvius: for example, the directions for locating the main plaza use almost Vitruvius's language about central or riverfront placement. There are provisions specifying suitable locations for cities, dimensions

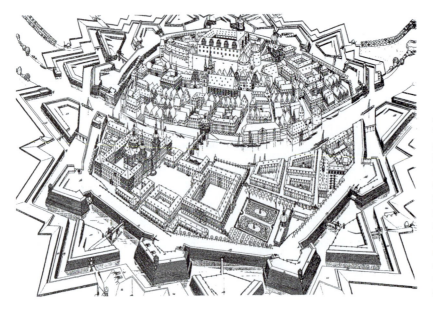

4.8
The fourth Gruber drawing showing the same city in 1750 illustrating the effect of the Thirty Years War on urban fortifications and the new Renaissance concepts of city design that have reorganized and transformed the city. However, it is still recognizably a pre-industrial city, with the same systems organization that it had some six centuries before.

Systems city design

for individual properties, and guidance for street layout in relation to the central plaza reflecting Vitruvius's admonitions about wind direction:

> From the plaza shall begin four principal streets: One [shall be] from the middle of each side, and two streets from each corner of the plaza; the four corners of the plaza shall face the four principal winds, because in this manner, the streets running from the plaza will not be exposed to the four principal winds, which would cause much inconvenience.[15]

Another provision stated that the frontage on the central plaza should be reserved for civic buildings like the cathedral and the governor's official residence. There are no provisions for fortifications, as Spain did not anticipate rivals for the control of these new cities.

It is likely that the people who laid out cities in the Spanish colonies of the new world carried with them an image of what a city should be that was guided by the official code but supplemented the sometimes opaque instructions of the code itself. Several cities in Spain had been founded by the Romans, including Merida and Zaragoza, and had originally been based on grid street plans, and the new city of Santa Fe de Granada, begun in 1491 by Ferdinand and Isabella, was designed very much like the Roman prototypes recommended by Vitruvius. Although nothing in the code specifies a street grid, there is a discernable similarity of plans among cities built by Spain in the Americas, from New Orleans, which was founded by the French early in the eighteenth century but actually developed by Spain after 1763,[16] and where the central plaza is on the riverbank, to Santa Fe, an inland city with the plaza in a central location, to Mexico City where the central plaza occupies the space once used for Aztec ceremonies. All the cities founded by Spain started from rectangular grid plans.

A summary of the pre-industrial urban system

The pre-industrial city was usually located near a river or harbor because the best way of moving freight in pre-industrial times was by water. Successful cities were built in healthful locations. The city often begins as a grid of rectangular streets, although the street configuration could be modified over time into a much more irregular pattern. There are main streets that divide the city into districts and meet in a central square, which is the location of the market and the principal religious and governmental buildings. Usually the city is surrounded by fortifications, which make expansion difficult and lead to intense development within the walls. Fortified cities usually have a citadel as military headquarters and storage for essential supplies. You can test the accuracy of this generalization by looking at maps of pre-industrial cities in different countries and cultures. Every pre-industrial city is unique, but they have many features in common, which suggests common causes.

Urban systems after the industrial revolution

The industrial revolution began, mostly in England and to some extent in France, around the middle of the eighteenth century. The first phase was a proto-industrial period, where pre-industrial technology was stretched to its limits to meet the needs of increasing trade and growing populations. Sailing ships grew larger, as international trade increased. Land owners in England enclosed the farms that had been worked by tenants for generations, raising sheep instead of crops to meet the rising demand for wool cloth. The first factories for weaving cloth were located not in cities but where their machinery could be driven by water power. Systems of canals grew up to link waterways and create a network for freight. Charcoal was used for smelting iron. Coal mines supplied fuel for city fireplaces, with coal delivered by canal barge. The horse-drawn stage coach was the first mass transit and a way of speeding mail delivery. The main effects of the proto-industrial revolution on cities were overcrowding, bigger ports and warehouse districts, and increasing numbers of rich people's houses and shops for luxury goods.

The coal-fired steam engine set off the next stage of the industrial revolution, powering railway engines and steam ships, and enabling factories to be located in cities. Rails had been used in coal mines to allow carts full of coal to be pushed, usually by children who could stand up in the mine tunnels, out to the mine entrance.[17] Steam engines were used in mines to pump out water. Railroads put these two technologies together.

The first use of a steam engine for transportation is Robert Fulton's paddle-wheel steam boat, tested in 1803, with a first voyage on the Hudson River in 1807. The first operating railroad is usually considered to be the Stockton and Darlington line in England which began operation in 1825. The speed with which railroads became the dominant force in urban development rivals the speed of acceptance of computers after World War II. Within fifty years a new system of urban organization had been created.

Early trains could travel at 15 miles per hour, and by 1850 trains could achieve speeds of 60 and 70 miles per hour, with trips averaging, including stops, around 30 miles per hour.[18] Walking speed for a person is about 3 miles per hour, a horse can trot with a light load at perhaps 15 miles per hour; horses walk at about 6 miles per hour. Canal boats pulled by horses, the proto-industrial solution to freight movement, moved at about 6 miles per hour, and there would be delays at locks and from working the canal boats under bridges.

The railroad thus drastically altered the relationship between time and distance, so that cities were days closer together than they had been, as were any stops along a railway line. Railroads increased the intensity of development in urban centers, bringing with them industry and industrial pollution, plus the negative influences of the trains and tracks themselves. Railroad also spread the area of urban influence by bringing more distant places within commuting distance, and by making easy connections from industry to industry.

The completion of the transcontinental railroad in the United States in 1869 immediately reduced the travel time across the country from six months to less than six days. However, in the early days of railroads, once you alighted from the train at a station you were back in the world of horse-drawn carts and carriages. Local passenger travel also began to be converted to rails, first using a proto-industrial solution of horse-drawn cars moving down the street on rails, then cable cars, then subway trains and electrified street railways. By the early twentieth century there was a network of trains covering most countries, connecting to local transit systems that radiated out from urban centers.

The result was a star-shaped system of urbanization. Local development radiated out from the traditional center along transit corridors. Street railways connected inner suburbs; rail transit systems reached farther destinations. Corridors of factories stretching out from the central city were supported by freight lines and sidings. Land values at the center rapidly increased, creating the demand for larger and taller buildings. The first two locations for skyscrapers were Lower Manhattan, a junction point for nearly all New York City's transit lines, and inside the Loop in Chicago, the Loop being a downtown elevated line that connected the long-distance rail terminals and served as a distributor for suburban transit lines.

The rationalization of building by systems

The standardization of building components, which had produced the cast-iron—and later, steel—rails that made train travel possible, also created the building systems which allowed urban development to achieve the new densities enabled by trains.

One of the changes set in motion by the French Revolution was the adoption of a new system of standardized weights and measures, the metric system. Another initiative towards standardization brought on by the French Revolution deprived the Ecole des Beaux Arts, the old architectural academy, of its official position, although it continued to function at a reduced level. A new school was created, L'Ecole Polytechnique, whose professor of architecture from 1795 to 1830 was Jean-Nicolas-Louis Durand. The Polytechnique was primarily an engineering school, born partly because the revolutionary government, surrounded by hostile monarchies, needed a great many military engineers in a hurry. J.-N.-L. Durand's course at the Polytechnique and his textbook, *Précis des leçons d'architecture,* first published between 1802 and 1805, undertook to simplify and codify the nature of architecture. Instead of architecture as Leone Battista Alberti had written about it at the end of the fifteenth century, where the building's organization and proportion became a subtle attempt to embody what were believed to be the underlying harmonies of the universe, Durand classified the design of buildings according to type and created a system of arrangement for the parts of a building that was based on a simple, modular grid based on the spans possible in masonry construction, arches, vaults, and domes.

Perhaps Durand was motivated by the need to jam as much architecture as possible into the heads of his engineering students, but—at least in its early years—the Polytechnique was seen as providing a revolutionary alternative to the architectural design pursued by the *ancien régime*. Durand's course, with its clearly articulated rules and easily repeated patterns, was well suited to the temperament of the late eighteenth and early nineteenth centuries. This was an important period in the development of modern science and engineering, and also the time of the proto-industrial revolution when changes in cities were happening at a rapid pace and on an unprecedented scale (Figure 4.9).

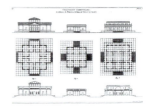

4.9
An illustration by J.-N.-L. Durand of how to reorganize masonry buildings into a modular system.

At the time Durand was formulating his curriculum, modular building products were also being created out of cast iron. Iron had been used by the Romans to fasten stones together; placed between the stones, the iron elements were protected from the weather. Iron chains were also used as tension rings for domes made of masonry. But iron did not become a reliable exterior building material until the end of the eighteenth century when new techniques were perfected in England for smelting iron using coal. Cast iron components could now be used not only for rails, but also for bridges and train shed components, frames for greenhouses, and even for prefabricated buildings.

Cast iron and glass were the materials for the Crystal Palace that was constructed in London's Hyde Park for the Great Exhibition of 1851. It was a greatly enlarged version of the greenhouses, train sheds, and shopping arcades that its architect, Joseph Paxton, and others had already designed from cast-iron frameworks and large panes of glass. However, the scale of the Crystal Palace and the speed with which its modular construction was carried out were both something new. It was 1,848 feet long by 408 feet wide; its central transept was 72 feet wide and 108 feet high. The whole structure was bigger than the palace of Versailles and was built in a little more than half a year (Figure 4.10). The term "Crystal Palace" was coined not by the architect but by the magazine *Punch,* whose recognition of the palace tradition in a building that was not at all obviously like a palace is significant. It was a structure on the scale of an enclosed city street with buildings on both sides, a third of a mile long. Not only was it built in a short time, but its modular parts permitted it to be taken down and rebuilt at Sydenham, south-east of London, when the exhibition in Hyde Park was over.

The idea of a city enclosed by a building, and the concept that the components of such a city might be demountable, were both to become important city-design ideas a century later. The immediate influence of the Crystal Palace seems to have been on shopping arcades and other exhibition buildings. The Galleria Vittorio Emanuele, designed by Giuseppe Mengoni and constructed in Milan in 1865, is a famous example of an enclosed shopping street with a glass roof, a concept that suggests that it could be extended into a system. Shopping arcades of an analogous design were constructed in most major cities.

The influence of the Crystal Palace may also be seen in the project for "Aerodomes" published by the French engineer Henry-Jules Borie in 1865. A system

4.10
Joseph Paxton's design for
the Crystal Palace,
constructed for an exposition
in 1851, was a modular
system of cast-iron and glass
1,848 feet long by 408 feet
wide; its central transept was
72 feet wide and 108 feet
high.

of glassed-in galleries thousands of feet long is surrounded by buildings connected at midheight by pedestrian bridges that establish a secondary means of circulation. The newly invented safety elevator permitted Borie to postulate buildings twice the height of the typical structures of his time. This proposal was intended as a prototype design for the centers of all major cities, where high land values would require a more efficient use of land.

Arturo Soria y Mata began advocating the construction of linear cities in 1882, as a repetitive modular system. The key element of Soria's proposal was a wide street with room in the center for trains and streetcars, all utilities, and enough additional land that public buildings could be provided at intervals. Smaller streets would provide access to development on either side of this central spine, and the system would be capable of almost infinite extension. Soria saw linear developments ringing existing cities or stretching across Europe and even to the Orient. An actual linear housing district was constructed according to Soria's principles in the Madrid suburbs starting in 1894, but the scale and density of the development were comparatively modest (Figure 4.11). The idea of linear cities would later be picked up by Le Corbusier and would ultimately become a component of mid-twentieth-century megastructure designs.

Something like a linear city concept had been suggested by Joseph Paxton as well, in his 1855 proposal for the Great Victorian Way, a circular road that would link all the railroad stations in central London, much as the underground Circle Line

4.11
Plan of an urban district
designed according to the
linear city principles of
Antonio Soria y Mata.

was later to do. The road was to have been enclosed by a gigantic glassed-in arcade, flanked by rail lines on either side, with the portion of the arcade between the City and Regent Street forming a linear shopping center. This application of the Crystal Palace concept may well be the origin of the "crystal palace" proposed forty years later by Ebenezer Howard as a linear, circular shopping center at the heart of each garden city.

Modular steel construction and tall buildings

The ultimate modular component has been the steel structural member, produced in factories in standard sizes that can be ordered and shipped to the building site. Steel began to replace the far less reliable cast iron after 1855, when Henry Bessemer patented a process for mass producing high-quality steel. Steel had been used for armor, swords, and knives for centuries, but had been far too expensive to be used as a building material. Another important invention was the safety device for stopping an elevator from falling if the hoist system broke, invented by Elisha Graves Otis and exhibited in 1853.[19] Iron and steel-frame construction, with exterior walls suspended from the structural frame, is the essence of modern architecture. Particularly as used in tall buildings with elevators it was a way of designing buildings that had previously not been possible. As we have seen in the first chapter, the steel-framed building was an essential part of the modernist city. But other systems were equally important in creating the modern city: inter-city railway systems, engineering systems to deliver drinking water to places that had outgrown their local water supplies, sewer systems essential to support high-density living, telephone and electricity lines, modern concrete and asphalt paving, the street car, local commuter lines.

Walter Christaller's central place theory and Homer Hoyt's sector theory

German geographer Walter Christaller published in 1933 a theory about systems of cities[20] that was founded on observation of the systematic connections created by railroads and transit and other modern engineering systems in southern Germany. Christaller postulated a uniform area of influence around each major city, with each city connected to the others in a master network in which some centers can be more significant than others, and can have larger areas of influence. In diagrams, the area of influence is drawn as a hexagon, rather than a circle, so that they fit together. There are also sub-areas that are connected radially to the central city, which are drawn as smaller hexagons that fit into the larger one. The smaller areas may each also have hexagonal sub-areas (Figure 4.12). This representation of a system corresponds well to commuter and freight distribution patterns when rail

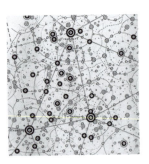

4.12
Diagram of Walter Christaller's central place theory that shows the hierarchical organization of urban areas determined by railroad systems.

was the dominant means of transportation. Goods would be shipped from major center to major center, then trans-shipped to branch lines going to less important centers, and then possibly trans-shipped again to an even smaller destination. Workers would commute to the central city from sub-areas on transit lines, possibly changing trains as they went from a small place to a larger one, and then into the center.

Christaller's central place theory continues to receive respectful attention because it is one of the earliest statements about systems of cities and it lends itself to mathematical models, but it corresponds to a reality that was already outmoded in 1933, because automobiles and trucks don't need to follow the hierarchical system established for railroads and because the areas around city centers are not in fact uniform.[21]

In 1939 Homer Hoyt, an economist for the Federal Housing Administration, published a study showing that the area of influence around the central city was divided into sectors radiating out from downtown. There were industrial corridors along railway lines and residential sectors along arterial roads or transit lines. Low-income residents lived close to industrial corridors, different ethnic groups tended to form sectors, and those with high incomes lived along the most desirable directions, such as the Chicago Lake Front north of the city center.[22] Hoyt's sectors are a corrective to Christaller and also to the concentric zone theory of city development—city center, zone of transition, outer suburbs—put forward by Robert Park, Ernest W. Burgess, and other professors at the University of Chicago, where Hoyt had completed his doctorate.[23] The sectors researched by Hoyt are still observable today, but they were created primarily by trains and transit and are partly superseded by newer patterns created by cars and trucks.

Modern urban systems and the multi-nuclear city

The automobile and truck were invented just in time to save cities from a breakdown of local, horse-drawn transportation systems, as the new urban densities required more horses, and created more horse manure, than cities could manage. Within fifty years automobiles had evolved from playthings of the wealthy to necessities for almost everyone, and trucks had moved on from local deliveries to a freight system that rivaled the railroads, and in some ways superseded them.

The capital cost for new streets and roads was far less than for rails. Effectively cars and trucks could go almost anywhere. Instead of the orderly hierarchical pattern and limited radius or urbanization characteristic of rail transportation, urban growth began to spread outwards from centers. This pattern is often called sprawl, but it is a system, although often wasteful and inefficient.[24] New centers grew up in former suburban downtowns and locations which were suitable for industry. By 1945 this new pattern of multiple centers was recognized by geographers Chauncy D. Harris and Edward L. Ullman in an article, "The Nature of Cities."[25] Harris and Ullman were describing a phenomenon which was just becoming visible, and which has since become dominant.

The construction of limited access highways turned the access points where traffic gets on and off the highway into locations that were likely to generate urban uses like shopping, restaurants, and offices as well as apartments and town houses. Sometimes these locations, called "edge cities," in a 1991 book by Joel Garreau,[26] could become larger and more important than many traditional city centers.

A look at a map of urbanization in the United States shows that development has been reshaped by the Interstate Highway System, begun in 1956. Cities that have only one interstate connection, like Sioux City, Iowa, are at a disadvantage compared to places where two Interstates meet, like Sioux Falls, South Dakota (Figure 4.13).

While highways were causing cities to decentralize, airports were becoming centers. Early airports were built close to existing downtowns, but, as the number of take-offs and landings grew, and as planes needed longer runways, airports were built in outlying areas where they would, at least initially, cause less disturbance. Airports in turn generated hotels and conference centers, and created factory locations for businesses where shipping by air was important; the larger airports also became locations for office parks.

By the later part of the twentieth century cities had become city regions, with multiple centers such as near the airport and at important highway intersections, and the automobile and truck had become the dominant systems of transportation.

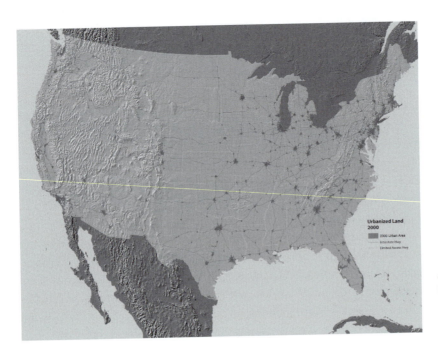

4.13
Map of urbanized areas in the United States in the year 2000 overlaid on the Interstate Highway System.

Systems city design

Megastructures: cities and districts as building systems

While this process of urban decentralization was going on, from the late 1950s up until about 1970, the idea of urban areas as highly centralized, interconnected buildings dominated much of the design thinking about cities. The city would be organized by structural and mechanical systems that had once been hidden within buildings and would now determine their form. The street would become a weather-protected corridor or bridge, the plaza an interior atrium, the building an incident within a larger framework. These ideas seemed to appeal especially to designers in Great Britain and Japan, but soon were promoted in various forms in Europe and North America and could be found being studied in architecture schools almost everywhere. Visions of the city as a gigantic structure were almost always tied to a future in which the imperfections of modern cities would be swept away by the force of new technology.

These ideas were drawn from diverse sources. One was the drawings made by Antonio Sant'Elia for his Città Nuova project, exhibited in Milan in 1914, where tall, streamlined shapes define a city of rapid travel and technological purity. The most famous drawing shows a railroad station rather like a great dam, with a stream of railway traffic beneath it and cliff-like rows of buildings on either side, not the conventional streets and buildings, but what appears to be a city as a single, linear structure (Figure 4.14).

Another source was Le Corbusier's sketches for Rio de Janeiro, São Paulo, and Montevideo which showed elevated highways running through each city, with buildings underneath them. This idea was elaborated by Le Corbusier in 1930 in the much better known plan for Algiers, which included an elevated highway whose supporting structure would have provided a framework for 180,000 dwelling units. Another influence: science fiction books and comics with illustrations of space colonies and the cities of "advanced civilizations" from other planets, which had in turn been strongly influenced by Buckminster Fuller and by the work of industrial designers like Raymond Loewy, who had sought futuristic imagery for industrial products. Other powerful images were petroleum refineries and cracking plants with their acres of complex piping, offshore platforms, giant dams that transform entire landscapes, and rockets capable of space travel.

Japanese architect Kenzo Tange's first megastructure project was done with MIT students for Boston Harbor in 1959. The next year saw the publication of Tange's similar plan for Tokyo Bay, which was organized around two highways carried on huge suspension bridges across the water. Between the two highways was to be a long, densely populated island which would contain the commercial center of the new city, while at right angles to the highways were causeways leading to residential structures created by huge slanting buildings back to back, like Japanese temple roofs on a gigantic scale.

4.14
Drawing made by Antonio
Sant'Elia for his Citta Nuova
project, exhibited in Milan in
1914.

Metabolism 1960—A Proposal for a New Urbanism was published in connection with the 1960 World Design Conference in Tokyo. The authors were the architects Kiyonoru Kikutake, Masato Otaka, Fumihiko Maki, and Kisho Kurokawa, and the graphic designer Kiyoshi Awazu. The Metabolist theory postulated cities designed to grow and change with time and different conditions. The underlying structure would be permanent, but units of the city would be attached to the structure as flowers to a stalk or leaves to a tree.

Kikutake made a series of projects of cylindrical residential towers built over water from 1958 to 1962, of which his "Ocean City" project, with collars of bug-eyed apartment units surrounding cylindrical concrete support shafts, is the most remembered image.

Kurokawa prepared a concept for an agricultural city at the invitation of the Museum of Modern Art in New York City, and the project was exhibited there in 1961. This city was a grid suspended from towers a story above the ground, in theory leaving valuable agricultural land undisturbed.

"A City in the Sky," following a somewhat similar design, was developed by Arata Isozaki between 1960 and 1962. His best-remembered presentation drawing of his City in the Sky shows cylindrical concrete towers supporting bridge-like buildings that span between them. This concept is shown in collage over a photograph of a ruined Greek temple, with the cylindrical towers—which should certainly be something like a hundred feet high—drawn so that they are the same size as individual ruined columns, which clearly must be much smaller. In the foreground is an elevated highway, and what seems to be a ruined bridge-like structure, which has fallen from one of the concrete supports—or alternatively is under construction and has yet to be hoisted into place. Whatever Isozaki intended by this drawing is protected by so many layers of irony that it remains obscure. Is this a serious proposal comparable to the cities as space-frame trusses being drawn by Yona Friedman in France at the same period? Other drawings and an elaborate model are testimony that Isozaki was indeed seriously developing this idea. Is this particular drawing a commentary on the triumph of modern technology over ancient civilization or is it meant to indicate that all structures and cities are similar and will meet the same fate?

In any event, the idea that new cities could be built over old, and that they would take the form of a permanent system that supports adjustable and temporary units, became a major ingredient in the development of theoretical cities designed as buildings.

A permanent supporting structure combined with relatively temporary capsules, which can be plugged into one location and later moved to another, lies behind much of the work of the Archigram Group, which started at London's Architectural Association School when most of its members were still students and began publishing their own magazine during 1961. The Archigram program was not so much to create the city of the future as to shake up the British architectural establishment. They wanted their readers to look at Bruno Taut's expressionistic Alpine architecture, at Buckminster Fuller's domes and capsules, at Fuller associate James Fitzgibbon's 1960 circular city on the water, as well as at the cities envisioned in space comics and illustrating stories in science fiction magazines (Figure 4.15).

Archigram 4 takes its readers on a tour of cities portrayed in space comics: "A respectful salute in the general direction of Roy Lichtenstein and we're off." Some of the best-known city images created by Archigram Group members themselves include the Interchange Project of 1963 by Ron Herron and Warren Chalk, Peter Cook's Plug-In City of 1964, and Ron Herron's Walking City, also of 1964. Herron and Chalk's urban interchange is a building in the shape of a flattened sphere where monorails, vehicles running along highways on guides, and railroads meet. The interchange is connected by long, telescoping tubes that contain moving sidewalks to surrounding cylindrical towers, which resemble the vacuum tubes that were used in radio receivers in the days before transistors.

The principal Plug-In City drawing was an axonometric that showed a vast agglomeration of cylindrical towers, inverted pyramids of plug-in, modular housing, and linear stepped-back terraces of housing, all served by tubular connectors. At the

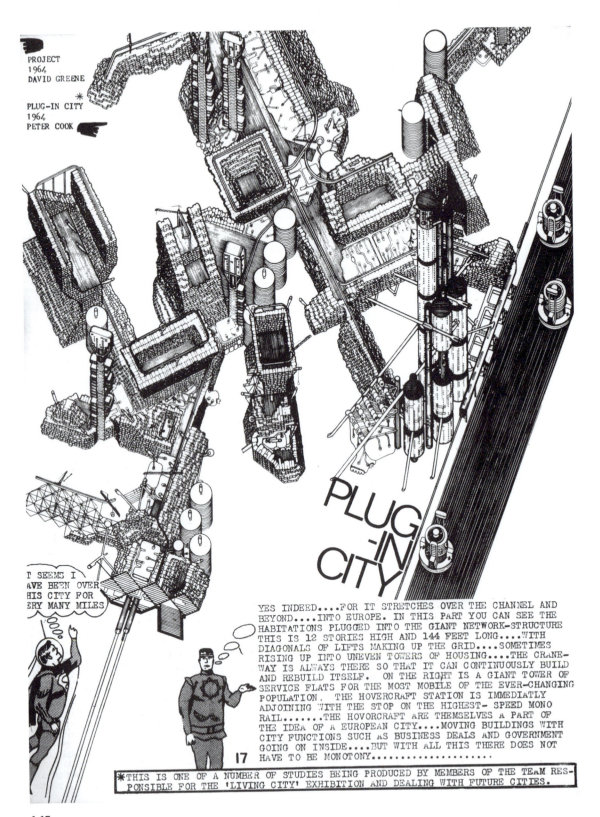

PROJECT
1964
DAVID GREENE

PLUG-IN CITY
1964
PETER COOK

PLUG
-IN
CITY

IT SEEMS I
HAVE BEEN OVER
THIS CITY FOR
VERY MANY MILES

YES INDEED....FOR IT STRETCHES OVER THE CHANNEL AND
BEYOND....INTO EUROPE. IN THIS PART YOU CAN SEE THE
HABITATIONS PLUGGED INTO THE GIANT NETWORK-STRUCTURE
THIS IS 12 STORIES HIGH AND 144 FEET LONG....WITH
DIAGONALS OF LIFTS MAKING UP THE GRID....SOMETIMES
RISING UP INTO UNEVEN TOWERS OF HOUSING....THE CRANE-
WAY IS ALWAYS THERE SO THAT IT CAN CONTINUOUSLY BUILD
AND REBUILD ITSELF. ON THE RIGHT IS A GIANT TOWER OF
SERVICE FLATS FOR THE MOST MOBILE OF THE EVER-CHANGING
POPULATION. THE HOVERCRAFT STATION IS IMMEDIATLY
ADJOINING WITH THE STOP ON THE HIGHEST- SPEED MONO
RAIL.......THE HOVORCRAFT ARE THEMSELVES A PART OF
THE IDEA OF A EUROPEAN CITY....MOVING BUILDINGS WITH
CITY FUNCTIONS SUCH AS BUSINESS DEALS AND GOVERNMENT
GOING ON INSIDE....BUT WITH ALL THIS THERE DOES NOT
HAVE TO BE MONOTONY.....................

17

✱ THIS IS ONE OF A NUMBER OF STUDIES BEING PRODUCED BY MEMBERS OF THE TEAM RES-
PONSIBLE FOR THE 'LIVING CITY' EXHIBITION AND DEALING WITH FUTURE CITIES.

4.15

Plug-in City from *Archigram 4*.

edge of the city giant hovercraft, drawn as cylindrical buildings, provided a regional transportation link. The whole composition was deliberately irregular, to suggest that building on this scale did not necessarily mean a regimented environment.

The plug-in concept was meant to be a method of permitting structures to be tailored to the needs of individuals, with endless permutations creating cities of infinite variety. As drawn, however, their high densities and complex interdependent structures would have required an unprecedented degree of social regimentation.

Plug-In City was worked out to show, among other details, how cranes at the top of structural frames would lift capsules into place, how services operated, and the way balloons could be inflated to seal off bad weather. One drawing, made to resemble a weather map, showed England as a series of high- and low-pressure development zones, with Plug-In City eventually filling in all the high-pressure zones.

Walking City was an arresting image of ovoid megastructures on huge telescoping legs. While the individual parts of the megastructure have an architectural character, the overall effect is of gigantic insectile creatures. There was always an element of jokiness in Archigram proposals, no matter how serious its proponents actually were about the main points they were making. The drawing "The Walking City in New York," by which Ron Herron's Walking City proposal is generally known, has more jokiness than usual. It shows the Walking City buildings arriving in New York harbor, with the Manhattan skyline in the background. Even if you are willing to accept the idea of sixty-story buildings moving on gigantic legs, it is hard to believe they can walk on water (Figure 4.16).

As the decade of the 1960s continued, the work of the Archigram group became more ecologically minded, more interested in underground cities, and at the same time more involved with demountable structures and environments for entertainment.

An interest in ecology is supposedly the motivating force behind a series of projects by Paolo Soleri, dating from 1959 and continuing through the 1960s, for huge underground, spherical or tower cities that would concentrate population and urban activities to protect the landscape. Soleri, a graduate of the Ecole des Beaux Arts during its last days who also spent some months studying with Frank Lloyd Wright at Taliesin, is able to combine monumental architectural compositions in the tradition of Boullee with the kind of "organic" engineering that Wright had used for

4.16
Ron Herron's "Walking City in New York."

Systems city design 181

the S.C. Johnson and Son administration building: forms in reinforced concrete that appear to have been designed by analogy with plants.

Soleri began construction on Arcosanti, a prototype for a megastructural city, in the Arizona desert in 1970. Progress has proceeded by slow, craft methods, mostly with volunteer student labor, and to date has achieved nothing beyond the scale of a small village. Soleri alone of the megastructuralists of the 1960s seems to have retained an unbroken faith in the concept, and the gap between his visions and their realization does not seem to deter him. Another powerful megastructure image is the space-frame drawn by Yona Friedman, in studies dating from 1960, to spread over existing cities. The idea is that existing urban activities would be drawn up into the space-frame, and the outmoded and now disused structures at ground level could later be demolished.

Hans Hollein's aircraft carrier projects of 1964 took the final steps toward relating Le Corbusier's polemic in favor of engineering imagery for architecture to a program for city design. Where Le Corbusier urged the ocean liner as an example of a new architecture already achieved, Hollein constructed collages showing aircraft carriers on dry land or buried in the landscape to demonstrate that habitable structures at the scale of the city already existed.

Megastructures actually implemented

Expo 1967, the world's fair held in Montreal, was the first occasion for a large public to see megastructural city-design ideas in built form, including a large Buckminster Fuller dome that housed the US Pavilion. A monorail train that ran through the Expo arrived at a station inside the dome in true space-age fashion. Perhaps the best-known component of this exhibition was Habitat, the housing project designed by Moshe Safdie. Habitat consisted of prefabricated concrete apartment capsules that were hoisted into position on a reinforced-concrete armature. The capsules were neither standardized nor removable; as they helped support each other, an apartment near the bottom needed quite a different wall structure from one at the top of the eleven-story complex. The resulting building had some of the picturesque qualities of a Mediterranean hilltop village blended with the promise of new technology, a potent combination. The high cost and idiosyncratic character of Habitat was to deny it the prototypical influence that Safdie had hoped for it, although a recent project by Rem Koolhaas for Singapore takes a comparable concept up an order of magnitude, using whole apartment buildings as components (Figure 4.17).

The Place Bonaventure which was completed in Montreal the year of Expo, has megastructural characteristics, although from the outside it appeared only to be a very large building. Built over railway tracks and a connection to the metro system, it had a shopping concourse, a convention hall of more than 200,000 square feet, six floors of merchandise mart, and then a hotel built around courtyards at the top of the structure. The exterior of the Place Bonaventure showed the influence of

4.17

Habitat designed by Moshe Safdie and built as part of Montreal's Expo 1967. This building looks like megastructure projects of a few years earlier but the construction of its modular design is conventional.

Paul Rudolph's architecture and art studio building at Yale, completed in 1964. It, in turn, can be compared with megastructures like those from the central portion of Kenzo Tange's Tokyo Bay project. Each tower of the Rudolph building, actually only the size of a small classroom, can be read as a scaled-down version of a massive separate building, with the bridges between them the size of whole town centers.

Rudolph used megastructure imagery in other buildings, such as the Boston Government Center designed in 1963, which contains elevated bridge-like elements; and the University of Massachusetts Dartmouth campus, which was designed the same year and, as a group of similar elements in a linear arrangement, effectively was a megastructure. Rudolph also designed several megastructure projects on an even larger scale, including, in 1967, a graphic arts center and housing in lower Manhattan, which was meant to be built of prefabricated apartment-elements similar to mobile home units; and a continuous residential structure to be built over the then proposed lower Manhattan expressway, also designed in 1967. Some large housing developments of the period were actually built as megastructures. The Byker estate at Newcastle in the north of England, by the Anglo-Swedish architect Ralph Erskine, was the largest of several continuous structures that Erskine designed with one elevation almost blank and the other opening out generously with windows and balconies. Originally devised to ward off north winds, this design in Newcastle screens the housing from an adjacent highway. The whole complex was planned to be almost a mile long.

The Brunswick Centre in London, with its Sant'Elia-like towers, was a housing project for the Camden Borough Council designed by Leslie Martin and Patrick Hodgkinson. It is like a megastructure because its architectural arrangement is capable of infinite extension: two parallel rows of buildings, designed in a terraced or stadium section, with a shopping concourse and garage in between.

Because the 1960s and early 1970s were a period of great expansion for colleges and universities, there were many opportunities to design a whole new campus or large groups of college buildings. Some of these new colleges were housed in megastructures, notably Scarborough College near Toronto by John Andrews, with its almost industrial silhouette, and Simon Fraser University at Burnaby, British Columbia, by Arthur Erickson, with its internal street covered by a space-frame. It can be argued that many large regional shopping centers are in fact megastructures, descended both from the Crystal Palace urban arcade tradition and from the internal controlled environment of megastructure projects, with the storefronts representing something like the interchangeable plug-in elements suggested by Archigram.

The Archigram aesthetic of bridge-like structures, much visible piping, and articulation of space into capsules is also seen in Renzo Piano and Richard Rogers' 1970 winning competition design for the Centre Pompidou in Paris and carried over into the completed building. The Expo 1970 world's fair in Osaka—a festive array of spaceframes, capsules, and robots—marked a kind of climax for the megastructure movement. Also in 1970, Kenzo Tange published a plan that treated the entire Japanese archipelago as a megastructure. By 1972 the Nakagin Capsule Tower by Kisho Kurokawa was completed in Tokyo. Extremely compact prefabricated living units, looking like elongated clothes dryers, were attached to concrete supports. Here was a plug-in structure actually completed. But the Nakagin tower was not a precursor of plug-in cities; it was an isolated and idiosyncratic building.

International airports built since the 1960s often have megastructural characteristics, as they house a large, self-contained, if somewhat limited community. Sometimes the architects have emphasized the likeness, as at the terminal building of Charles de Gaulle Airport near Paris, where inclined tubes connecting across a central circular space could owe some of their inspiration to Ron Herron and Warren Chalk's Archigram Interchange project. The new airport in Hong Kong is a megastructure by any definition (Figure 4.18).

4.18
The new airport at Hong Kong, a massive megastructure, designed by Foster + Partners.

4.19
A recent group of apartment
buildings in Beijing designed
by Steven Holl, linked to
suggest a megastructure.

China seems to be one place that can afford to implement office and residential buildings on a megastructural scale. The China Central Television Tower (CCTV) in Beijing by Rem Koolhaas and Ole Scheeren of the Office of Metropolitan Architecture (OMA) is composed of two leaning towers joined at the top and bottom by other large building elements (see p. 48). The building defies conventional structural and economic logic through the expert guidance of Arup, the engineers who have made many unusual buildings possible. Another recent Chinese megastructure is a group of eight apartment towers and a hotel, also in Beijing, designed by Steven Holl. The spectacular bridges which turn the group of towers into a megastructure form a kind of elevated shopping street, but do not really have a clear economic purpose (Figure 4.19).

Why most megastructure concepts failed

The megastructure as a vision of an entire future city had never overcome awkward practical problems. Most city development is financed in increments over time; it is rarely feasible to build structures for hundreds of thousands of people in just a few years. If such an undertaking is to be privately financed, the real-estate market will not absorb so much new development; if government-supported, the municipal power to finance needs to be spread over a larger period of time, and the political problems of governmental projects increase geometrically with size.

The structural framework of a megastructure is also a new element that is not required by conventional buildings; it is needed to hold up the equivalent of conventional buildings that will be built at a later time. The real-estate market is not accustomed to financing the non-income-producing cylindrical towers or mile-square space-frames that can receive individual dwelling capsules at some time in the future. Rai Okamoto's urban design plan for midtown Manhattan, proposed by the Regional Plan Association in 1969, ran aground on this problem. The concept was to control new growth by causing future buildings to be constructed in clusters. To make the clusters happen, elevators, fire stairs, vertical ductwork, and other service elements for future buildings would be constructed first. But the question of who would pay was never answered (Figure 4.20).

4.20
The horizontal and vertical transportation systems of midtown Manhattan imagined as a megastructural framework for development in a design by Rai Okamoto and Frank Williams for the Regional Plan Association.

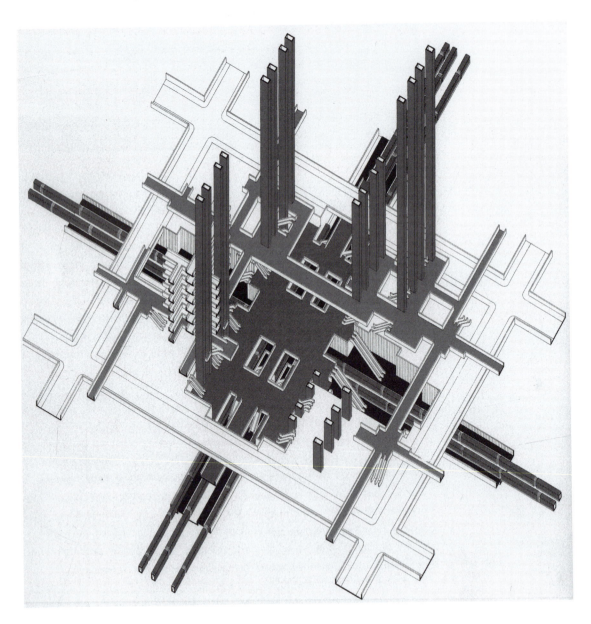

Many megastructure concepts were based on the assumption that people should be able to move their complete house or office from one location to another. It is usually more flexible, however, for people to simply move their belongings to another space, whose location and size are more suitable for their current needs.

The only strong argument in favor of the future city as a gigantic building was that it represented an orderly and efficient means of growth. But taking the order and efficiency of a building up to the scale of a city can actually create serious inefficiencies. The notorious Pruitt-Igoe housing development in St. Louis, which was so unsuccessful that parts of it were ultimately dynamited, was built in 1955 on something like a megastructure scale (2,764 apartments), and with access galleries for the apartments that were a version of the street-in-the-air concept of Le Corbusier.

The problems with Pruitt-Igoe may well have been administrative as well as architectural, as projects of comparable size and similar design have been more successful in other cities, but it illustrates the dangers of projects where the individual dwelling is an anonymous capsule in a large, impersonal framework. Pruitt-Igoe became an important symbol for those who questioned the assumptions that lay behind much of the enthusiasm for megastructures.

One of these assumptions was that cities were centralized and congested. But the 1960s and 1970s turned out to be the period when the automobile, the truck, the limited access highway, and outlying airport locations created the enormous extension of cities and the decentralization of many functions that had once existed only in the congested downtown area. These trends had begun before World War II but had been interrupted by economic depression and then the war itself. The new pattern came about more quickly in North America and Australia than in Europe or Japan, but it was visible everywhere. The automobile made many of the previous requirements for urban concentration irrelevant, and— by removing industry from the city center—had set the stage for the re-creation of the center as a preserve for business, tourism, and high-income residents. A primary purpose of the megastructure was to create a vast increase in density within the confines of an existing city, or as a system of new cities. But by the 1960s and 1970s many people neither needed nor wanted to live at this kind of density.

The 1970s also saw the replacement of old ideas about the advantages of rapid growth and large-scale urban development with ideals that came close to being the opposite. Jane Jacobs inverted Daniel Burnham's famous axiom and advised communities to make no large plans. Historic preservationists have successfully argued that the existing city should not be replaced by towers in parks, or gradually phased into a space-frame, but preserved and restored. Architects rediscovered the virtues of historic buildings once despised as outmoded and retrograde. The energy crisis has suggested that conservation of existing structures and modest modifications to cities were more sensible than wholesale rebuilding, particularly conversion to structures as subject to energy loss as highly articulated capsules or vast controlled environments. Rapid inflation has also often made renovation better structural economics than new construction. In short, every trend of the late 1970s contradicted the premises that made the city as megastructure seem a reasonable prediction a few years earlier.

Christopher Alexander and incremental systems of city design

Christopher Alexander's reaction to his experience as an architecture student at the University of Cambridge in the 1950s was that there had to be a more systematic and intellectually defensible way of understanding and teaching architecture. Alexander's doctoral thesis at Harvard, developed into his 1964 book, *Notes on the Synthesis of Form*,[27] used the computer techniques then available to sort a list of functions for a building, or a city, into clusters of relationships. In theory it would then be possible to synthesize these clusters into a design with sound functional relationships. The difficulty was that Alexander had only devised a method of analysis, not synthesis. He had not found a way of putting together his functional clusters to form a building. Interestingly, the account of the "worked example" in *Notes on the Synthesis of Form* is not about a building, but about a village in India, written while Alexander was staying at the home of his architecture-school classmate Kamal Mangaldas in Ahmedebad. Villages, from their origins in prehistoric times, had already evolved into something like a design system.

Notes on the Synthesis of Form generated great interest among designers when it was published.[28] A Design Methods Group grew up to build on the approaches that Alexander had created; the DMG published a newsletter and held annual conferences. The American Institute of Architects awarded Alexander a medal for research. Alexander refused to accept the medal in person at the Institute's annual conference in 1967, instead sending a letter questioning whether the architectural profession had any idea what research was.[29] Soon afterwards, Alexander decided that the methodology in his book was a dead end. Instead he took to studying examples of clusters of functions that could be observed in buildings already constructed, most of them pre-industrial. Borrowing from linguistics, he called his new research product *A Pattern Language*, published in 1977 by the center he had created at the University of California in Berkeley.[30] This book has also been widely influential. It is full of interesting and useful insights, but it is a dictionary or vocabulary, not a language. As in Alexander's previous thesis, there is no syntax. Various case studies published by Alexander describing the way he used his pattern language in actual buildings demonstrated that his patterns took him only part of the way; that he incorporated the patterns into his buildings as intuitively as any other architect.

The Linz Café is an account Alexander wrote about the process he followed for a small restaurant he was asked to design as part of an exposition, Forum Design, held in Linz during the summer of 1980. Although the materials are mostly wood and the scale is modest, the form of this building resembles a traditional basilica or church, with restaurant booths organized as if they were side chapels, and the other tables in the central nave with its high-pitched roof and clerestory windows. Like other architects, Alexander reduced the synthesis process to a problem in simplicity so he could solve it, and then fitted the program into the resulting form.[31] His description of designing and building the Linz Café highlights a central problem in Alexander's methods: all functions, and all patterns, are not equally important. Treating each issue equally makes the design much more sensitive to matters of detail, but also makes it much harder to resolve into a coherent concept.

Alexander's new theory of urban design

A Pattern Language shows a marked preference for pre-industrial construction and building forms, which had been generated by centuries of incremental improvements to similar buildings within relatively stable societies—which is why they had become patterns. They were fragments of building systems which had once been accepted as the only way to build. Alexander's reliance on traditional design systems is especially marked in *A New Theory of Urban Design*, an account of a studio Alexander directed at the University of California at Berkeley.[32] The studio is interesting as a study of systems city design because Alexander sought to have the form of a waterfront district in San Francisco emerge from the collective efforts of the eighteen student participants. Alexander set the studio the objective of creating the quality of wholeness or coherence to be found in pre-industrial cities.

To guide the students, Alexander had to address syntax. He sets out seven rules to achieve wholeness. The first is that no building increment can be too large, with a sub-rule that there should also be a variety of building sizes. The second rule is that each building should contribute to the growth of a larger whole. Third rule: each building should somehow correspond to people's inner vision of what the building should be. Four, each building must create coherent and well-shaped public space next to it. Five: the interior arrangement of large buildings must be connected coherently to the exterior places around the building. Six: buildings should be made up of a coherent system of substructures. Seven: each increment of development should be in itself a center of a symmetrical subsystem, but not rigidly so.

These seven rules are all derived from the norms of pre-industrial cities. Pre-industrial structural systems set limits on the size of most buildings, and wood and stone roof structures imposed differing dimensions. Fortifications enclosing a city limited available sites, imposing a need to consider the whole city in making renovations or additions to any part. The restricted range of building types possible in pre-industrial societies meant that design ideas were familiar to most people in a general way. Coherence of public space in the western European tradition was a Renaissance innovation which shows up in the last stage of Gruber's drawings of a pre-industrial German city on p. 168. The connection of interior and exterior spaces was also a Renaissance innovation, as is the effort to achieve symmetry within subsets of the city. Modularity of structure is implicit in Renaissance architecture, but became more systematic in the teachings of Durand during the French Revolution.

In a final section of the book reviewing the relative success and failures of the studio, Alexander concludes that some improvements were needed in how the rules were stated but that the big problem was that "The process we have outlined is incompatible with present day city-planning, zoning, urban real-estate, urban economics, and urban law." This is a clear exposition of the reasons why Alexander's new theory of urban design has not been widely accepted.

Alexander's timeless way and the nature of order

Christopher Alexander's response to both the need to create grammatical rules for his pattern language and to convince society to accept his conclusions about design was to dig deeper into the nature of the results he was trying to create.

The Timeless Way of Building is meant to be an introduction to *A Pattern Language* although it was published two years later.[33] The timeless way cannot be attained "but it will happen of its own accord, if we will only let it." "It is thousands of years old, and the same today as it has always been." To say that the objectives for constructed environments should remain the same as they have always been is to say that the industrial and communications revolutions, globalization, or any other factor that distinguishes modern life should not have any effect on what is a desirable building or city. On the contrary, all these innovations have gotten in the way of the connections that people should have to nature and community. However, Alexander is not advocating a return to the economic and social conditions which produced most of the scenes of buildings and landscape portrayed so beautifully in the photographs he includes in his book.

The timeless way creates "the quality without a name," which is the essential element of good buildings and good places. The gateway to the timeless way is through understanding patterns. The patterns have a structure as a language because there are interconnections among them. When all these interconnections are resolved completeness results and the quality without a name is attainable. Alexander gives step-by-step accounts of the formation of a building and of a group of buildings from patterns. What he will not do is lay out a procedure for design so it would be possible for the reader to reconstruct all the reasoning behind the steps Alexander records. For Alexander design is a mystical process in which order and coherence are gradually revealed.

Where does this order and coherence come from? This question occupied Christopher Alexander for some twenty-seven years as he worked on his four-volume series, *The Nature of Order*.[34] Alexander is convinced that there is a scientific basis for what he calls wholeness and the quality of aliveness. He has concluded that there are fifteen properties that underlie the patterns that make up *A Pattern*

Language and these properties create the coherence needed to put the patterns together into a meaningful language. The list:

1. Levels of scale
2. Strong centers
3. Boundaries
4. Alternating repetition
5. Positive space
6. Good shape
7. Local symmetries
8. Deep interlock and ambiguity
9. Contrast
10. Gradients
11. Roughness
12. Echoes
13. The void
14. Simplicity and inner calm
15. Non-separateness

Alexander goes far beyond asserting that these qualities might be a useful way of thinking about architecture or cities. He has become convinced that they are indicators of a pervasive order that underlies all of nature. Like Michael Batty he believes there are "deeper theories to be discovered about the forms and structures that develop," although he is coming at them from observation and inference not from mathematics.

As noted on p. 93, Rudolph Wittkower wrote in *The Architecture of Humanism* of Pythagoras's discovery that harmonic relationships in music corresponded to the length of the strings that produced the notes according to the ratios of small whole numbers, and "that this staggering discovery made people believe that they had seized upon the mysterious harmony which pervades the universe."[35] Maybe there is a harmony that pervades the universe and Christopher Alexander and Michael Batty in their different ways are heading towards discovering it. Certainly, if such harmony exists, finding ways to emulate or re-create it would be the key to architecture and city planning. Right now, however, this key is not available.

The role of codes in shaping cities

Planning and building codes were a response to the breakdown of the systems of city design that had evolved up to the nineteenth century, the invasion of cities by railroads and industry, industrial pollution and industrial slums, big increases in traffic, the segregation of cities into new sectors, and the dispersal of urban functions across the landscape. Detailed codes have become particularly well developed in the United States where the Constitution leaves most decisions about the management of urban growth to the states, which in turn delegate most such decisions to local governments. To harmonize approval practices the Federal government has prepared model codes and the individual states pass enabling legislation for codes that outline how the delegated powers should be used. The codes tend to be written as systems that favor explicit requirements over discretionary review, from a well-founded distrust of the use of discretionary authority by local governments.

Building codes are primarily concerned with preventing fires, structural collapse, unventilated rooms, and similar threats to public safety. The history of building codes goes back to the pre-industrial city. For example, after the Great Fire of London, masonry walls were required between attached houses. In the nineteenth and early twentieth century new building codes were needed not only for fire safety in new types of buildings, but to regulate ventilation and sanitation and the structural soundness of new materials. Today, because so many building components are manufactured, there has been a movement towards standardizing building codes. While local authorities have the ability to write any provision they wish, most have adopted standard requirements for wiring, plumbing, fire resistance, insulation, elevators, and many other building components. Architectural elements such as windows and doors have also become standardized. As the building industry has become more systematized, it requires a serious effort by an architect to prevent a building from looking like many other buildings.

Planning codes also began in the pre-industrial city. One of the most powerful codes has been the height limits in Paris that are related to the width of the streets and have been in force since the mid-eighteenth century. This one simple provision is a principal reason why the development of Paris has been so coherent. Builders who wish to construct the most space permitted must build to the front property line and then straight up to where the front wall meets the mandatory setback plane that is drawn from the center of the street (Figure 4.21). This requirement produces a uniform street frontage that is usually a more powerful design element than the architecture of the individual buildings. The 1916 New York City zoning code drew on the Parisian regulatory system as a way of controlling the height and bulk of elevator buildings (Figure 4.22). This rule also produced a uniform street frontage, although not as uniform as Paris, as can be seen in this view of the buildings facing Central Park from the 1960s just before New York City adopted a different type of code (Figure 4.23). Washington has also used a Parisian type of code to control building height, which produces downtown business streets with coherent street facades, as shown in this photograph of K Street (Figure 4.24).

Height and setback controls in US zoning ordinances are examples of simple rules that influence complex behavior. Another such simple rule with sweeping consequences is the separation of land uses. Laws confining industry to separate zones began to be passed in Germany and the Netherlands in the late nineteenth century. New York City's 1916 code, which was the most comprehensive enacted

4.21
These diagrams show the evolution of regulations in Paris that relate the height of buildings to the width of the street.

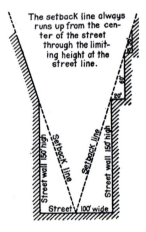

4.22
A diagram from New York City's 1916 zoning regulations shows how a "sky exposure plane" drawn from the center of the street at an angle set by the rules governs the height of the building, a similar method to those long-used in Paris.

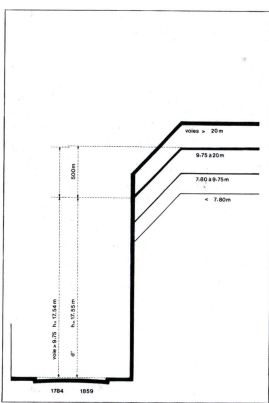

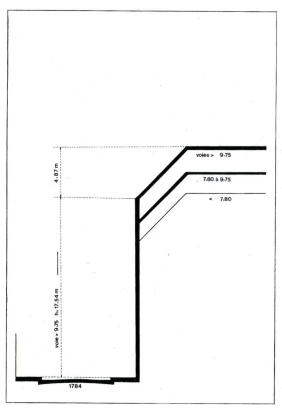

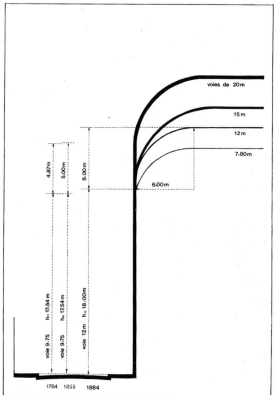

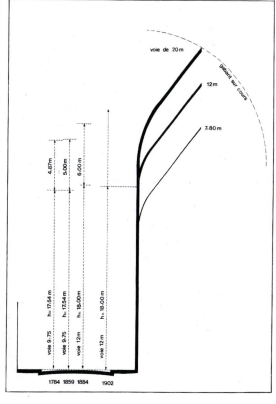

4.23
This photograph of Central Park in New York City taken just after the code was changed in the mid-1960s shows how the Sky Exposure Plane regulations from the 1916 zoning were a powerful influence on city design by encouraging building to the front of the site and creating a uniform setback line.

4.24
This photograph of K Street in downtown Washington, DC, shows the controlling effect on city design of the height limits in the District of Columbia.

in the United States up to that time, also included separate industrial zones, and protected residential zones, a response to the encroachment of the garment industry on the fashionable precincts of Fifth Avenue.

US neighborhoods which date from the early twentieth century usually have a mix of different sized houses and apartments, and it is likely that a grocery store, a drug store, plus restaurants and other services can be found on a shopping street within easy walking distance. As local governments adopted zoning codes, however, they began separating houses from apartments and segregating houses by zones based on the size of the lot. The building industry responded by creating districts where every house was the same size and price, and other districts where there were only garden apartments. Commercial zoning districts often did not permit residences at all; local shopping was zoned along arterial streets which were often out of walking distance from the new residence districts.

Negative influence of modern codes on cities

Zoning took the concept of a main street lined with shops on either side and extended it along arterial highways far out into the countryside, a major factor in creating the automobile-based commercial shopping streets now found everywhere in the US. The combination of large parking fields, chain stores, and franchised businesses in these commercial zones makes it hard to distinguish one such place from another.

The commercial strip is an example of effective systems city design; unfortunately the system is not a good one. The design is dysfunctional because it mixes through-traffic on the major street with drivers making turns against traffic to enter and leave commercial establishments. Parking lots, signs, and overhead utility wires create the dominant design impression. Most people consider such places the unavoidable result of the market at work, but in reality they are the closely determined results of defective codes.

Commercial strips are often the product of land-use provisions in zoning interacting with the related provisions of the subdivision code, which governs how large tracts of land are divided into smaller lots, and also sets standards for the width and configurations of new streets, and requirements for grading the land to keep streets from being too steep.

An unexpected consequence of large-scale application of subdivision codes has been regrading and the stripping of vegetation to meet grading requirements, leading to increased storm-water run-off, and much more frequent serious flooding. As described in Chapter 3, environmental zoning ordinances are attempts to preserve the existing ecology, and counteract the most serious consequences of subdivision codes that do not consider the environment as an ecosystem.

Another systems change in land-use regulation which has had unexpected negative effects has been the change from Parisian style height and setback requirements to regulating the bulk of buildings by floor area ratios. The floor area ratio is a multiple of the size of the property. For example, a floor area ratio of 10 would permit 10,000 square meters of development to be built on a 1,000 square meter lot. The ordinances based on floor area ratios usually also included provisions limiting coverage of the land to offset the potential height of the towers. The rationale for the change is that floor area is an occupancy control, a means of relating the potential population of a building to the transportation systems and other supporting infrastructure, and is thus more precise than simply limiting the height and bulk of a building. The unexpected consequence has turned out to be that floor area ratio is one of the simple rules that lead to random consequences, as the size of properties, development decisions about building height, and choices about where to place buildings on lots are all highly variable.

The reaction to the buildings produced when codes switched to floor area ratios has often been dismay: low-rise residential neighborhoods suddenly invaded by apartment towers generally react unfavorably; the passage of a floor-area-ratio ordinance for downtown San Francisco was soon followed by a huge public battle to reimpose height limits. In New York City, Boston, and many other places, the introduction of floor area ratio as the dominant control caused the cities to enact additional rules to regulate the size and placement of buildings and preserve historic districts.

Form-based codes: build-to lines and maximum block perimeters

As described in Chapter 2, form-based codes have been the method used to try to relate modern buildings to traditional concepts of city design, but that is not the only way they can be used. Form-based codes recognize that codes shape buildings. The legal rationale for zoning and subdivision codes has been to protect neighboring owners and investors from negative consequences of a new development, such as pollution, noise, traffic congestion, and blocking light, air, and views. Instead of building and city forms being a by-product of legislation to prevent the worst effects of new development, why not envision desirable development and write the code to facilitate it?

Early form-based codes enacted in New York City during the 1960s were intended to counteract the randomization of building design introduced by the 1965 zoning resolution which used floor area ratios as the basic building bulk control. The new codes included a Special Theater District, the Lincoln Square Special District to shape the form of development around Lincoln Center, a Special Fifth Avenue district intended to preserve retail street frontages, as well as zoning that limited height in a designated historic district in Brooklyn Heights (Figure 4.25). The most important provision to come out of these districts was the build-to line, the opposite of the more familiar setback line. Build-to requires that a high percentage of a building's front facade be constructed at the front property line, or at another uniform line designated by the code. This concept formalized the effect of the Parisian height

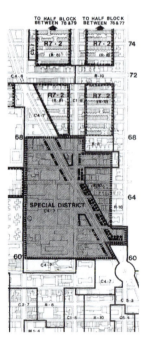

4.25
The zoning map for the Lincoln Square Special District in New York City, an early example of form-based coding.

limits in creating a coherent wall along street fronts, in situations where there might not be the same economic incentive. A more conventional setback line can be used to control the height of the building at the build-to line.

Build-to lines were an important part of the Battery Park City code completed in 1979, which used the build-to line not only to create street walls, but to control the placement of towers. The code at Battery Park City differed in an important way from codes that are part of zoning or subdivision ordinances. The Battery Park City Authority owned the land, and anyone wishing to develop had to accept the design guidelines as part of the purchase agreement. The code has been an important factor in making Battery Park City one of the most completely realized large-scale urban design projects. The codes at Seaside and the Kentlands referred to on p. 103 also were enforced through property deeds, which permitted the extension of the code into areas of building design, such as the style of architecture to be used for each building, that would be hard to control through zoning.

The Smart Code developed by Andres Duany, who with his partner Elizabeth Plater-Zyberk were the planners for Seaside and the Kentlands, has taken their experience in writing codes for planned developments under one ownership and seeks to apply it to zoning, a much more random situation, as there are many owners in a community and they may or may not be planning to develop their properties. The Smart Code is directed towards specific formal results, but the method is primarily prescriptive. The Smart Code seeks to anticipate each possible situation and write a rule for it, and a community which wants to make use of the code needs to adopt it in its entirety to be effective. Conventional zoning and subdivision are more like systems, in that a variety of results can emerge from rules, although sometimes the results may not be desirable.

One concept devised by Duany that has strong possibilities as a design system is the Maximum Block Perimeter, a simple method for insuring a walkable environment in a new development which could easily be incorporated into existing subdivision ordinances. A maximum block perimeter of 1,800 feet, for example, means that a block could be 700 feet by 200 feet, a good size for houses, or 450 by 450 for a larger building, or many other combinations of dimensions. Coupled with requirements for building sidewalks and reasonable limits for the widths of streets, this one simple rule can insure the creation of a connected grid of walkable streets which can be adapted to the building types, terrain, and boundaries of many different developments, without prescribing the design in advance.

The build-to line and the maximum block perimeter are indicators that it should be possible to invent a system that improves upon existing zoning and subdivision codes and will permit a variety of desirable environments to emerge while still meeting regulatory objectives. One important feature of the Smart Code that is transferrable to other kinds of zoning is promoting mixed use rather than the separation of land uses. Modern artificial ventilation and insulation make it much easier to mix land uses than it was when such codes were first being written, leaving only heavy industry and activities which are massive traffic generators to be segregated in special districts. It also should be possible to mix house sizes in walkable neighborhoods, using build-to and setback lines to unify the presence of diverse house types.[36]

Spatial Analyst in GIS as a city-design tool

The Spatial Analyst program in ArcGIS now allows designers to work with the kinds of issues that Jane Jacobs, following Warren Weaver, defined as problems in disorganized complexity, in ways far less abstract than the procedures that Jacobs criticized for favoring formulas over reality. This program enables a designer to arrive at the most suitable locations for urban functions, population centers, conservation districts, and other elements of regional planning and design by ranking cells within a map—a cell could be an individual hectare, for example—into categories of high and low desirability using the weighted overlay modeling process in the computer program. Data is classified into categories related to the problem being solved on a scale of, say, 1 to 10. Weights are assigned to each category of a dataset from the most desirable, 10, to the least desirable, 1. The computer program can respond to many different sets of issues and arrive at an optimal location based on the various sets of criteria. The criteria can be based on subjective judgments. The procedure is a means of relating variables too numerous and complex to be understood as a system without the help of powerful computation.

Urban Design Studios at the University of Pennsylvania have used this procedure to create projections of development in the seven-county Orlando region according to current trends and in an alternative scenario postulating improved public transportation and more comprehensive protection of natural resources to show how predicted new population would then be more likely to choose compact communities over sprawl. The maps of these alternatives helped generate a major public decision-making process.[37]

Another studio used comparable GIS techniques to propose a network of conservation lands for the entire State of Florida taking into account preservation of habitat, conservation of water resources, protection of wetlands, encouragement of agriculture, and creating contiguity with lands that had already been preserved in their natural state (Figures 4.26, 4.27). Another PennDesign studio used Spatial Analyst to predict the location and number of present and future residents and businesses in the Delaware River Basin that would be at risk from a one-meter rise in sea levels.

4.26
The layers of analysis that form the basis for the Ideal Conservation Network for Florida. They are, from top to bottom: Habitat, Water, Wetlands, Agriculture, and Contiguity.

Regional and super-regional systems

Patrick Geddes observed more than seventy years ago that groups of cities were forming what he called "conurbations," so that city planning and design had become

4.27
A map of the ideal
conservation network for
Florida which uses the
computer to synthesize the
priorities for different types of
conservation criteria shown in
the previous illustration.

a regional problem. The urban geographer Jean Gottmann published his famous *Megalopolis* study in 1961. Megalopolis was the name Gottmann gave to the continuous strip of urbanized area that stretches from Washington, DC, to Boston, Massachusetts, and which today would probably be defined as stretching from Richmond, Virginia, to Portland, Maine. The definition of a megalopolis has since been applied to other urbanized corridors, such as the Randstad in the Netherlands; Tokaido, which includes the cities of Tokyo, Yokohama, Osaka, Nagoya, and Kobe; or the whole of the upper midwestern United States from Pittsburgh to Chicago.

Rural areas within a megalopolis are not what they seem to be. For example, in a state like Connecticut almost every resident makes a living from non-farm employment, despite extensive tracts of open country and the places where woodlands have grown back over what were once fields and pastures. Rural areas outside a megalopolis are often not what they seem to be, either. The presence of a sophisticated restaurant or a designer clothing boutique often shows that a seemingly pastoral village is really a summer or winter vacation colony for city people. Even in agricultural areas today's well-traveled farmer-executive operating a computer and complex farm machinery is hardly a country bumpkin. The whole idea of provincialism is difficult to maintain when an entire population watches the same

Systems city design **199**

television programs, reads the same national news magazines and newspapers, looks at the same websites, and can be connected by social networking sites.

A study at the University of Pennsylvania in 2004 showed that 62 percent of the US population lives in nine super-city regions, and that these areas were likely to account for 71 percent of the US population by 2050.[38] This work has been refined by Armando Carbonell and Robert D. Yaro,[39] by Robert E. Lang and Arthur C. Nelson,[40] and by Catherine L. Ross and Myungje Woo.[41] There is still some disagreement over what to call this phenomenon: multi-city regions, megaregions, or megapolitan regions, and whether there are nine or ten of these regions. If there are ten, the proportion of the US population that may be included in them could be as high as 80 percent.

These multi-city regions grew together in the era of suburban sprawl, but new influences tend to push urban development in these regions towards centralization, countering the decentralizing influences of automobiles and trucks. These influences include international container shipping to and from big regional container ports on increasingly large ocean-going freighters, the worldwide network of jet aircraft, increasing use of high-speed rail for regional transportation, and improvements in local transit. Containers not only create centralized freight depots but revitalize the railroads that are needed to trans-ship containers efficiently over long distances. Airports continue to generate airport-related development which can sometimes justify the term "airport city." High-speed rail can unify geographic regions and strengthen existing city centers, which may include recent developments near airports or the locations characterized as edge cities as well as traditional downtowns. Fixed-rail rapid transit lines also strengthen central locations.

The influence of globalization on city-region development

Malcolm McLean started the first containership line in 1956 using standardized metal containers that could be transferred directly from trucks or railway cars at either end of their sea voyage, instead of individual shipments which had to be loaded and unloaded from the ships by stevedores, and then transferred, also by hand, to trucks or railway box cars. Earlier versions of container shipping had been used in World War II and trucks had been loaded on ships before, but the use of modular containers that could be transferred from one form of transport to another greatly facilitated international trade. A factory in northern China can supply parts to a manufacturer in the central United States, or finished merchandise to a US warehouse. A container can be loaded at the factory in China, shipped by rail or truck to a container port, let us say in Tianjin, and loaded directly from the railway to a ship bound for, as an example, San Pedro, California. At San Pedro the container can be transferred to a train for Dallas, where it can be loaded on to an inter-state truck bound for its ultimate destination in Kansas City. The whole journey is facilitated by automation, using bar codes on the side of the container. The use of containers, plus the rise in fuel costs for containers transported by truck, has helped revive railroads, while requiring improvements along the lines to permit containers to be double-stacked.

Jet airliners came into operational use in the late 1950s, were two to three times as fast as propeller-driven aircraft and had longer ranges, making inter-continental air travel much more feasible. A professor at MIT can jet to a consultancy with an electronics firm in California, or an international banker or lawyer based in New York can spend a week out of every month in Shanghai or London. Parisian families live all summer in East Hampton, New York; New York families spend the summer in the south of France, or Tuscany. As a result, it not only becomes more and more difficult to distinguish between rural and urban areas; it is no longer as clear where one city's influence ends and another's begins. Many more people now have personal experience of distant countries, which has led to increased international business, educational, and professional relationships, and also means that disease and terrorism can cross boundaries much more easily.

High-speed rail as the main street of multi-city regions

Construction began on the Shinkansen high-speed rail line in Japan in 1959 which now links almost all of Japan except the northern island of Hokkaido. Japan has an integrated rail passenger transportation system with inter-city travel linked to local transit and commuter lines. This system is the prototype. The TGF high-speed rail started in France in the 1960s; the map now shows the links among European capitals with train speeds of more than 200 kilometers per hour (Figure 4.28). Eventually much more of the European rail network will be upgraded to some kind of high-speed rail.

4.28
Map of the rail links among important centers in Europe. Many of these links now use high-speed rail technology.

China is upgrading its rail network to have high-speed rail service from Harbin in the north to Shenzen and Hong Kong in the south in a system that will link most of the major cities.

The United States is belatedly recognizing the importance of high-speed rail for regional transportation. The Federal government has identified potential high-speed rail locations (Figure 4.29). These systems would connect destinations within multi-city regions; most long-distance trips would still take place by air.

How the new systems of multi-city regions relate to a global system of interconnected cities will be a central city-design problem for the first half of the twenty-first century.

4.29
The Federal Railroad Administration's map of potential high-speed rail systems. No one thinks high-speed rail is the way to go from Los Angeles to New York, but among centers in the multi-city regions it is more efficient to travel by high-speed rail than by car or airplane.

Conclusion

The fifth way of city design

Modernist ideas of city organization have helped create public housing projects and downtown urban renewal districts, as well as the design of tall office buildings, low-rise office parks and massive hospital complexes. Traditional city design has given form to groups of civic and cultural buildings, created public parks and boulevards, and provided a heritage of actual monuments: columns, obelisks, even triumphal arches. Groups of traditional buildings are also to be found in the older parts of the local university campus, in historic districts, and have been revived in new urbanist suburban developments. The garden city and garden suburb, early forms of what is now called green city design, have shaped fashionable residential districts and, in a more diluted form, the newer suburban subdivisions. Infrastructure and engineering systems designs are what make modern cities possible. The concept of the city as a structural system has helped shape regional shopping centers, airports, and the places where office buildings, hotels, and shops are connected by interior atria and networks of pedestrian bridges or tunnels.

There are at least four ways to look at every city-design problem: not mutually exclusive, but clearly distinguishable. A logical conclusion would be that designers are free to choose the city-design approach, or combination of approaches, that best fit the city and problem at hand. But passionate partisanship can get in the way of logic. Modernists continue to describe traditional city design as retrograde and unsuitable for life today. The new urbanists, currently the principal partisans for traditional city design, scorn modernism as mechanical and an affront to everything that makes cities livable. Green urbanists assert that landscape will replace architecture as the basic building block of contemporary urbanism, while other environmentalists often oppose development as irresponsible interference with the balance of nature. Designers who believe in the primacy of systems look to the future to deliver them from the inefficiencies and incoherence of the present.

Relationship to older buildings

The idea that a design must be original is part of the ideology of modernism itself. When applied to city-design problems, rejecting the past can lead to the rejection of the surrounding urban context. For the modernist, past buildings need only be preserved, if at all, for "sentimental" reasons, such as being the scene of an important historical event. The traditional urbanist looks to the past for guidance, so the precedents set by earlier buildings are accepted; and preserving and relating to the existing context becomes important. If an earlier city-design concept sets up design expectations for streets and building placement, the traditional urbanist is likely to honor them. If the expected pattern is not there, the traditional urbanist will seek to create it. Green city design gives pre-eminence to the natural landscape, terrain, and microclimate, but accepts that existing buildings are often the more sustainable alternative to building something new. Past and proposed buildings become incidents in the larger natural framework. The green city designer sees the environmental context first even in an area that has already been largely urbanized. Systems city design overlays past and future development with a comprehensive system which may be structural, geometric, based on services, or on a series of instructions; but is also always abstract and self-consistent. Past buildings can be included in the system, but need to be made consistent with it: new development is expected to emerge from the system.

Design composition

The basic organization of new development, the arrangement of streets, the public spaces, and the building forms are determined differently by each of the design approaches. Modernist composition is balanced but asymmetrical, symmetry is consciously avoided; streets are separated from buildings. Traditional urbanism sets up progressions of spaces that are symmetrical along axes. Buildings are used to define the space of streets and other public places. Green city design is informal and naturalistic, while systems city design controls both buildings and landscape.

Open space and the natural landscape

Open space in modernism is abstract, a picture-plane on which buildings are arranged and thus often a level, paved platform. Exterior spaces are residual, the by-product of the arrangement of the buildings. In traditional city design the buildings define and enclose a succession of public spaces, and the design system often extends its geometries into the landscape. Trees and plants can be ruthlessly reshaped in pursuit of a traditional geometric ideal. In green city design the landscape is dominant and the building arrangements are informal and in accord with the land contours, while in systems city design building and open space become integral parts of the same system, which means that open space may be included within a structural framework that also encloses buildings.

Building form

Building form in modernist city design is always abstract, free of applied ornament, and usually planar and unarticulated. Sometimes the building has a simple geometric shape, and sometimes significant or iconic form, usually based on engineering, but today sometimes based on an algorithm. Traditional city design uses building forms that are articulated to emphasize corners and mid points, and to create elements that terminate vistas. Sometimes traditional colonnades and arcades are evoked. Green city design seeks buildings that are informal in their organization, often constructed of natural materials, and designed to fit into the landscape. In systems urban design, the system, often structural or mechanical, dominates the building form and experiments are taking place using algorithms or emergence to create a city-design system.

Streets

In modernist design, streets are widely spaced: a supergrid designed for automobiles. There may be streets within the superblock, but they are likely to be located to prevent connections to the subsidiary streets in the next superblock. In traditional city design the streets form a connected network with multiple routes to go from one destination to the next. Traditional streets are designed to encourage pedestrians, with ample sidewalks, small blocks, and the shortest possible crosswalks at corners. Green streets are landscaped and make use of natural systems for storm drainage; the street systems are related to the land contours and so are often curved. In systems city design, the street is the channel for all infrastructure; and may be conceived as a movement system rather than as an urban space.

Who is correct?

Le Corbusier and Rem Koolhaas are both correct in saying that we can't go back to designing only the kinds of buildings that were possible before modern construction materials were invented. Tall buildings, abstract forms, and inventive structures are a permanent part of city design. Leon Krier and Andres Duany are right to remind us that there is still much to be learned from the traditional design of streets, public spaces, and the organization of groups of buildings; and the historic preservation movement is right that the older parts of cities are valuable and should not be written off. Ebenezer Howard, Ian McHarg, and Charles Waldheim are all correct in saying that city design today must begin with the natural landscape, particularly as we learn that today's environment may be subject to change with relatively little notice. City design today also continues to require the transportation networks, infrastructure, codes, and other systems that make the modern urban region possible.

Patrik Schumacher, a partner of Zaha Hadid Architects, has defined an alternative to modernist city design which appears to be based on systems design and which he calls Parametric Urbanism:

> There is a global convergence in recent avant-garde architecture that justifies its designation as a new style: parametricism. It is a style rooted in digital animation techniques, its latest refinements based on advanced parametric design systems and scripting methods. Developed over the past 15 years and now claiming hegemony within avant-garde architecture practice, it succeeds Modernism as the next long wave of systematic innovation. Parametricism finally brings to an end the transitional phase of uncertainty engendered by the crisis of Modernism and marked by a series of relatively short-lived architectural episodes that included Postmodernism, Deconstructivism and Minimalism.[1]

On closer inspection, the projects Schumacher illustrates, drawn from his practice at Zaha Hadid Architects, are not solutions to problems of organized complexity, the subject of ongoing research in systems urban design. They are examples of the familiar modernist strategy of creating significant or iconic forms, brought up to date by digital generation techniques applied at the scale of urban design. Schumacher asserts that these forms are examples of a new style, accepting that the essential problem of architecture and urban design is to create a style that will exert "hegemony." This view, introduced into the discourse of modernism by Henry-Russell Hitchcock and Philip Johnson in their 1932 exhibition at the Museum of Modern Art, and reinforced by partisan historians like Nikolaus Pevsner and Sigfried Giedion, is based on the belief that architectural history can be told as a progression of distinctive styles.

If a single style has characterized each historical period, future historians can be expected to look back on what is happening now and discern the dominant style not yet visible to contemporaries. The designers who have chosen right will be remembered and honored; the others will be scorned and forgotten. Stating this expectation explicitly ought to be enough to expose its absurdity. It may still be possible to describe earlier periods as a progression of styles: Renaissance, Mannerist, Baroque, Rococo, and, eventually, Modern. Using the same method today to define such categories as post-modern, neo-modern, rationalist, or the new something or other is viewed with skepticism by most art historians, who have concluded that assumptions about the nature of time, intention, and influence are not easy to make in a world of diverse cultures and instant communication. However, descriptions of the history of art and architecture progressing towards a specific objective persist in textbooks still being read by generations of architecture and landscape architecture students, and thus continue to foster a belief that history is looking over the designer's shoulder, prepared to reject the unworthy.

It is not necessary to accept Schumacher's claims of historical inevitability to appreciate that Zaha Hadid Architects have created an abstract formal language at an urban design scale which is one way to solve the problem of creating an ensemble of modern buildings to be built by different owners and architects over an undetermined period of time—the problem whose solution eluded the architects competing to rebuild the World Trade Center.

An early example of Zaha Hadid Architects' urban design strategy can be seen in their winning competition proposal for the One North development in Singapore. The design begins by creating a second landscape, a curved and sloping plane, representing the roofs of all the buildings. This second landscape is dissected by the streets, which form a loose grid plan, using only curves, no straight lines or right angles. The Jurong Town Corporation, or JTC, the Singapore government's development agency, has worked out a set of design guidelines to implement the plan concept. They rely on a traditional street plan that defines relatively small blocks, using build-to lines to control the street facades of the individual buildings. The height of each building is set—not by Parisian-style ratios to the width of the street—but by the shape of the second landscape as it applies to the individual block. The JTC has introduced more open space preservation than was shown in the original design and wider streets, but they should be able to implement the concept if they can keep control of the roof planes. This roof plane is conceptually different from the angled tops of buildings proposed by Daniel Libeskind for the World Trade Center site because the plane provides continuity from building to building.

The One North plan, at least as defined by the guidelines, represents a synthesis of modernist buildings, traditional street and block design, the naturalistic form of green city design, and the digitally generated shapes of systems city design.

Some suburban planned communities are based on a synthesis of traditional formal public spaces and axial building relationships for the town center, with the naturalistic parks and winding streets of green city design in the residential neighborhoods. Modernist city design is still dominant in many places because parking requirements are inescapable; and modern building types like distribution centers, factories, hospitals, high schools, shopping centers, and tall buildings, are hard to fit into traditional concepts of city design. Regional highway, transit, water, sewer, electrical, and information systems shape both regional and local city designs.

The city has become so vast and encompasses so many different densities of development, so many different kinds of activity and such a variety of communities that it is unlikely that any single design concept could emerge to give form to a metropolitan area in the way that Renaissance theorists might draw an idealized Vitruvian city as a polygonal street plan surrounded by ramparts. Attempts to reshape the city to a static pattern failed even during the Renaissance, as economic and social change were too rapid and too complicated to be contained. It would be vastly more difficult to accomplish the same task today. What is needed now is not a new all-purpose city-design concept, but new ways of integrating city design with the process of economic and social change and the need for a sustainable relationship with nature.

Begin with the natural landscape

All city design today needs to begin with natural systems, even for sites which are within an already urbanized region. Adaptation to climate change means that the latest hundred-year flood plain maps must be investigated and, in coastal areas, the latest sea-level rise predictions. Adapting to higher storm surges and other climate changes may require regional design solutions. Any city design should also promote sustainability by minimizing adverse effects on the environment. Good storm-water management suggests that no more water should drain from a site after development than left it before. Building and landscape design should fit the natural systems and topography of the site rather than attempt to subdue them through engineering. Air circulation and microclimate effects like heat islands need to be considered, as well as the potential for on-site energy generation.

Enhance connective transportation systems

Near universal automobile ownership had a profound decentralizing effect on cities. Low oil prices encouraged trucking as an alternative to railroad freight. Today the congestion on highways and arterial streets has revived the construction of transit systems, and higher costs of fuel and the invention of containerization are bringing back railroads as freight carriers. The many destinations in today's decentralized regions are also creating a demand for high-speed passenger rail as a way to reduce congestion on highways and at airports. Airports are a strong centralizing influence, creating related hotel, office, and warehouse development around them, and becoming a destination for high-speed rail and transit systems. City design, while it must continue to deal with automotive access and parking requirements, must now respond to the new centralizing influences of rail and air transportation. This puts an emphasis on creating larger ensembles of apartment, retail, hotel, and office buildings that usually have been separated by parking requirements and decentralized access.

Understand the design implications of new economic systems

New functional patterns are being created as metropolitan areas grow together to create regional cities and super-regional urbanized areas, and respond to the global market place by specialization in the economic areas where the region has the greatest competitive advantage. Preconceptions about cities as all-purpose downtowns surrounded by suburbs have to be replaced by an understanding of the location and specialization of centers in a multi-city region. The old downtowns may continue to have significant functions as office, cultural, entertainment, and administrative centers, but there may well be other important office and retail centers, a new center near the airport, a medical research center, other research parks related to universities, employment concentrations related to different industries, resort concentrations, and specialized agriculture. The social geography of the region has also changed, with high-density residential locations in what were once suburbs or even rural areas. The city designer has to understand what the city is becoming, and make design proposals that relate to current economic realities.

Promote compact business centers and walkable neighborhoods

Walking is the most efficient form of short-distance transportation, as well as the most productive of pleasant experiences. The places that attract the most tourists are almost always walkable. One of the great defects of modernist city design was its romantic belief in the viability of speeding to destinations in fast cars. This concept may have seemed plausible in the 1920s, when car ownership was still confined to a relatively small group, but the speed goes away in urban areas when everyone has a car. As Jane Jacobs, Jan Gehl, and William H. Whyte have documented, the casual interactions among people that are among the greatest advantages of urban life, are lost when cars are the only way to go from place to place. The automobile has conferred great mobility and freedom which no one is prepared to give up, but business centers should be designed so that people can walk to other offices, to health clubs, or places to have lunch, and neighborhoods should be designed so that people can walk or bicycle to schools or convenience stores, and can visit informally. The re-emergence of local transit and the creation of high-speed rail also strongly suggest the need for walkable places around stations as the means of access to the concentrated development that is the usual consequence of a railroad or transit station.

Design for modern building types and parking requirements

Advocates of traditional city design sometimes produce detailed plans, and accompanying codes, filled with building types that have rarely been constructed since the 1920s. It is true that most modern building types assume an auto-based sprawl configuration, but it is not productive to try to correct this problem by expecting developers to go back to historic economic and social conditions. The challenge is to design modern buildings that will fit into a walkable public open space system. Another challenge is to design for groups of modern buildings that can adapt to topography and other existing site conditions rather than relying solely on engineering. Systems city designs also have to accept building typologies the real-estate industry is willing to construct; and infrastructure must be associated with something that produces income if it is to be feasible.

At-grade parking spaces are an enemy of urbanity. City designers can reduce parking requirements by sharing parking among uses which have demand peaks at different times of the day. An obvious example is the parking lot for the football stadium that is only used a few times a year, usually on weekends, and could easily provide parking for a substantial office concentration. Shopping centers and hotels also have peak parking demand at different times from workplaces. Smaller businesses can share parking also, if the parking on individual properties is part of a larger access system. Garage parking can become feasible if the development is sufficiently intensive. The land cost for a hotel, office, or residential building on a shopping center property could be the cost of decanting the retail parking into a garage.

The city designer has to meet the requirements of real-estate investors while creating the benefits of superior city-design configurations.

Make the big public design decisions through a public process

Just having a series of big public meetings where people take votes is not an effective way to guide a decision-making process about city design. A public meeting is much better at articulating what is wrong with a city-design proposal than inventing an alternative. Also, some of the people most concerned, rival property investors, elected public officials, administrative personnel worried about their employment future, may not say what they really think in a large public meeting. There need to be two component parts to the public process. There should be a working committee of no more than thirty people which can meet without the public and the press, and the public meetings where the tentative conclusions of the working committee are reviewed and either rejected or endorsed.

The working committee needs to include representatives of all the constituencies—often described as stakeholders—whose agreement will be needed if the city design is to be implemented. The committee must include representatives of the developer or developers who will build according to the design, representatives of the government bodies that must approve the design, civic advocates, design experts, and community leaders. As noted in the Introduction, not having such a committee as part of the public process for rebuilding the World Trade Center site was a significant reason why the process failed.

However, if the working committee proceeds to conclusions without checking each step with the public, the process can also fail. So a public meeting should present each step in the working committee's decision process, and members of the committee should attend the public discussion to hear what people have to say.

The decision-making process needs to follow a logical order. It requires consultants to prepare the materials for discussion and also a strong chair for the working committee and the public meetings who has the respect of the important players and can pull the proceedings back from incoherence and irrelevance. A logical first step is to seek a definition of a desirable outcome that everyone can agree to support. The definition will inevitably be general in order to embody consensus, but it becomes a means of measuring the desirability of various proposals as they come up in discussion. The next step can be a systematic survey of potential design concepts that go some way towards fulfilling the definition of a desirable outcome. It is important to present a wide range of design alternatives at this point to reassure the participants that the process is an open one. The alternatives can include different design approaches as well as different programs and objectives. The next step is to narrow the alternatives to those that should be developed further. Next a preferred alternative has to be selected, and then there needs to be a discussion of how the design proposal should be worked out in detail.

This process can be messy, but if followed conscientiously it usually does work. There will never be unanimity, but those in the minority will understand the position of the others even if they don't agree. Completely unresponsive participants, who will never change their initial position, will eventually be marginalized. Making a significant city-design decision this way, about a revised code, the alignment of a new road or transit system, the construction of a new business center, or the rebuilding of an urban neighborhood, can easily take a year. Success is achieved when committee members and the public understand the issues thoroughly and want to stop talking and make a decision. The result will be faster and less controversial official approvals, and a much greater likelihood that developers will follow the design, rather than start the whole process over again.

City design decisions affect everyone. The public should participate and be able to make an informed choice.

Notes

Introduction

1   For a comprehensive discussion of the complex interaction of global demographics and technological change see *The Scale of Urban Change Worldwide*, by David Satterthwaite, International Institute for Environment and Development, 2005.

2   *Shadow Cities: A Billion Squatters, A New Urban World*, by Robert Neuwirth, Routledge, 2006.

3   Source: The National Association of Home Builders, statistics from 1978–2008.

4   The US Army Corps of Engineers released a report admitting these failures on June 1, 2006.

5   See for example, *Six Degrees, Our Future on a Hotter Planet*, by Mark Lynas, Fourth Estate, 2007.

6   The local effect of sea-level rise is modified by whether coast lines are rising or subsiding, and whether the land is in an earthquake zone.

7   *New York Times* editorial, July 17, 2002.

8   *Up From Zero*, by Paul Goldberger, Random House, 2004, and *Imagining Ground Zero: Official and Unofficial Proposals for the World Trade Center Site*, by Suzanne Stephens with Ian Luna and Ron Broadhurst, Architectural Record, Rizzoli, 2004.

9   Designers of the Battery Park City Plan were Alexander Cooper and Stanton Eckstut. The plan is discussed in Chapter 3.

10 *Design with Nature* by Ian McHarg, originally published by the Museum of Natural History Press, 1969.

1 Modernist city design

1   Peter Gay's *Modernism, The Lure of Heresy*, Norton, 2007, a discussion of modernism in all the arts, gives a good overview of modern architecture's cultural context.

2   *The CIAM Discourse on Urbanism, 1928–1960*, by Eric Mumford, MIT Press, 2002, provides the most complete history of the CIAM, its deliberations, and its policy prescriptions.

3   For an excellent discussion of the origins and progress of modern architectural theory going back even before the eighteenth century, see *Modern Architectural Theory: A Historical Survey, 1673–1968*, by Harry Francis Mallgrave, Cambridge University Press, 2005.

4   Mumford, as previously cited, p. 18.

5   Frederick Etchells, English designer and painter, lived in Paris during the experimental days of modern painting before World War I and was associated with Roger Fry, Vanessa Bell, and Duncan Grant in the Bloomsbury-connected Omega Workshop and then with Wyndham Lewis, Ezra Pound, and other Vorticists. He later became an architect.

6   A good account in English is *Weissenhof 1927 and the Modern Movement in Architecture*, by Richard Pommer and Christian F. Otto, The University of Chicago Press, 1991. The participating architects in addition to Mies were Peter Behrens who had been an employer for both Mies and Le Corbusier before World War I; Belgian architect Victor Bourgeois, whose building was technically on an adjacent site; Richard Docker from Stuttgart who was the executive architect for the whole project; Josef Frank from Vienna; Walter Gropius, head of the Bauhaus in Dessau; Ludwig Hilberseimer, a good friend of Mies; Le Corbusier; Dutch architect J.J.P. Oud, who was briefly considered a leading proponent of modernism; Hans Poelzig, a prominent architect, like Behrens, from an older generation; Adolf Rading, included for political reasons; Hans Scharoun, a somewhat surprising inclusion as he was a proponent of a more expressionistic architecture; Adolf Schneck, a local Stuttgart architect best known for his furniture design; young Dutch architect Mart Stam; Bruno Taut, often unfairly overlooked in histories of modern architecture; and Max Taut.

7   Sigfried Giedion, "L'Exposition du Werkbund a Stuttgart 1927" and "La Cité du Weissenhof" in *Architecture Vivante*, Paris, 1928 as translated and quoted by himself in *Space, Time and Architecture*, 3rd edition, enlarged, Harvard University Press, 1954, page 549 and ff. On page 550 is an aerial photo of the Weissenhof houses vignetted within a curved, free-form shape, helping to disguise the banality of the actual plan.

8   *Richard Neutra and the Search for Modern Architecture*, by Thomas S. Hines, Rizzoli, 2005 is a readable, thoroughly researched and well-illustrated account of Neutra's buildings and career. An earlier version was published in 1982. The information about the number of copies of *Wie Baut Amerika?* is on p. 83 of the 2005 edition.

9   For a somewhat convoluted discussion of what lay behind Hilberseimer's projects, see *Modernism and the Posthumanist Subject*, by K. Michael Hays, MIT Press, 1992.

10   The English translation is by Gropius himself from the version of his CIAM presentation that he published in a collection of his essays, *Scope of Total Architecture*, Allen & Unwin, 1956, chapter 10, pp. 114, 115.

11   For an illuminating discussion of the way that Bauhaus architects dealt with the Nazi regime see "Bauhaus Architecture in the Third Reich," by Winfried Nordinger in *Bauhaus Culture from Weimar to the Cold War*, edited by Kathleen James-Chakraborty, University of Minnesota Press, 2006, pp. 139–152.

12   Mies continued to practice architecture, mainly exhibition design, in Nazi Germany until he moved to the United States in 1937. For an account of the last days of the Bauhaus and of Gropius's version of Bauhaus history as presented at the Museum of Modern Art in New York City in 1938, see "The Bauhaus, 1919–1928, Gropius in Exile and the Museum of Modern Art, 1938," by Karen Koehler in *Art, Culture and Media Under the Third Reich*, edited by Richard A. Etlin, University of Chicago Press, 2002.

13 The quotes from Gropius are again from his own translation published in *Scope of Total Architecture*, chapter 11.

14 This chronology comes from *The International Style: Exhibition 15 and the Museum of Modern Art*, by Terence Riley, Rizzoli, 1992, which is the definitive account of the exhibition as Riley had access to the archives of the Museum of Modern Art. There is an introductory note to the book by Philip Johnson, who was then eighty-six, saying that his recollections were sometimes different but that Riley must be correct. For more about the interesting life of Philip Johnson, including his youthful admiration for Huey Long, Father Coughlin, and the Nazi regime and his later role as a leader of US architectural discourse, see *Philip Johnson, Life and Work*, by Franz Schulze, Knopf, 1994.

15 *The International Style*, by Henry-Russell Hitchcock and Philip Johnson, Norton, 1966, p. 11. This is a reprint of the original 1932 edition with a new foreword and appendix by Hitchcock.

16 Ibid., p. 19.

17 Giedion illustrates this plan and writes approvingly about it in *Space, Time and Architecture* but does not mention van Eesteren.

18 Published by the Harvard University Press, and by the Oxford Press in England. Despite the apocalyptic title, the book has nothing to do with World War II. It may have already been in production when the Japanese bombed Pearl Harbor, although the war in Europe had begun in 1939.

19 There is an account of the genesis of Le Corbusier's version of the Charter in Eric Mumford's book, previously cited, pp. 154–155, and Robert Fishman analyzes Le Corbusier's attempts to serve the Vichy government in *Urban Utopias of the Twentieth Century*, MIT Press, 1977, pp. 243–253.

20 The comparison of Parkchester with New York City's existing zoning is discussed by Simon Eisner and Arthur Gallion in *The Urban Pattern*, 3rd edition.

21 See the chapter by Winfried Nordinger cited under 11, above.

22 Mies was originally hired by Armour Institute of Technology in 1937 which merged with Lewis Institute to become the Illinois Institute of Technology in 1940.

23 *The New City: Principles of Planning*, by Ludwig Hilberseimer, Paul Theobald, Chicago, 1944.

24 "Brutalism" was a pun on *beton brut*, French for unfinished concrete, often with the marks of the formwork showing. This was a favorite material of Le Corbusier in his later work and influenced other architects for a time, particularly in the 1960s. Peter Smithson, Reyner Banham and others sought to popularize the terms *brutalism* and the *new brutalism* as epitomizing an architectural philosophy. Why they thought either the architecture or the philosophy would have wide appeal is a mystery.

25 The original Catalan spelling of his name is Josep Lluis Sert; in the US during his lifetime Sert tended to use the anglicized spelling, as on the title page of his book *Can Our Cities Survive?*

26 The definitive account of the whole history of CIAM is Eric Mumford's book, cited above.

27 A substantial transcript of the conference was published by *Progressive Architecture*, August, 1956. *Harvard Design Magazine* devoted its Spring/Summer issue in 2006 to essays about the significance of this conference as seen fifty years later.

28 Aline Saarinen in a discussion at Yale in 1962 attended by the author.

29 *Art*, by Clive Bell, 1913. Bell was married to Vanessa Stephen, Virginia Woolf's sister.

30   *Eero Saarinen On His Work: A Selection of Buildings Dating 1947–1964*, by Aline B. Saarinen, Yale University Press, 1962.

31   *Changing Ideals in Modern Architecture 1750–1950*, by Peter Collins, McGill University Press, 1965, pp. 272 and following.

32   The illustration from the Chicago History Museum is included in a catalog of built work and projects in New York City, 1934–1968 in *Robert Moses and the Modern City*, edited by Hilary Ballon and Kenneth T. Jackson, Norton, 2007. Mies's involvement in the project ended when the developer, Herbert Greenwald, who had also been the developer for other projects by Mies, was killed in a plane crash in 1959.

33   Ole Scheeren in a presentation at Tong Ji University in Shanghai in 2005 attended by the author.

34   For an interesting discussion of possible ways to use and understand algorithms in architecture see *Algorithmic Architecture*, by Kostas Terzidis, Architectural Press, 2006.

35   Maxwell Fry's recollections about the design of Chandigarh can be found in *The Open Hand: Essays on Le Corbusier*, MIT Press, 1977.

36   *Edge City, Life on the New Frontier*, by Joel Garreau, Doubleday, 1991.

2 Traditional city design and the modern city

1   Honors received by Richard Rogers include the Gold Medal of the Royal Institute of British Architects, the Stirling Prize, the Pritzker Prize, and, from the British government, a knighthood, followed by a life peerage, making him Baron Rogers of Riverside, and then designation as a Companion of Honour.

2   *Guardian*, June 12, 2009.

3   Architects Dixon, Jones with Michael Squire, and Kim Wilkie, landscape architect.

4   *The Times*, June 4, 2009.

5   John Summerson's *Sir Christopher Wren*, Archon Books, 1965 is both readable and informed by a deep knowledge of art history. A more recent account, supported by extensive documentation, is *His Invention So Fertile, A Life of Christopher Wren*, by Adrian Tinniswood, Oxford, 2001. *London Rising, The Men Who Made Modern London*, by Leo Hollis, Walker, 2008, is an account of the rebuilding of London after the Great Fire that uses Wren's life as a principal focus.

6   First published in 1537.

7   Lewis Mumford, *The City in History, Its Origins, Its Transformations, and Its Prospects*, Harcourt, 1961, p. 370. "The rich ride, the poor walk . . . Insolence battens on servility."

8   Earl of Bedford is the correct title for the period. The head of the family owning the Covent Garden properties did not become the Duke of Bedford until 1694.

9   John Summerson, *Inigo Jones*, Penguin Books, 1966 and also *Georgian London*, originally published 1945, revised edition, Pelican Books, 1962.

10   John Summerson, "John Wood and the English Town Planning Tradition," in *Heavenly Mansions*, Cressett Press, 1949.

11   John Wood published an illustrated *Description of Bath* in 1749 including his theories about its history going back to the days of the Britons and the Romans.

12   *Washington, The Making of the American Capital*, by Fergus M. Brodewich, Amistad, 2008 is a good account of the political and financial background for the development of Washington. Brodewich describes how important the location of the City was to the backers of slavery, and how important slave labor was to its early construction.

13 A good account of L'Enfant's life and struggles is *Grand Avenues, The Story of the French Visionary who Designed Washington, DC*, by Scott W. Berg, Pantheon 2007.

14 Elbert Peets, "The Genealogy of L'Enfant's Washington," *Journal of the American Institute of Architects*, April, May, June, 1927.

15 But the axis at the University of Virginia was closed by Cabell Hall, designed by Stanford White, in 1899, much as White's partner, Charles McKim, and Daniel Burnham closed L'Enfant's axes with the Lincoln and Jefferson Memorials in the 1903 McMillan Plan for Washington; see page 84.

16 The Louisiana Purchase, 1803.

17 Tristan Edwards, *Good and Bad Manners in Architecture*, Philip Alan, 1924. See also John Summerson, *The Life and Work of John Nash, Architect*, MIT Press, 1980.

18 See the account of Parisian height limits by Norma Evenson in, *Paris: A Century of Change, 1878–1978*, Yale University Press, 1979.

19 An excellent description of the transformation of Paris in the mid-nineteenth century can be found in Sigfried Giedion's *Space, Time and Architecture*, published by the Harvard University Press, originally in 1941. A more recent account is *Haussmann, His Life and Times, and the Making of Modern Paris* by Michael Carmona, translated by Patrick Camiller, Ivan R Dee, 2002. *Les Promenades de Paris* by Haussmann's collaborator, the landscape architect, Adolphe Alphand, was reissued by the Princeton Architectural Press in 1985.

20 Robert Moses, "What Happened to Haussmann?" *Architectural Forum*, July, 1942.

21 See Richard Chafee, "The Teaching of Architecture at the Ecole Des Beaux Arts," *The Architecture of the Ecole Des Beaux-Arts*, edited by Arthur Drexler, Museum of Modern Art, MIT Press, 1977. Students were required to follow the sketch design they produced at the beginning of a project to help prove that the final design was the student's own work, but the requirement took for granted that the concept could be established from the beginning of the design process, rather than being created as the product.

22 See *Daniel H. Burnham, Architect, Planner of Cities*, by Charles Moore (Burnham's long-time assistant, not the architect Charles W. Moore), originally published 1921, Da Capo Press, 1968; also *Burnham of Chicago*, by Thomas S. Hines, Oxford University Press, 1974. A more sceptical view: "Toward an 'Imperial City': Daniel H. Burnham and the City Beautiful Movement," by Mario Manieri-Elia, translated by Barbara Luigia La Penta, in *The American City from the Civil War to the New Deal*, MIT Press, 1979. The 1909 *Plan for Chicago*, by Daniel H. Burnham and Edward H. Bennett was reissued by Da Capo Press in 1970.

23 Washington, DC, enacted a height limit in 1894, soon after elevator buildings came into use, initially because of neighborhood protests over a tall apartment house. The law limited apartment buildings to a height of 90 feet and office buildings to 110 feet. This local law was confirmed by acts of Congress in 1898 and 1910 which were more restrictive as maximum heights could only be realized on wide streets. With minor modifications these height limits continue in effect.

24 For Canberra, see Walter Burley Griffin's *The Federal City*, and James Birrell's monograph, *Walter Burley Griffin*, University of Queensland Press, 1964.

25 Robert Grant Irving's *Indian Summer, Lutyens, Baker and Imperial Delhi*, Yale University Press, 1981 is an extensive and well-illustrated account of the design of the new capital.

26 Camillo Sitte, *Der Stadte-Bau nach seinen Kunsterischen Grundsatzen*, originally published in Vienna in 1889, was translated by George R. Collins and Christiane C. Collins

and published by Random House in 1965 under the title: *City Planning According to Artistic Principles*. See also, by the same authors, *Camillo Sitte and the Birth of Modern City Planning*, Random House, 1965.

27   See Kenneth Frampton's "A Synoptic View of Architecture of the Third Reich" in *Oppositions* 12 (Spring, 1978). The same issue also contains an interview with Albert Speer by Francesco Dal Co and Sergio Polano.

28   See *The Third Rome 1870–1950, Traffic and Glory*, an exhibition catalogue by Spiro Kostoff, Berkeley, 1973.

29   Volume 19 of *Studies of the Warburg Institute*. The articles on the *Principles of Palladio's Architecture* collected in this volume had originally been published in Volume VII, 1944, pp. 102–122 and Volume VIII, 1945, pp. 68–102, of the *Journal of the Warburg and Courtauld Institutes*. Other material in the book had been published earlier in the same journal.

30   The Tiranti edition was published in 1952.

31   Wittkower's *Architectural Principles of the Age of Humanism*, p. 93 of the 1952 Tiranti edition.

32   "The Mathematics of the Ideal Villa" was first published in *The Architectural Review* in 1947, and later in *The Mathematics of the Ideal Villa and Other Essays* by Colin Rowe, MIT Press, 1976.

33   Published in French in 1948 and 1955; in English in 1954 and 1958. In an opening chapter, Le Corbusier describes a long chronology for the development of his Modulor theory.

34   Le Corbusier, *Le Modulor*, on p. 63 of the first English edition, Faber, 1954.

35   According to music critic Harold Schonberg writing in the *New York Times* in 1959, as quoted by Franz Schulze in *Philip Johnson, Life and Work*, 1996, p. 260.

36   Lincoln Center is currently being remodeled, beginning with a radical transformation of Belluschi's Julliard School buildings designed by Diller Scofidio + Renfro. It will be interesting to see if a coordinated modern design for the whole complex can emerge from this process.

37   See the account by Christopher Gray, "A 1960's Protest That Tried to Save a Piece of the Past" in the *New York Times*, May 20, 2001.

38   Herbert Gans, *The Urban Villagers, Group and Class in the Life of Italian Americans*, Free Press, 1962.

39   William H. Whyte, *The Last Landscape*, Doubleday, 1968.

40   William H. Whyte, *The Social Life of Small Urban Spaces*, The Conservation Foundation, 1980, and *City, Rediscovering the Center*, Doubleday, 1988.

41   Penn Central Transportation Co. v. New York City, decided June, 1978.

42   Colin Rowe and Fred Koetter, *Collage City*, MIT Press, 1978. An earlier version appeared in the *Architectural Review*, August, 1975.

43   "Roma Interrotta," *Architectural Design Profile* 49(3–4) (March, 1979).

44   As described in the opening sections of *Seaside: Making a Town in America*, by Keller Easterling and Thomas Mohony, Princeton Architectural Press, 1996.

45   Peter Katz, *The New Urbanism, Toward an Architecture of Community*, McGraw Hill, 1994. The six founders of the Congress were Peter Calthorpe, Andres Duany, Elizabeth Plater-Zyberk, Stefanos Polyzoides, Elizabeth Moule, and Daniel Solomon.

46   An illustrated book, *Charter of the New Urbanism*, was published by the Congress for the New Urbanism, McGraw Hill, 1999. I wrote an introduction "What's New about the New Urbanism?," and contributed a section on "Neighborhood, District and Corridor."

47   From the text published on the Driehaus Prize website.

3 Green city design and climate change

1   Melting sea ice does not raise sea levels because the ice displaces an equivalent volume of liquid, just as melting ice cubes do not raise the level in a glass of water.

2   "A semi-empirical approach to projecting future sea-level rise," by S. Rahmstorf, *Science* 315, pp. 368–370, 2007.

3   See *Six Degrees, Our Future on a Hotter Planet*, by Mark Lynas, Fourth Estate, 2007. Lynas marshals a convincing array of scientific papers to show that humanity should do everything possible to control greenhouse gas emissions before the world gets too hot for us. He also argues that this is not necessarily something that could happen only in several centuries; there is a chance it could happen in the lifetimes of people already alive.

4   Robin M. Mills, *The Myth of the Oil Crisis*, Prager, 2008.

5   Geoffrey and Susan Jellicoe, *The Landscape of Man*, Thames & Hudson, 1987, p. 27.

6   Loraine Kuck, *The World of the Japanese Garden: from Chinese Origins to Modern Landscape Art*, Weatherhill, 1980.

7   *Het gezantschap der Neerlandtsche Ost-Indische Compagnie, aan den grooten Tartarischen cham, den tegenwoordigen keizer van China*. The Dutch Head of State, William of Orange, also became King of England in 1688, and there were close connections between the two countries during this period.

8   Prince Charles has published a book of his own watercolor landscapes entitled *HRH. the Prince of Wales: Watercolours*, Little Brown, 1991.

9   According to David Watkin in *The English Vision, The Picturesque in Architecture, Landscape and Garden Design*, Icon Editions, Harper & Row, 1982.

10   A remarkable website which permits you to make an extensive virtual tour of the gardens at Stowe is http://faculty.bsc.edu/jtatter/stowe.html, maintained by John D. Tatter of Birmingham-Southern College.

11   *Designs of Chinese buildings, furniture, dresses, machines, and utensils: to which is annexed a description of their temples, houses, gardens, &c*, London, 1757 and *A Dissertation on Oriental Gardening*, by Sir William Chambers, London 1772. The second edition of Chambers' *Dissertation* has been digitized and can be read on line. It includes a fictional account ostensibly written by a Chinese garden designer, and is an interesting example of the polemic that surrounded English garden design in the eighteenth century.

12   Brown's actual first name was Lancelot. It is said that he invariably told his prospective clients of the great capability of their land for improvement. As he was not from the upper classes, and his clients were, the slightly derisive nickname became how he was known.

13   This is the origin of the term according to Horace Walpole, amateur architect and historian, novelist, and prolific letter writer, in his essay "The Modern Taste in Gardening" in volume four of his *Anecdotes of Painting in England*, 1771. The reference is from David Watkin's *The English Vision* as cited above.

14   The first version of Price's essay was published in 1794.

15   Also published in 1794, as quoted by David Watkin in *The English Vision*, cited above. Knight, a wealthy eccentric, also published his *Analytical Inquiry into the Principles of Taste* in 1806, giving his opinions on just about everything including his disagreements with Uvedale Price and Edmund Burke's essay on *The Sublime and The Beautiful*.

16   But not by Knight, who also criticized Repton in *The Landscape*, but for different reasons. A readable history of the origins and competing elements of picturesque theory is

The Picturesque, Studies in a Point of View, by Christopher Hussey, G.P. Putnam, 1927. Hussey was for many years the architectural editor of the English periodical, *Country Life*.

17   A good account of early suburban development can be found in the opening chapters of Robert Fishman's *Bourgeois Utopias: The Rise and Fall of Suburbia*, Basic Books, 1989.

18   Alphand documented his work in a book, *Les promenades de Paris*, originally published between 1867 and 1873, and reprinted by the Princeton Architectural Press in 1984.

19   Frederick Law Olmsted to Riverside Improvement Corporation in *Civilizing American Cities: a Selection of Frederick Law Olmsted's Writings On City Landscapes*, edited by Sharon B. Sutton, MIT Press, 1979, pp. 292–305.

20   Anne was Queen of England from 1702 to 1714, roughly in the middle of the much longer period of work that inspired the term.

21   An early National Park, designated in 1890.

22   *The Landscape Urbanism Reader*, edited by Charles Waldheim, Princeton Architectural Press, 2006.

23   Walter Creese, in his book *The Search for Environment*, suggests that Ebenezer Howard may have seen Olmsted's design for Riverside being implemented while he was living in Chicago, and Creese also speculates that Howard might have been aware that Chicago before the fire had been known as the "Garden City," because of its tree-lined streets and well-cared-for yards.

24   As quoted by Frederic J. Osborn in his preface to the 1945 Faber and Faber edition of *Garden Cities of Tomorrow*.

25   A reprint of *Town Planning in Practice* was published by the Princeton Architectural Press in 1994.

26   As quoted in *The Housing Book*, by William Phillips Comstock, Comstock, 1919, p. 14.

27   The planning of Norris is described in Mel Scott's *American City Planning since 1890*, University of California Press, 1971, pp. 312–315. For a more general discussion of the TVA see Walter L. Creese, *TVA's Public Planning, the Vision, the Reality*, University of Tennessee Press, 1990.

28   "The City in Agrarian Ideology and Frank Lloyd Wright: Origins and Development of Broadacres" by Giorgio Ciucci in *The American City from the Civil War to the New Deal*, translated by Barbara Luigia La Penta, MIT Press, 1979.

29   *Crabgrass Frontier, The Suburbanization of the United States*, by Kenneth T. Jackson, Oxford, 1985.

30   An interesting, if somewhat censorious, description of the evolution of Levittown house plans can be found in "The Levittown Look" by Robert Schultz in *Architecture of the Everyday*, edited by Steven Harris and Deborah Berke, Princeton Architectural Press, 1997.

31   See, for example, the chapter "The Misplacing of America" in *Changing Places, Rebuilding Community in the Age of Sprawl*, by Richard Moe and Carter Wilkie, Henry Holt, 1999, and *Edge City: Life on the New Frontier*, by Joel Garreau, Doubleday, 1988.

32   This seemingly paradoxical situation is explained in *Nixon and the Environment*, by J. Brooks Flippen, University of New Mexico Press, 2000.

33   *Design with Nature*, by Ian L. McHarg, with an introduction by Lewis Mumford, was originally published by the Museum of Natural History in 1969. This book is still in print in a John Wiley edition of 1995.

Notes

34   For a discussion of the historical importance of Ian McHarg and the development of the relationship between ecology, planning, and design, see *Ecological Planning: A Historical and Comparative Synthesis*, by Forster Ndubisi, Johns Hopkins, 2002.

35   *Performance Zoning*, by Lane Kendig with Susan Connor, Cranston Byrd, and Judy Heyman, Planners Press, 1980.

36   For a discussion of trends worldwide in evaluating energy use and other sustainability factors see "Sustainability Assessment in a Global Market," by Ali Malkawi and Fried Augenbroe, *Wharton Real Estate Review*, Fall 2009.

37   The maps come from a study of the Seven-County Orlando Region prepared by the Urban Design Studio at the University of Pennsylvania in 2005 under the direction of professor Jonathan Barnett.

4 Systems city design

1   Warren Weaver was a mathematician who for many years was the director of the Rockefeller Foundation's Program for the Natural and Medical Sciences. Jane Jacobs writes that she is quoting from an essay by Weaver published in the Foundation's Annual Report for 1958. Two Rockefeller Foundation grants supported the writing of Jacobs's book, *The Death and Life of Great American Cities*. Weaver's initial writings about complex problems were published in the 1940s as "Science and Complexity," *American Scientist* 36, p. 536 (1948) based on material presented in Chapter 1 of *The Scientists Speak*, Boni & Gaer, 1947.

2   Jane Jacobs, *The Death and Life of Great American Cities*, Random House, 1961, chapter 22, "The Kind of Problem a City Is."

3   Herbert Gans, *The Urban Villagers, Group and Class in the Life of Italian-Americans*, The Free Press, 1962. Gans's method was to actually live in the West End and observe and get to know his neighbors. One of Gans's conclusions was that the place worked for the people who were living there, despite physical deficiencies. The real reason the West End was torn down was probably to obtain the land for redevelopment, for which the statistical diagnosis of slum conditions was a justification, but one that was accepted as standard practice.

4   Steven Johnson, *Emergence: The Connected Lives of Ants, Brains, Cities, and Software*, Scribner, 2002.

5   "Swarm Urbanism," by Neal Leach in *Architectural Design*, July/August, 2009.

6   Stephen Wolfram, *A New Kind of Science*, Wolfram Media, 2002.

7   Wolfram, as previously cited, pp. 24–30.

8   Michael Batty, *Cities and Complexity: Understanding Cities with Cellular Automata, Agent-Based Models and Fractals*, MIT Press, 2005.

9   Batty, as previously cited, p. 457.

10   "A Digital Breeder for Designing Cities," by Michael Batty, *Architectural Design*, July/August 2009.

11   For a good summary of current research about human development before historical records began, and the relationship of that development to natural resources, see Jared Diamond's *Guns, Germs, and Steel*, Norton, 1996. Another good summary can be found in the opening pages of Jeffrey Sachs, *Common Wealth: Economics for a Crowded Planet*, Penguin Press, 2008. Lewis Mumford also addresses the first steps in the development of human settlements in *The City in History*, Harcourt, 1961. Mumford's book is a brilliant work of synthesis and interpretation, but his early chapters rely on

now-outdated research about prehistoric settlements. Mumford also tries to convince the reader that village life was inherently peace-loving and that wars did not begin to take place until cities grew up and required centralized organization under despotic leaders. The notion of prehistory as an age of innocence has a long literary pedigree but unfortunately is not very likely.

12   The edition of Vitruvius (Marcus Vitruvius Pollio), *The Ten Books on Architecture*, consulted is the translation by Morris Hicky Morgan, completed by Herbert L. Warren, published by the Harvard University Press in 1914, and republished by Dover in 1960.

13   The importance of this "armature" in Roman cities is stressed by William MacDonald in his *The Architecture of the Roman Empire, volume II: An Urban Reappraisal*, Yale, 1986.

14   Karl Gruber, *Eine deutsche Stadt: Bilder zur Entwicklungsgeschichte der Stadtbaukunst*, Bruckmann, 1914.

15   The quotation from the Law of the Indies as promulgated on July 13, 1573 is from *Spanish City Planning in North America*, by Dora P. Crouch, Daniel J. Garr, and Axel I. Mundigo, MIT Press, 1982, p. 14.

16   The French did fortify their cities in North America, as memorialized by Rampart Street in New Orleans which had been founded by the French. Napoleon took New Orleans back from Spain in 1801, but then sold it to the United States two years later as part of the Louisiana Purchase.

17   Historians of rail systems point out that the Greeks used wooden rails when they pulled ships across the Isthmus of Corinth in classical times.

18   Statistics from *Railway Economy: A Treatise on the New Art of Transport, its Management, Prospects and Relations, Commercial, Financial, and Social*, by Dionysius Lardner, Harper, 1850, p. 177.

19   Sigfried Giedion's *Space, Time and Architecture, the Growth of a New Tradition*, originally published by the Harvard University Press in 1941, includes an excellent history of the development of modern building technology.

20   Walter Christaller, *Central Places in Southern Germany*. Translated by Carlisle W. Baskin from *Die Zentralen Orte in Süddeutschland*, originally published by Gustav Fischer in 1933, Prentice Hall, 1966.

21   Christaller, a member of the Nazi party, worked for Heinrich Himmler replanning territories conquered by the Nazi regime. This history has caused some to view central place theory as authoritarian, but simplistic and outmoded would be better descriptions.

22   Homer Hoyt, *The Structure and Growth of Residential Neighbourhoods in American Cities*, Federal Housing Administration / US Government Printing Office, 1939.

23   *The City*, by Robert E. Park, Ernest W. Burgess, Roderick D. McKenzie; with a bibliography by Louis Wirth, University of Chicago Press, 1928.

24   See the discussion on page 141.

25   *Annals of the American Academy of Political and Social Science* 242(1), p. 7–17 (1945).

26   Joel Garreau, *Edge City: Life on the New Frontier*, Doubleday, 1991.

27   Christopher Alexander, *Notes on the Synthesis of Form*, Harvard University Press, 1964.

28   I prepared a condensation of the book that was reviewed and approved by Alexander and published in the *Architectural Record* in 1965.

29   I was present at the American Institute of Architects Conference in New York City in 1967 when Alexander's letter was read to the assembly. Alexander now prominently lists the award in his curriculum vitae.

30 Christopher Alexander, Sara Ishikawa, Murray Silverstein, with Max Jacobson, Ingrid Fiksdahl-King, and Shlomo Angel, *A Pattern Language, Town, Buildings, Construction*, Oxford, 1977.

31 Christopher Alexander, *The Linz Café, Das Linz Café*, Oxford University Press and Locker Verlag, 1981.

32 Christopher Alexander, Hajo Neis, Artemis Anninou, Ingrid King, *A New Theory of Urban Design*, Oxford University Press, 1987. The studio at UC Berkeley on which this book is based took place in 1978.

33 Christopher Alexander, *The Timeless Way of Building*, Oxford University Press, 1979.

34 Christopher Alexander: *The Phenomenon of Life: Nature of Order, Book 1:* Center for Environmental Structure, 2001; *The Process of Creating Life: Nature of Order, Book 2:* Center for Environmental Structure, 2003; *A Vision of a Living World: The Nature of Order, Book 3*, The Center for Environmental Structure, 2004; *The Luminous Ground: The Nature of Order, Book 4*, Center for Environmental Structure, 2003.

35 Wittkower's book was a hot item in British architectural circles when Christopher Alexander was an architecture student at Cambridge.

36 I have written a more extended discussion about urban codes in the United States in a chapter of *Urban Coding*, edited by Stephen Marshall, Routledge, 2011. See also my "Regional Design: Local Codes as Cause and Cure of Sprawl" in *Planning for a New Century*, edited by Jonathan Barnett, Island Press, 2001.

37 See "Alternate Futures for the Seven-County Orlando Region," by Jonathan Barnett in *Smart Growth in a Changing World*, edited by Jonathan Barnett, Planners Press, 2007.

38 *Smart Growth in a Changing World*, as cited previously, pp. 7–16.

39 Armando Carbonell and Robert D. Yaro, "American Spatial Development and the New Megalopolis," *Land Lines* 17(2), 2005.

40 Robert E. Lang and Arthur C. Nelson, "Metropolitan America, Defining and Applying a New Geography" in *Megaregions, Planning for Global Competitiveness*, edited by Catherine L. Ross, Island Press, 2010.

41 Catherine L. Ross and Myungje Woo, "Identifying Megaregions in the United States" in *Megaregions, Planning for Global Competitiveness*, as cited previously.

Conclusion

1 Patrik Schumacher, "Parametric Urbanism," *Architectural Design*, July/August, 2009.

Illustration credits

Introduction

I.1 2008 Model photo
Model photo by Joe Woolhead, courtesy of Silverstein Properties.

I.2 Memorial Plaza model photo
Memorial Plaza by Beyer Blinder Belle, Cooper Robertson, courtesy Lower Manhattan Development Corporation.

1 Modernist city design

1.1 Aerial perspective of Garnier's Cité Industrielle
From *Une Cité Industrielle* by Tony Garnier, A. Vincent, Paris, 1918.

1.2 Le Corbusier 1922
From *Towards a New Architecture* by Le Corbusier, translated by Frederick Etchells, Rodker, London, 1927.

1.3 Le Corbusier Plan Voisin Paris
From *Le Corbusier*, edited by Willy Boesiger, Praeger 1972, © 2010 Artists Rights Society (ARS), New York/ADAGP, Paris/FLC.

1.4 Le Corbusier Domino
From *Towards a New Architecture* by Le Corbusier, translated by Frederick Etchells, Rodker, London, 1927.

1.5 Original study for Weissenhof
From *Modern Architecture* by Bruno Taut, London, the Studio, 1929.

1.6 Weissenhof as built
From *Modern Architecture* by Bruno Taut, London, the Studio, 1929.

2 Traditional city design and the modern city

2.1 Chelsea Barracks, Rogers

From press release materials provided by Rogers Stirk Harbour + Partners.

2.2 Chelsea Barracks, Rogers

From press release materials provided by Rogers Stirk Harbour + Partners.

2.3 Alternative sketch by Quinlan Terry

From press release material provided by Quinlan and Francis Terry LLP.

2.4 Wren's Plan for London

From *Civic Art* by Werner Hegemann and Elbert Peets, 1922.

2.5a Teatro Olimpico plan by Bertotti Scamozzi 1776

From *Le fabbriche e i disegni di Andrea Palladio* by Ottavio Bertotti Scamozzi.

2.5b Part of permanent set

Photo released into the public domain by Peter Geymeyer.

2.6 Fresco Vatican Library

From the University of Pennsylvania Library Image Collection.

2.7a Plan of the Piazza del Popolo

Plan is from a drawing by Ernest Farnham Lewis in *Landscape Architecture*, April 1914.

2.7b Piazza del Popolo today

Photographer, WolfgangM, licensed under Creative Commons Attribution 2.0.

2.8 Serlio Comedy

From *Sebastiano Serlio* Book II, University of Pennsylvania Library.

2.9 Serlio Tragic

From *Sebastiano Serlio* Book II, University of Pennsylvania Library.

2.10 Serlio Satyric

From *Sebastiano Serlio* Book II, University of Pennsylvania Library.

2.11 Michelangelo's Capitol at Rome

Engraving by Letrouilly from *Civic Art* by Werner Hegemann and Elbert Peets, 1922.

2.12 Plan for Versailles

Map by the Abbé Delagrive from 1746 from *Civic Art* by Werner Hegemann and Elbert Peets, 1922.

2.13 Leghorn, Peets

Sketch by Elbert Peets from *Civic Art* by Werner Hegemann and Elbert Peets, 1922.

2.14 Place des Vosges

Photo by AlNo, permission granted under GNU Free Documentation License.

2.15 Covent Garden

From the image collection of the University of Pennsylvania Library.

2.16 Circus and Royal Crescent at Bath

Drawing from *Civic Art* by Werner Hegemann and Elbert Peets, 1922.

2.17 Royal Crescent at Bath

Photo by Christophe Finot, permission according to Creative Commons.

2.18 Edinburgh from Unwin

From Raymond Unwin, *Town Planning in Practice*, London, 1909.

2.19 Jefferson Washington Plan

From the image collection of the University of Pennsylvania Library.

2.20 L'Enfant Plan for Washington

From *Civic Art* by Werner Hegemann and Elbert Peets, 1922.

2.21 Peets, Geneology

From the *Journal of the American Institute of Architects*, April, May, June, 1927.

2.22 Nash, Regent Street

From *Civic Art* by Werner Hegemann and Elbert Peets, 1922.

2.23 Nash, Regent's Park as built by 1833

Photograph of 1833 map by User Pointalist, released into the public domain.

2.24 Original design guidelines, Rue de Rivoli

From *Civic Art* by Werner Hegemann and Elbert Peets, 1922.

2.25 Progress report of 1867

From *Civic Art* by Werner Hegemann and Elbert Peets, 1922.

2.26 Haussmann boulevard

From Shepp's *Photos of the World*, 1892, collection of the author.

2.27 Haussmann and Alphand, promenades

From *Les Promenades De Paris* by Adolphe Alphand, 1867–1873.

2.28 Ringstrasse

From *The Art of Town Planning* by H.V. Lanchester, 1925.

2.29 Idelfons Cerdà 1859 map

From the image collection of the University of Pennsylvania library.

2.30 Paris street furniture

From *Les Promenades De Paris* by Adolphe Alphand, 1867–1873.

2.31 Court of Honor Chicago World's Fair

From the Goodyear Archival Collection, The Brooklyn Museum.

2.32 McMillan Plan for Washington

From *The Art of Town Planning* by H.V. Lanchester, 1925.

2.33 Burnham Plan for Chicago

From *The Plan for Chicago* by Daniel Burnham and Edward Bennett, Commercial Club of Chicago, 1909.

2.34 Burnham Plan height limits

From *The Plan for Chicago* by Daniel Burnham and Edward Bennett, Commercial Club of Chicago, 1909.

2.35 Chicago River

From *The Plan for Chicago* by Daniel Burnham and Edward Bennett, Commercial Club of Chicago, 1909.

3 Green city design and climate change

4 Systems city design

4.3   Wolfram page 25

Pages from Stephen Wolfram, *A New Kind of Science*, Wolfram Media, 2002, used by permission.

4.4   Michael Batty image

Graphics by Michael Batty from M. Batty (2009) "A Digital Breeder for Generating Cities," *Architectural Design* 79(4), July–August, Profile No. 200, 46–49. Used by permission.

4.5   Gruber 1

From Karl Gruber, *Ein Deutscher Stadt*, collection of the author.

4.6   Gruber 2

From Karl Gruber, *Ein Deutscher Stadt*, collection of the author.

4.7   Gruber 3

From Karl Gruber, *Ein Deutscher Stadt*, collection of the author.

4.8   Gruber 4

From Karl Gruber, *Ein Deutscher Stadt*, collection of the author.

4.9   Durand, *Précis des leçons*

From J.-N.-L. Durand, *Précis des leçons d'architecture*, collection of the author.

4.10 Crystal Palace

From a contemporary engraving, collection of the author.

4.11 Soria y Mata Linear City

From *The Art of Town Planning*, by H.V. Lanchester.

4.12 Christaller diagram

Diagram from Walter Christaller's *Die zentralen Orte in Süddeutschland*.

4.13 Map of urbanization on the Interstate

Map by Kyle Gradinger from a studio at the University of Pennsylvania, 2004.

4.14 Sant'Elia 1914

Drawing by Antonio Sant'Elia, from *Antonio Sant'Elia* [exhibition catalog] Como, 1962.

4.15 *Archigram 4*

From *Archigram 4*, collection of the author.

4.16 *Walking City*

From *Archigram 5*, collection of the author.

4.17 Habitat Montreal

From de Bild Habitat permission under GNU Free Documentation License.

4.18 Hong Kong Airport

From Maccess Corporation assigne of Alex Timbol permission under GNU Free Documentation License.

4.19 Steven Holl, linked hybrid

Lu Hou Photo.

4.20 RPA diagram

Courtesy Regional Plan Association.

4.21 Parisian height limits

From Paris Projet # 13–14.

4.22   New York zoning diagram

Diagram from New York City 1916 zoning regulations.

4.23   Central Park

Jerry Spearman Photo.

4.24   K Street

NM Photo.

4.25   Zoning map for Lincoln Square

From the New York City Zoning Resolution in 1974.

4.26   Conservation analysis

From the CPLN 702 Studio, University of Pennsylvania, 2005.

4.27   Ideal conservation network

From the CPLN 702 Studio, University of Pennsylvania, 2007.

4.28   High-speed rail Europe

Map by Bernese Media, permission under Creative Commons license.

4.29   Designated high-speed rail corridors

Courtesy US Department of Transportation.

Every effort has been made to contact and acknowledge copyright owners. If any material has been included without permission, the publishers offer their apologies. The publishers would be pleased to have any errors or omissions brought to their attention so that corrections may be published at later printing.

Index

Note: page numbers in *italics* refer to illustrations; those followed by 'n' refer to information in the Notes.

New Orleans 97, 169, 221n16; Hurricane
    Katrina 3, 4–5, 156
New Theory of Urban Design (Alexander)
    189
New Towns After the War (Osborn) 135
New Urbanism 11, 102–104
New York City 3, 80, 99–100; Central Park
    28, 90, 116, 137, 192, *194*; garden
    suburbs 132, *132*; Landmarks
    Preservation Commission 97, 100; and
    Le Corbusier 28–29, *30*; Lincoln Center
    94–97, *96*, 100, *100*; Pennsylvania
    Station 97; Williamsburg Houses 33,
    33; World Fair (1939–40) 29, 31, *32*;
    zoning code 12, 33, 43, 86, 90, 97,
    99–100, *194*, 196–197, *196*
New York Regional Plan (1929) 42
Noise Control Act (1972) 146
Nolen, John 133, 137
Norris, T.N. 140, *140*
Notes on the Synthesis of Form
    (Alexander) 188
Nothing Gained by Overcrowding (Unwin)
    135
Nouvel, Jean 53, *53*

Office of Metropolitan Architecture (OMA)
    48, *48*, 53, *53*, 185
Okamoto, Rai 186, *186*
Olmsted, Frederick Law 82, 116, 117, 118,
    118, 128
Olmsted, Frederick Law Jr. 83, 132, *132*,
    133
Olympic Games, Beijing 54, 55
One North, Singapore 207
open space 204–205
Oregon 149–150
orientation of buildings 11, 20, 33, *33*
Orlando, Florida *154*, *155*, 198
Osborn, Frederick J. 135
Oud, J.J.P. 18, 24, 26, 213n6

Palladio 61, *61*, 94
Panama canal 119
Parametric Urbanism 206–207
Paris 12, 76, *77*, 78, *79*, 80, 143, 184;
    decline of Parisian city design 90–91,
    91; influence on city design 80–81, *80*,
    81, 82–6, *82*, *83*, *85*, *86*; and origins of
    modern city planning 86–89, *88*, *89*
Parkchester 31, 33, *33*
Parker, Barry 119, *119*, 126–130, *127*, *129*,
    135–136, 138
parking 209–210
parks 27, 80, 116–117, *117*; Central Park,
    New York City 28, 90, 116, 137, 192,
    194; national 119–120; Paris 78, *79*,
    116, *117*

Pattern Language, A (Alexander) 188, 189,
    190–191
Paxton, Joseph 117, *117*, 172, 173,
    173–174, *173*
pedestrians *see* walkable urban
    environments
Peets, Elbert *65*, 70–72, *71*
Penn, William 67
Penn Center, Philadelphia 41–42
Pennsylvania 132, 148
Pennsylvania Station 97, 104
Performance Zoning (Kendig) 148
Perry, Clarence 27, 137–138, *138*
Peterson/Littenberg 6, 7, 8
Philadelphia 41–42, *42*, 43, *43*, 67
Piano, Renzo 184
Piazza del Popolo, Rome 61, *62*, 64
picturesque landscapes 112, 114, 115, *116*
Place de Vosges, Paris 65, *66*
planning, origins of 86–89, *88*, *89*
planning codes *see* codes
Plater-Zyberk, Elizabeth 102, 103, *103*,
    105–106, 197
plazas 64, 95, *96*
Plug-In City 179, *180*, 181
Population Bomb, The (Erlich) 146
Port Authority of New York and New
    Jersey 5, 6, 8
Port Sunlight 118, *118*, 125, 126
Portland, Oregon 150, *150*, *151*
post-modern architecture 104
post-modernism 47–48, 51
pre-industrial cities 164–167, *165*, *167*,
    168–169, *168*, 189–190
prehistoric cities 162–164
Prince Charles *see* Charles, Prince of
    Wales
Prince Regent (King George IV) 73, 74
proportion 93–94
Pruitt-Igoe housing project, St. Louis 51,
    187
public participation in city design 5, 6–7,
    103, 210–211
Public Works Administration, New York
    City 33, *33*
Pythagoras 93, 191

Qatar 52, *52*; Chelsea Barracks
    development 56–58, *57*
Quayside Neighbourhood, Vancouver 107,
    107, *108*
Queen Anne style 118

racial segregation in housing 31, 33, 144,
    145
Radburn, New Jersey 26, 129, 137, *137*
railroads 170–171, 174–175; high-speed
    200, 201–202, *201*, *202*